AFRICAN FOOD PRODUCTION SYSTEMS

AFRICAN FOOD PRODUCTION SYSTEMS

Cases and Theory

Edited by

PETER F. M. McLOUGHLIN

THE JOHNS HOPKINS PRESS
BALTIMORE AND LONDON

Copyright © 1970 by The Johns Hopkins Press
All rights reserved
Manufactured in the United States of America

The Johns Hopkins Press, Baltimore, Maryland 21218
The Johns Hopkins Press Ltd., London

Library of Congress Catalog Card Number 72-107092
ISBN 0-8018-1075-2

In Memoriam
S. B. W. de E.
1969

PREFACE

Although a great deal has been written on agricultural production in recent years, the subject of food has received relatively little isolated and specific attention. Food production, quite rightly, is increasingly receiving world attention. The purpose of this collection of original articles is to focus on the food problem in an African environment.

We just do not know enough about the nature of food crop production to permit rational decisions and policy-making at either the national or the local level. Statistics are inadequate concerning production, consumption, size and direction of crop flows and markets, the effects on production of labor migration and transport development, and so on. It is often difficult to know if there are genuine food shortages, what causes them, and what their magnitude is at the local, let alone the national level. Nor do we have statistics that relate changing levels and distributions of national income to changing demands for foods or that tie these relationships to the problems of food imports and exports.

In much of Africa, under both colonial and independent governments, food crop policy has been essentially one of self-sufficiency. Because domestic systems for marketing food crops are relatively underdeveloped and production is insufficiently specialized by region, this policy has served, for the most part, to maintain the typical rural householder's objective of food self-sufficiency. For long established and justifiable reasons the rural family, particularly the women of the household, generally insists on producing as much of its basic food requirements as possible. This fact has pronounced effects on land use, attractiveness of cash crops, income levels, and so on. The keeping of livestock for food products has equally significant ramifications. No two areas will have identical food production problems, and each therefore requires individual policy-making attention.

Based almost entirely on field work in rural communities, the case studies presented here describe in some detail the food production of seven African societies. Both anthropologists and economists are contributors. The study of African food production systems and problems requires attention from all sciences. No one discipline has all the questions or all the answers. Historically, much of the failure to analyze properly the problems of raising food crop output and to devise acceptable and effective strategies may be attributed to an almost purely technical approach to these problems. An agronomist, particularly one from a developed country with highly specialized agricultural activities, is normally not trained to view the broader aspects and constraints of food production systems.

While long germinating, this book had its real start when I noted the positive reactions from both operational and academic people to a two-volume work on African agriculture published recently for the World Bank.* The detailed case studies presented there have been widely used by planners, extension personnel, researchers, teachers and others. Though these studies tend to deal with a broader range of agricultural subjects than food production systems, the interest in using such detailed material demonstrates what is, in my view, an urgent need for specific case material.

I have contributed the introduction and the conclusion to the work. Between are the seven case studies. The introductory chapter provides framework for the case studies: my discussion covers the reasons for studying food crop production and the theoretical efforts that have been made in the social sciences toward defining and solving the problems of rural African development. The concluding chapter pulls together the characteristics of these food production systems and discusses some of their implications for policy.

I wish to thank my friends the contributors for their hard work and patience. I am also grateful to the School of Business and the Department of Economics of the University of Santa Clara; they provided long hours of typing and other assistance. Particular thanks are also due to David Brokensha, Thayer Scudder, and George Dalton, whose comments assisted greatly with drafts of the theoretical discussion in the Introduction.

P. McL.

---

* John C. de Wilde et al., *Experiences with Agricultural Development in Tropical Africa*, 2 vols. (Baltimore: Johns Hopkins Press, 1967).

CONTENTS

Preface	vii
Introduction, by Peter F. M. McLoughlin	1
Social Factors and Food Production in an East African Peasant Society: The Haya, by Priscilla Reining	41
The Food Production System of a Semi-Nomadic Society: The Karimojong, Uganda, by Rada and Neville Dyson-Hudson	91
Zande Subsistence and Food Production, by Conrad C. Reining	125
Food Production by the Yalunka Household, Sierra Leone, by Leland Donald	165
Agriculture and Diola Society, by Olga Linares de Sapir	193
The Introduction of the Ox Plow in Central Gambia, by Peter M. Weil	229
The Food Economy of Ba Dugu Djoliba, Mali, by William I. Jones	265
Conclusions, by Peter F. M. McLoughlin	307
Index	317

Metric-English Conversion Table

Length

1 millimeter	= 0.04 inches	25 millimeters	= 1 inch
1 meter	= 40 inches		
1 kilometer	= 0.6 miles	1.6 kilometers	= 1 mile

Area

1 hectare	= 2.5 acres	0.4 hectares	= 1 acre

Weight

1 kilogram	= 2.2 pounds	0.45 kilograms	= 1 pound
1 metric ton	= 1.1 short tons	0.91 short tons	= 1 metric ton

Yield

1 kg./ha.	= 0.9 lbs./acre	1.1 kg./ha.	= 1 lb./acre
1 MT/ha.	= 0.45 short tons	2.3 MT/ha.	= 1 short ton/acre
$1/ha.	= $0.40/acre	$2.50/ha.	= $1/acre

AFRICAN FOOD PRODUCTION SYSTEMS

CHAPTER 1

INTRODUCTION

Peter F. M. McLoughlin

Food production is Africa's most important activity. The vast majority of Africa's peoples, regardless of physical, social, or political environment, devote most of their effort to production of their basic food supply, though they may have other economic activities as well. They live in what are called subsistence societies.[1]

FOOD POPULATION PROBLEM

Perhaps the most important problem in the world today is the continuously unfavorable relationship between changes in population and changes in food supply. Given the normal difficulties of marketing and transportation in Africa, one must deal with this relationship at a rather local level. The question "Can Africa feed itself?" is not meaningful. Except for urban areas, which contain only a small percentage of Africa's peoples (though they have increased at an annual rate of 5 to 7 percent over the last 10 to 15 years),[2] we must look at the issue in terms of particular societies in specific areas.

Some societies experience extremely low net rates of population growth yet have great difficulty in feeding this increase. The difficulty is particularly evident in many livestock societies where grazing areas are limited. It is also true of numerous shifting-cultivation societies where new mouths cannot be fed adequately because of declining yields. In many places, population density is too great, at present levels of technology, to permit fields to lie fallow long enough to restore soil fertility.

At the other extreme, there are examples of food production keeping up with high rates of population growth partly through expansion of cultivated area and partly through rising yields per acre. Such areas tend to have better soils and rainfall, and more tree crops and other cash crops as well. But how long such areas can maintain this pace is uncertain. Evidence is accumulating that even those areas where food has kept pace with population are beginning to lose the race. Production can expand only so far under limited technology. Beyond that the system must change completely to get more.

It is probably realistic to state that 20 to 30 percent of Africa's

---

[1] This rather awkward word "subsistence" will be discussed briefly later in the chapter.
[2] These demographic data and those that follow are from Economic Commission for Africa, *Size and Growth of Urban Population in Africa* (Addis Ababa, 1960).

rural peoples are currently experiencing difficulty in feeding themselves. Famines and hunger are a bit more widespread and occur more often than they used to. But this is not a bad record, in one sense. Africa's population has roughly doubled in this century, and the rural economy, with these exceptions, has fed that population.

But what about the next 30 years? There will be twice again as many to feed by the turn of the century. Can the agricultural sector more than double its food output over the next generation? The solution cannot be sought in expansion of farmland. The best areas are already overcrowded. In many places, even highly marginal land is eagerly sought, and cash crops often compete with food crops for space on the same farm. To feed itself, Africa must raise its yields per acre.

The problem is compounded by Africa's burgeoning urban population. The Economic Commission for Africa estimates that the population in cities of 100,000 or more, while only 5 percent of the total population in 1950, was 9 percent in 1960. By now this could be 13 to 14 percent of the total. Smaller communities are also growing quickly. The equivalent figures for localities of 20,000 or more were 10 percent in 1950 and 13 percent in 1960. Today this may be 15 to 17 percent of the total population. There are indications that the rate of flow to the cities is accelerating, though the rate varies considerably from country to country. Thus, aside from the strain to feed itself, the rural economy is being asked to help feed a constantly growing nonagricultural sector.

In countries like Kenya and Uganda, the rural economy generally copes with the urban market, though prices are sometimes rather high for the ordinary wage earner. But in countries like Zambia the supply of food to the industrial areas is sometimes difficult. Many West African countries are already importing grains such as wheat and rice, and the volume is steadily expanding. Some countries, particularly those that are English-speaking, have devised complicated marketing-board systems to regulate and usually subsidize the production, collection, and domestic sale of basic foodstuffs, particularly maize. Most such countries attempt to keep a reserve for the recurrent drought years or to provide a surplus for the cities and towns. In spite of these efforts most African societies will be hard pressed to maintain per capita food output over the next generation.

But to come to grips with Africa's food production problem, it is important to recognize that the continent manifests dozens of different agricultural systems under widely contrasting ecological, demo-

INTRODUCTION

graphic, social, political, and economic conditions. Each of these systems is unique and requires individual research and policy attention for development. In view of the limited human and financial resources for assistance, how does one determine priorities? Does one focus on food economies that simultaneously provide crops for export or for urban areas, or those containing significant numbers of people, or those that are the poorest, or those with the highest rates of population growth, or those with the most restricted opportunities for earning income by other means, or those with the best agricultural conditions? Political considerations, and the nature and strength of ongoing programs as well, will have an important role in establishing such priorities. Governments usually do not select one of these criteria and ignore the rest. Sensible development programs work on a variety of fronts simultaneously.

Labor migration is a major issue intimately connected with food production. A considerable volume of literature has accumulated regarding the reasons for migration from rural areas;[3] most of it suggests that a deteriorating family food supply is a critical factor in pushing people out to attempt to earn more income.

Many of these studies also indicate some of the effects of the absence of able-bodied men on the food economy. The ability of the remaining household to maintain per capita food output often falls, particularly where the system requires continuous bush clearing, which normally is men's work. In some cases the absent workers send back money to enable the family to buy food, but in others a not inconsiderable volume of food is sent *from* the rural household to the absentees. In some areas migration has continued for so long that the community no longer regards improvement of its farming as a solution to the problem of maintaining the desired level of physical welfare. Farming there has become an occupation for women, children, and the old. For economies that do not grow very rapidly, labor migration can be expected to be a permanent feature.

At the same time, since the migration to cities is greater than the increase in jobs, unemployment and underemployment in towns and cities have been increasing. After months or years in a slack labor market, a would-be wage worker, often a relatively aggressive and motivated person, is forced to seek other ways to earn income. Some turn to trading, but most return to farming. Many areas where this is true and where food production systems have remained

[3] The closest thing to a documented theory and classified typology of labor migration has been developed by R. M. Prothero, Professor of Geography, University of Liverpool. The work is as yet unpublished.

undeveloped are now experiencing pressures for change from these relatively younger and more capable men. Examples are the Kano Plains of Kenya and parts of Malawi.[4] These men are insisting that the local authorities and extension officers provide them the means to improve their agriculture—fertilizers, better seed, credit, and the like. Sometimes this is possible, sometimes it is not. There are also situations in which one nation, because of its own unemployment problems, closes its borders to migrants from other countries. This has had particularly serious effects on nations like Malawi. Half of her adult males historically have worked in Zambia, Rhodesia, South Africa, and elsewhere, but their labor markets have closed or are closing.

Land use and the effort to develop more cash income from agriculture are closely related to food production systems. There are many examples of African farmers expanding the production of export crops. Sometimes entire regions, often in the earlier stages dragging government with them, have expanded the production for export of cacao (especially in Ghana), coffee, cotton (in Sukumaland, Tanzania), groundnuts, and so on. The production of food and industrial crops for export has provided—usually with considerable government assistance—the engine for economic growth in many areas, especially since World War II.

But world markets are not expanding particularly quickly for these major food and industrial crops, even though the African smallholder can normally produce these items at lower costs than plantation systems. The production and export of most of these crops will expand slowly, and unit production costs will decrease. But the decline in world prices and the slow rate of expansion of world markets will ensure that the typical African producer who is growing these crops will not be able to expand his earnings quickly. In any case, most African farmers and herders have been participating only marginally, if at all, in export production.

Thus production for domestic markets must expand. What concerns us here is the need to articulate production systems to provide basic food crops for the increasing nonagricultural population as well as industrial crops for an expanding (hopefully) industrial sector. Each ecological zone within a country must specialize in the crops it can grow best; usually this will also be the area that produces the crop most cheaply. For instance, let the somewhat drier areas (with, say, 24 inches to 40 inches of rainfall a year) that can-

[4] See, for example, my article "Some Aspects of Land Reorganization in Malawi (Nyasaland), 1950–1960," *Ekistics* (September, 1967).

not raise horticultural crops provide the maize, and purchase their other food from the market, food produced as a cash crop by some other farmer.

The implications of this objective are profound. They come down to the need of the typical farming household to devote more of its land to the production of crops for sale. Given the normal size of farms, levels of technology, and seasonal labor requirements, this almost invariably requires the cash crop to be increased at the expense of crops for family consumption. And this most African housewives just will not tolerate at present.

Women are normally responsible for feeding the family. To expend scarce labor and (usually) scarce land for crops expressly for sale—that is, to make the farm somewhat more specialized—thus requires some form of understanding between the man and his wife. She will want to be sure of a share of the cash proceeds, which usually go to the man, sufficient to maintain her obligation to provide food for the family. As yet one sees this understanding in only a very few households. A critical element in arriving at a solution to this problem is the need to guarantee, through experience, the availability in the local marketplace of the right kinds of food at the right time and at reasonable prices. When the housewife can trust such a marketplace, the whole process will move forward more easily.

This aspect is intimately connected with the need to maximize output by using every acre to its full capacity. But what does one see? Especially in East and Central Africa, a significant percentage of the best land, which could be producing tea or other valuable export crops or yielding high levels of food crops under improved management and technology, is producing basic food crops under more traditional production systems. On the same farm one sees the man tending a crop (usually for export) with improved management systems and technology. Next to it, his wife is growing maize and other crops traditionally for household consumption. This is carried to extremes in some areas. For instance, parts of upland Kenya could be devoted to vegetables, tea, dairying, and so on, but instead they are used by housewives for grains that take 9 to 11 months to mature.

Generally speaking, innovations affecting cash crops have spread much more quickly than those suggested for basic food crops. There is a high correlation between the successful cash-crop programs and the labor supplies available at particular times. The labor demands for tree crops often are relatively easy to meet compared with those of annual crops. It is unmistakably clear, for example, that in Sukumaland, Tanzania, the steady increase in cotton output has been possible because the crop's peak labor requirements can be adjusted so as not to conflict with food crop production. But when it comes to a choice, as it does from time to time when the rains are late or too erratic, then the food crops take precedence. Even on large capital-using irrigation projects such as the Gezira scheme in the Sudan, provision must be made for food crops in the rotation. Irrigation systems revolutionize partly because they *guarantee* food supplies.

In my opinion, the failure to recognize these technological, ecological, and economic aspects of innovation and the need for a complementary package of inputs has precluded the more rapid and general acceptance of innovation, rather than some cultural indisposition, as discouraged extension officers have often charged.

It should be clear that any program to enhance the productivity of the typical African farm must be built around, or in sympathy with, the maintenance of that farm's food output. Really successful programs make the raising of food-crop yields the center of the change and use this lever to discuss with the farmer the further intensification of his overall production system. The recent success with maize in Kenya is a case in point. Kenya is now having to contend with a surplus, produced mainly by smaller farmers.

TECHNICAL RESEARCH

Although food sufficiency has been recognized as a main priority, most research and extension efforts have been devoted to the enhanced production of both food and nonfood export crops that have been grafted onto basic food production systems. Only in recent years have many countries paid more technical attention to the raising of basic food output.

I have been impressed with the overwhelming need in particular areas to increase food crop productivity. In numerous parts of West Africa—for example, in the Eastern Region of Nigeria—population has doubled in the last 25 or 30 years but the productivity of the land has not kept pace because the technical inputs have not been available. Agricultural development is based on technological change consistent with the changing attitudes and capabilities of farmers and herders. Technical research must therefore be dynamic.

Technical deficiency is especially noticeable in African livestock societies. Virtually none of the multitude of projects and schemes for improving traditional livestock practices have achieved any sustained success. There are successful European ranchers, and there are African smallholders with high-grade dairy cattle introduced into their radically improved farming systems. But we apparently do not have the technology to raise productivity on a sustained basis for the tens of millions of animals managed in a more traditional manner on open ranges. What has been offered to herdsmen has failed to attract them technically and economically. There are a number of ranching projects now under way in East and Central Africa that show promise, but whether they are economic or not is another matter.

FOOD PRODUCTION AND DIET

Many African diets are deficient in the basic elements that affect a child's development. The urban population tends to develop a taste for a wide range of foods, many of which cannot be supplied from the local rural economy; but for the majority of Africans both a demand for and the supply of a more balanced diet have to be created. The demand will come, and indeed is coming, through adult education programs, migrant labor, schools, community development and related efforts, and the increased utilization of the mass media for education.

Balance may be provided by a more diversified cropping system on the farm itself. It may also come through the agricultural sector's becoming much more specialized, as discussed earlier, permitting the purchase of diet-balanced foods produced as cash crops elsewhere in the country or even abroad. Both cases require a revolutionized food production system, and this comes about, the farmer willing, only through the supply from the outside of a complementary and appropriate package of new inputs.

In many areas the ecological constraints preclude crop diversification after a certain point as well as the keeping of livestock in any numbers. Once again we are back to the housewife and how she views all this. And once again we return to the problem of having the theoretical, institutional, technical, and other information required to answer the questions of what is to be done when, where, and by whom.

WHAT CAN SOCIAL SCIENCE THEORY TELL US?

Unfortunately, there is no satisfactory theory of rural change for Africa. In fact, "... there is no generally accepted social science model of change and development."[5] The theoretician of change needs detailed examinations over time of an adequate sampling of societies. The basic data required do not exist.[6]

On the other hand, we do know quite a bit about African food production systems. A constant and reliable output of basic food crops is seldom found in most of Africa. While there are numerous local exceptions, particularly in the higher rainfall areas and in a few highland zones, the typical farming or herding household is not able to predict what physical conditions are in store. As these conditions vary, so do the volumes and types of food output. The physical conditions affecting the timing and volume of production include the time and amount of rainfall, groundwater supplies, pests, diseases, vermin, and the changing incidence of soil leaching and erosion.

Other factors influencing the range and volume of food production may also change from season to season. One of the most important is the labor force available for such critical tasks as ground preparation, weeding, and harvesting. The incidence of sickness, migrant labor, government employment, children in school, and other factors combine to change over time the amount and types of labor available.

The household has a complex relationship with its environment. Economic, social, political, and cultural activities affect and condition one another over time. The pace of change of any one element of this interrelated system, such as food crop production, is affected by and in turn influences other changes in the entire system (see the introduction of chapter 3 for more on the nature of these relationships). An examination of African food production systems must take these interrelationships into account; the approach must be systemic.

[5] Clifton R. Wharton, Jr., "Risk, Uncertainty and the Subsistence Farmer: Technological Innovation and Resistance to Change in the Context of Survival," mimeographed (New York: Agricultural Development Council, 1968), p. 17; also in *Subsistence Agriculture and Economic Development*, ed. Clifton R. Wharton, Jr. (Chicago: Aldine Publishing Co., 1969).

[6] A number of anthropologists and economists continue to stress the need for long-term studies. One of the few such studies is the Colson-Scudder work on the Gwembe Tonga (see note 30). Haswell returned to a Gambian village after ten years. Priscilla Reining has also revisited the Haya in Tanzania (see chap. 2). Gottfried Lang has been conducting long-term studies on the Sukuma (Tanzania), and there are others. But there are precious few that start out designed as long-term studies. Those who do involve themselves in field work should, it seems to me, be cajoled into considering their work as the first, or benchmark, phase of a continuing program.

Though we have no adequate general theory, we do have a rather diffuse but relatively voluminous body of literature describing and commenting on rural society. Some documentation deals with generalities at the continental, regional, and national levels. In the main, such broad spectra are of limited use in the development of theoretical models that will guide the more practical and effective policy-making for development at the local and farm level. At the other end of the spectrum, one has an amazing volume of detailed technical descriptions of agriculture, crops, soils, and the like.

By and large it is the agricultural economists who have advanced their development models the furthest, at least in presenting an organized and integrated picture of agricultural change and its requirements. But the model-building and theoretical discussion have almost invariably been based on studies of non-African areas. One of the best recent pieces on peasant motivation, covering dozens of cases, does not refer to any African situation.[7] This neglect relates to another issue: I strongly believe that most Africans are not the same sort of "peasants" that are being studied and theorized about in other low-output regions. Perhaps the closest thing here to peasants are the West Africans who live in what used to be the Divine Kingdoms. Even if the theorizing *is* valid elsewhere, does it hold for Africa?[8]

NEED FOR IMPROVED TECHNOLOGY

The basic goal of development is a progressively higher level of per capita consumption. This results, on a sustained basis, from a progressively higher level of per capita production. Productivity is a function of improved technology and a more capable worker, regardless of sector or type of activity being considered, regardless of institutions or decision-making processes, regardless of political or cultural environment, regardless of time or place.[9] Everything else

[7] Everett M. Rogers, "Motivations, Values, and Attitudes of Subsistence Farmers: Toward a Subculture of Peasantry," mimeographed, chapter for Wharton, ed., *Subsistence Agriculture.*

[8] The best and most recent example of the attempt to synthesize the literature of theories of change is George Dalton, "Theoretical Issues in Economic Anthropology," *Current Anthropology*, 10, no. 1 (February, 1969), 63–102. While I do not agree with everything Dalton says, the comments published with the article show how far many anthropologists and sociologists have to go before their work can really be useful for developmental problems.

[9] Robert A. Solo, in *Economic Organization and Social Systems* (Indianapolis: Bobbs-Merrill Co., 1967), goes into the qualitative contrasts between different types of decision-making systems. He sees the main development problem as an "incapacity for coherent social action" (p. vi).

may be propitious for sustained development, but without the farmer's or herdsman's acceptance of technological change development doesn't happen. Technological change is a social process. Technology is "a set of problem solving ideas, skills and devices."[10] The context for problem-solving is ecological, that is, the cultural and physical environments. Development is the integration of new technology into an already ongoing sociocultural process.[11]

What we are therefore concerned with is the means whereby technological change may be introduced into African food production systems. Change requires a package of improved technology and a farmer or herder willing to adopt and capable of managing it.

CONSTRAINTS ON THE ADOPTION OF NEW TECHNOLOGY

We come closer to theorizing by drawing up lists of factors influencing farmers' decisions. Clifton R. Wharton, Jr., among others, has provided a short list of the reasons for the failure of farmers to adopt new technology.[12] In the following list we use African examples with Wharton's classification headings.

I. *The Farmer*
  A. *The technology may not be known or understood.* Often the farmer has never heard of the particular innovation or, if he has, he does not comprehend its full application. A situation one encounters all too often is the farmer with a new implement that he has been trained to use but not to repair. Africa is cluttered with an enormous array of equipment for such tasks as cultivating, weeding, spraying, and decorticating.
  B. *The technology may not be within the farmer's managerial competence.* There is very little point in pressing the farmer

---

[10] Thomas R. De Gregori, "Technology and African Economic History: A Provisional Overview" (paper prepared for the meeting of the Society for the History of Technology and the American Association for the Advancement of Science, Dallas, December, 1968), p. 1. De Gregori traces the nature, sources, and effects of technological changes over several centuries. He also discusses economic development theory in terms of these processes, indicating that theory is not relating to this basic force. See his *Technology and the Economc Development of the Tropical African Frontier* (Cleveland: Press of Case Western Reserve University, 1969). I read the University of Texas doctoral dissertation from which the book stems, not the book itself.

[11] De Gregori, "Technology and History," p. 1.

[12] "Risk, Uncertainty", pp. 17–20.

to adopt a new technique or implement unless he is simultaneously given the skill to employ it. The standard displays, demonstrations, and other educational devices must provide the farmer with the required competence. The farmers' training centers in many parts of English-speaking Africa have become a rather effective educational tool, particularly in providing short courses on the production of export crops. Though research, and hence instruction, in general farm management has lagged, improvement is noticeable in a number of countries.

There are numerous examples of farmers' trying out something new and not being able to cope with it. Unfortunately, in most areas in Africa the extension agent who contacts the farmer is often not skilled enough to train or instruct the farmer. In addition, new innovations cannot be learned in isolation; any significant improvement comes through a package of new techniques and practices. The farmer must learn a number of new things simultaneously. Unless significantly more skilled than most, he may reject the package, even though he may be able to accept and handle particular elements of it.

C. *The innovation may not be socially, culturally, or psychologically acceptable.* There is considerable evidence indicating that changes are sometimes rejected because they would disrupt the community's or family's political, social, or economic patterns or power structure. One of the significant reasons for the failure of the land reorganization scheme in central Malawi (then Nyasaland) in the 1950's and early 1960's was the sustained resistance of women. The reallocation process divided sister from sister and mother from daughter, making it impossible for a woman to socialize with close kin while cultivating. Societies in these particular areas are primarily matrilinial and matrilocal.

We have already indicated the virtually automatic resistance of the housewife to any innovation that deprives her of enough space or time to provide the family's basic food supply. Men tend to resist land consolidation if they are used to a migratory labor system; individualization of farmland can deprive them of rights to land as well as its produce. Even the provision of cultivating equipment can meet strong resistance. Such equipment may make a younger household more independent of the wishes of the wider kin

group. The spread of such technology tends to be accompanied by an increased nucleation of families and hence more decision-making groups.
II. *The Innovation Itself*
   A. *The innovation may not be technically viable or adequately adapted.* Governments employ various techniques to test out a new idea, tool, practice, or whatever. The choice of technique depends on the item and the interpretation of the agricultural economy into which the innovation must be fitted. Often information on the system of production, and particularly its constraints, is especially weak. Then an innovation may be devised quite outside the technical framework in which the farmer or herder has to use it. Research stations may not have representative soils or climate, and they usually use wage labor, pure stands of crops, appropriate doses of fertilizer, insecticide, and pesticide, and so on—hardly typical conditions.

   One of the most commonly recommended techniques is early planting. Research stations frequently find a high positive correlation between earlier planting (earlier than a community is doing it) and much greater yields per acre and per input of labor. But the farmer often cannot plant earlier. His oxen are at their weakest at the end of the dry season and sometimes die in their traces. People are also at their weakest then, often having gone through the dry season on short rations. The rains also bring malaria and other fevers in many areas. Some of the men may not have returned from dry-season jobs or job-hunting elsewhere. One sees light tractors and equipment operating in heavy soils and enormous equipment on sandy, friable soils. Examples of such difficulties could be multiplied. It is small wonder that many African farmers turn down suggested innovations for technical reasons.

   It is also worth repeating that technically suitable innovations for food crop production, at least outside of irrigation schemes, are in terribly short supply compared with those devised for export crop production. This is gradually changing, but the chronic and, in most African countries, worsening shortage of skilled and innovative technicians continually hampers progress in this direction.
   B. *The innovation may not be economically feasible.* The most serious cause for farmers' or herders' resistance to new tech-

nology is their realization that it simply would not be profitable. Few research stations have an agricultural economist analyzing research designs and research results. Virtually all African research and extension work has been conducted by technical personnel, mainly agronomists. Though agronomic feasibility is of course the place to start, the failure to put research programs and research results to the economic test has been, I believe, the prime cause of rejection of even the simplest inputs, such as fertilizer.

One problem that research often does not surmount is the integration of one innovation with other required changes. Because agriculture is a system, any change in one segment of the system will affect all other elements to some degree.[13] To maximize the benefit of one change in technology, it is normally necessary to take a number of complementary inputs as well. The cost/benefit relationship for the entire package may be quite different from that of one individual input.

There are a number of reasons for the "one input at a time" approach, which many experts support strongly. Perhaps the most important is the feeling, rather outdated, that the average farmer can handle only one change in a season or over a few years.

But another serious aspect of this approach is the splintering of research effort, which is particularly severe in French-speaking Africa. A dozen or two separate agencies may be involved in research, each handling a different crop. There will be a cassava institute, a coffee institute, a maize institute, and many others. In the Ivory Coast, for example, when working there on a particular development project, I could find no one who was working on farming as such. Yet part of our particular task, and indeed a stated objective of the government, was to stabilize shifting cultivation in sections of the forested southern third of the country. That requires examination and change of the *system*.

Conversely, it is also in French-speaking areas that one encounters the most successful attempts at a unified service for farmers. French organizations are often employed to

---

[13] Some innovations require a minor adjustment and seem to be more readily acceptable. A higher-yielding seed strain (synthetic maize in Kenya, for example) is often welcomed by many farmers and causes little disturbance. But the introduction of oxen and ox-drawn equipment can be nearly revolutionary.

handle all activities in a particular area—research, extension, farmer training, supply of inputs, credit, marketing, everything. Such organizations are developing improved *packages* of inputs that integrate the innovations in food crop and cash crop production into more productive systems that lie within the farmer's labor, climatic, and other constraints but still are attractive enough economically to encourage the farmer to try them.

III. *The Externalities*
   A. *All elements in the new package may not be available.* It is so often the case that the farmer cannot get the quantity of the new item needed at the right time. He may know about the item or the package, but does not adopt it because he cannot trust the inadequate services to provide it. A new seed is usually of little use without added fertilizer; both have to be available.

PHASES OF RURAL DEVELOPMENT

Recognizing that technological change is the means to "modernize" and improve welfare, some analysts of rural development have developed "stage" concepts. John W. Mellor seems to have done this best. He posits three phases, recognizing that these are broad patterns of movement and may not always apply in any specific place.[14] He terms his phases traditional agriculture, technologically dynamic agriculture–low capital technology, and technologically dynamic agriculture–high capital technology.

Traditional agriculture, Phase I, "is a technologically stagnant phase in which production is increased largely through slowly increased application of traditional forms of land, labor, and capital. Thus, although expansion of production does occur in this phase, and the fact that it occurs through an essentially symmetrical expansion of all inputs or through increased input of already abundant low productivity resources results in either no increases or a decline in the productivity of resources. In other words, expansion of production in Phase I is accomplished by declining income and productivity per unit."[15]

[14] John W. Mellor, *The Economics of Agricultural Development* (Ithaca, N.Y.: Cornell University Press, 1966). See especially chap. 13. The book contains an excellent bibliography.
[15] *Ibid.*, p. 224.

INTRODUCTION

This phase must contain virtually all of Africa's livestock peoples and some 80 percent of its farm families. This does not mean that there are no attempts to improve agriculture in this phase—there may be some fertilizer, for example, or a new type of seed, or cash crops. But there is no "constant generation and application of technology," as Mellor puts it.[16]

As distinct from Phase I, Phase II does feature cumulative and constant technological change. Over most of Africa, this is the phase on which the agricultural effort as well as the theory-building must focus. Beginning with a few changes in a few areas, an increasing array of innovations spreads wider, mainly through the continuing improvement of the institutions serving agriculture. The emphasis is on yields per acre, not necessarily on output per unit of labor. The Phase I traditional agriculture tends to maximize returns to labor input; Phase II maximizes land input; Phase III tries to improve yields of all inputs, including labor. In Phase II, in other words, though increased capital use is still small, it is more widespread. Again at a guess, 10 or 15 percent of Africa's farmers may be in Phase II.

Of Phase III, Mellor says, "the key characteristic . . . is the substitution of capital in the form of large-scale machinery for labor."[17] This provides constantly increasing returns to labor. This phase is difficult to conceive of under current African conditions. Even where one finds heavy machinery (Ghana's state farms, low-density settlement schemes, irrigation projects), there is usually no shortage of labor. Costs per unit of output for the machinery often are higher than the labor it replaces—forced mechanization, almost invariably, is high-cost modernization.

What Mellor is referring to is the situation of the agricultural sector in developed countries like the United States, Canada, and the Soviet Union, where it has been essential to evolve machinery to replace labor needed by expanding industrial, service, and government sectors. With the *possible* exception of the European agricultural sector in South Africa, about which this writer knows little (and which is outside the geographic coverage of this discussion), I do not know of any Phase III situation in Africa. There is large-scale technology in many places, but not on a self-forcing cumulative basis.

[16] *Ibid.*, p. 226.
[17] *Ibid.*

CLASSIFICATION OF VARIABLES AFFECTING RURAL DEVELOPMENT

There is still the basic problem of how one gets from Phase I to Phase II. We know that there are any number of variables that affect the farm family's decision to move ahead. A number of attempts to classify these variables indicate how complicated the subject is. The following list, by Bruce F. Johnston, gives a breakdown of "proximate and conditioning" factors that influence agricultural productivity and output.[18]

I. *Proximate or Farm Level Factors*
  A. Increases in technical and managerial efficency
   1. *Adoption of technological innovations*: Adoption of improved inputs, e.g., higher-yielding plant varieties
   2. *Growth of managerial capabilities*: More efficient combination of inputs and products and better planning and organization of the farm work program
  B. Increased input of resources
   1. *Increased input of labor,* which may be the result of fuller utilization of the existing stock of labor, e.g., by increasing the number of hours worked per day or spreading out the work load so that labor is employed more fully through the year
   2. *Increased input of land* by bringing new land into cultivation, extending the period during which land can be cropped without excessive loss of soil fertility or risk of erosion, or enhancing the agricultural value of land by irrigation or other land improvements

---

[18] Bruce F. Johnston, "An Economic Framework for Considering the Choice of Measures for Agricultural Development" (paper from a seminar entitled "The Economic, Cultural and Technical Determinants of Change in Tropical African Agriculture," held at Stanford Food Research Institute, April 1 and 2, 1966), p. 84a.

Johnston explains that these categories are interdependent and to some extent overlapping. No sharp distinction can be made, he says, between the use of a new or improved input such as fertilizer or improved seed—a technological innovation—and increased use of working capital. Similarly, it is difficult to draw the line between increased input of labor and capital formation that is essentially an embodiment of nonwage family labor. The factors considered here, he says, focus on increasing output, but better storage practices, both on and off the farm, can be important in increasing supplies available for consumption.

3. *Increased input of capital*
    a. Nonmonetary capital investment using nonwage farm labor
    b. Biological-chemical inputs and other forms of capital complementary to existing resources of land and labor
    c. Capital that is mainly labor substituting
II. *Conditioning or Socially Determined Factors*
    A. Factors influencing the level of technical knowledge and skills
        1. *Agricultural research* to test, adapt, and develop improved production possibilities
        2. *Extension-education programs* to carry knowledge and understanding of improved technology to farmers and to transmit knowledge of farmers' problems back to experiment stations
        3. Modifications in the *institutional, cultural, and economic environment that leads to changes in attitudes and values*
    B. Factors influencing production incentives and the use of resource inputs
        1. The process of structural transformation as it affects the growth of monetary demand for agricultural products and the effective demand for purchased farm inputs
        2. Institutional arrangements and physical facilities for marketing agricultural products and supplying farm inputs
        3. The level (and variability) of product processes as influenced by domestic and export demand, market mechanisms, and government programs (e.g., a buffer-stock operation)
        4. Land-tenure arrangements, especially as they determine the share of farm receipts accruing to cultivators and whether farmers have sufficient security of tenure and control of a farm unit large and compact enough to encourage investment of labor and other resources in planting tree crops, land improvements, etc.
        5. Availability, design, and price of purchased inputs (and consumer goods)
        6. Availability of credit or subsidies for purchase of inputs
        7. Taxation (as it affects the resources available to farmers and incentives—negatively or positively)

The following classification of factors affecting agricultural development, though similar to Johnston's, slices the pie in a different way. It is a consensus from several disciplines.[19]

I. *Physical Input Factors*
   A. Nonhuman physical inputs
      1. Land
      2. Climate
      3. Seeds
      4. Water
      5. Fertilizer
      6. Pesticides
      7. Structures
      8. Work animals
      9. Other animals
     10. Tools and machinery
     11. Fuel and power other than animal power

II. *Economic Factors*
   A. Transport, storage, processing, and marketing facilities for products
   B. Facilities for the supply and distribution of inputs, including credit
   C. Input prices, including interest rates
   D. Product prices, including prices of consumer goods
   E. Taxes, subsidies, quotas

III. *Organizational Factors*
   A. Tenure, land
   B. Farm size and legal form
   C. General government services and policies
   D. Voluntary and statutory farmers' organizations for:
      1. Coordinating physical input use, e.g., irrigation associations, tractor stations
      2. Economic services, e.g., purchase, sale, credit associations, and cooperatives
      3. Social services, e.g., health centers, schools, family planning centers
      4. Local government
      5. Diffusion of knowledge, e.g., adult education classes, youth clubs

---

[19] David Hapgood, in David Hapgood, ed., *Policies for Promoting Agricultural Development: Report of a Conference on Productivity and Innovation in Agriculture in the Underdeveloped Countries* (Cambridge, Mass.: Center for International Studies, Massachusetts Institute of Technology, 1965), p. 13.

IV. *Socio-psycho-cultural Factors*
   A. Integration of agricultural institutions, practices, and values within the technical-social matrix of the nation
   B. Public administration factors, structure, values, mode of operation of the innovating bureaucracy
   C. Social structure, cultural values, and dynamics of peasant communities
   D. Processes of sociocultural change, barriers, and motivations in the innovative sequence, functional harmony or disharmony in society as its constituent parts change
V. *Knowledge Factors*
   A. Organization of basic and applied research
   B. Diffusion of knowledge relating to:
      1. Technical knowledge, e.g., agronomy, plant genetics, soil science, water management, agricultural engineering, pest control, home technology
      2. Economic knowledge, e.g., land economics, general economics, farm management
      3. Policy, e.g., politics, public administration, planning
      4. General education, e.g., literacy, adult education, mass communication

MODELS IN ANTHROPOLOGY

Anthropologists and sociologists also have their lists that are the product of extensive field work, research, and thought. Following is a list of data requirements for agricultural project areas by three behavioral scientists who attempted to develop theory regarding rural and agricultural development.[20]

I. Basic physical-demographic data
   A. Population, land settlement (size of units, dispersal, distances between, relations to market and administrative towns)
   B. Land tenure and attitudes toward same
II. Basic technologies, materials and their sources
III. Principal occupations
   A. Distribution by villages and areas
   B. Nature of vested interest groups

[20] F. M. Foster, M. L. Barnett, and A. R. Holmberg, "Behavioral Science Research and Its Potential Role in Agricultural Development," in Hapgood, *Policies for Promoting Development*, pp. 291–93.

IV. Social structure
   A. Families, nature of roles, obligations, size, extension; unilinear segments such as clans?
   B. Concept of friendship, fictive kinship, roles, obligations
   C. General nature of reciprocal obligations:
      1. Horizontal—between people of same status—traditional cooperative units
      2. Patron-client
      3. Other
   D. Caste and class patterns
V. Political structure
   A. Locus of authority; basic description of system
   B. Techniques by which political leaders achieve position
   C. Decision-making processes (election, council of elders, consensus, etc.)
   D. Relationship of local political structure to larger units; where does control really lie?
   E. Concept of authority—who legitimately exercises it?
VI. Law
   A. Nature and extent of conflict (e.g., factions, individual quarrels)
   B. Conflict-resolving techniques
   C. What constitutes settlement of a quarrel ("justice"? restoration of status quo?)
VII. Religion
   A. Leaders and influence
   B. Limitations stemming from dogma and doctrine (e.g., Catholics and birth control, Buddhists and pesticides)
   C. Basic cultural values stemming from religion
   D. Role of religious activities—entertainment, instrumental in curing, in farm magic?
   E. Superstitions, magic
VIII. Communications and mobility (behavioral science research)
   A. Literacy, radio, newspapers, etc.
   B. Possible language problems (multiple languages)
   C. Seasonal and other migration to mines, cities—do families have relatives in cities?
IX. Basic "patterns" of society and culture
   A. For example, "balance" in Latin America in wealth, folk medicine, etc.
   B. Cognitive orientation and world view (perception of role of government and individuals)

C. Basic "values," aspirations of people
X. Dynamics
   A. Patterns of innovation—motivations to change
   B. Resistances to change
   C. "Natural" leaders—who is a "respected individual"?
   D. Can innovation-prone individuals be identified?
   E. Can innovation-prone villages be identified?
XI. Health
   A. Folk medical beliefs and practices
   B. Vital statistics—basic indexes on health and morbidity
XII. Socialization
   A. Learning processes in context of this community
   B. Inculcation of dominant values; implicit assumptions about conditions of life of the group

The authors also pointed out that sociocultural systems are functional units and are characterized by patterned regularities and similarities. Knowledge of these patterns permits a considerable degree of success in predicting future reactions and the like. But no two systems are the same, these authors emphasize; what works in one place may not work somewhere else. This is particularly important for much of Africa, where a given region or country may contain considerable diversity of sociocultural systems.

The dynamics of agricultural change must take account of barriers (which we have already discussed) and incentives as well. In the literature, there seems to be a considerable degree of professional jealousy, or discipline guarding, on the whole issue of incentives. Anthropologists and other behavioral scientists deal with psychological, social, and cultural aspects of motivations and incentives; economists deal with the economic aspects, and apparently "ne'er the twain shall meet."[21] But anthropologists in particular, the three mentioned above and many others, are fairly sure that the following factors influence the process of change in rural societies (everywhere, not just in Africa):

1. Ongoing obligations to kinsmen and others usually mean that any net gain from the adoption of an innovation has to be shared with others (or approbation if the innovation fails to result in a net gain).

[21] This cross-disciplinary problem of communications is dealt with by Walter C. Neale in an untitled working paper prepared for a workshop on Peasant Motivation and Economic Behavior, sponsored by the American Universities Research Program of the Agricultural Development Council, New York, April, 1968.

2. "The size and composition of groups have a great deal of bearing on the kinds of activities that can be carried out. There is usually a critical mass, an optimum size that, if achieved, permits activities otherwise difficult to carry out."[22] This size will vary with the society, and to be most effective the change agent must find it.

3. Symbolic representations may have completely different meanings in different cultures. Extension personnel and educators must be aware of these.

In the opinion of these three behavioral scientists and others, there are also three motivations that are of virtually universal importance, though there are others found in particular societies:

1. Perceptions of economic gain, especially of the more enterprising farmer or herder.
2. The desire to achieve prestige and status.
3. The desire to please the change agent.

We also know, however, that change must come from within the rural society itself. One may alter the outside world in all sorts of ways, in all the areas we have listed, but unless the psychological and social chemistry changes *within* the society little will happen. Eric R. Wolf, among others, brought this out extremely well fifteen years ago for Latin America.[23]

Dr. Victor Uchendu, an anthropologist, has perhaps come closest to devising a body of theory that integrates the external and internal forces for change and draws on several disciplines in an African setting. In a number of documents, Dr. Uchendu reviews the models normally employed by anthropologists to classify African cultures.[24] Anthropologists have normally used these models to

---

[22] Foster, Barnett, and Holmberg, "Behavioral Science Research," p. 289.

[23] Eric R. Wolf, "Types of Latin American Peasantry: A Preliminary Discussion," *American Anthropologist*, 57, no. 3 (1955), 452–71, also found in *Tribal and Peasant Economies: Readings in Economic Anthropology*, ed. George Dalton (New York: Natural History Press for the American Museum of Natural History, 1967). Dalton's excellent collection includes a useful bibliographical essay. Many of Wolf's ideas may also be found in his *Sons of the Shaking Earth* (Chicago: University of Chicago Press, 1959).

[24] Victor C. Uchendu, "Socioeconomic and Cultural Determinants of Rural Change in East and West Africa" (unpublished). An earlier version of the paper was presented at a seminar on Research on Agricultural Development in East and West Africa in June, 1968, sponsored by the Agricultural Development Council and the Department of Agricultural Economics, Michigan State University. See also Uchendu's "Some Thoughts on the Socio-Cultural Determinants of Agricultural Change: The African Case," in "Proceedings of a Seminar at Stanford Food Research Institute, April 1 and 2, 1966, on the Economic, Cultural and Technical Determinants of Change in Tropical African Agriculture," ed. Bruce F. Johnston (mimeographed), pp. 1–27.

analyze their field work and for comparative analysis. The five main models are the culture area, kinship, policy, linguistics, and cultural focus.

Uchendu says: "These five models have their uses; but as theoretical tools in the hands of a student of economic development, their limitations are obvious. We cannot say on the basis of any of these models what will be the likely response of a given society to a given set of innovations. Or, put in another way, what set of innovations, or programs of directed change, will succeed in one area and not in another."[25] A number of ecologists, cultural anthropologists, and sociologists, such as Uchendu, Thayer Scudder, and Robert Netting, believe that much of Africa does not have the virtually "closed" peasant society that dominates the theoretical literature on farmers elsewhere. In any case, the demographic patterns vary so widely, as do ecological conditions, that generalizing is terribly difficult.

There is a consensus that Africans are acquisitive and that wealth, whatever its form, is often the basis of status distinctions. But Uchendu feels, probably rightly, that: "All over Africa the control over people is an ideal cultural goal—a goal that gives orientation to African traditional economies. The orientation of African traditional agriculture is not necessarily towards growth; it is a prestige-oriented economy—an economy where surplus produce is converted as soon as practicable into items that confer prestige: Plural wives, cattle, power, and—most important—the command over people."[26] For Uchendu and others, the "polity primacy" has made for social development but not economic; economic goals are secondary to political ones. It would appear to be true, and our own case studies bring this out, that African societies are not inflexible but that the flexibility is *not* oriented to growth.

The barriers to change that anthropologists like Uchendu and many other behavioral scientists who have studied African conditions consistently bring out in their case studies and other writings include:

1. Primitive technology. The hoe and the machete are the main tools virtually everywhere.

2. Very similar, the elementary nature of the scientific knowledge available, which is more in the form of an art than a science. Magic is an important element in explaining cause and effect, not science.

---
[25] Uchendu, "Socioeconomic and Cultural Determinants," p. 7.
[26] *Ibid.*, p. 12.

3. Religious beliefs, and not only in some aspects of Muslim societies. Prohibitions and practices in ancestor worship can interfere with production systems as well.

4. Restrictive institutions regarding resource use. The most popular in the literature is the issue of land rights and uses. This is unquestionably important, though perhaps too much is made of it as a problem in particular instances.

5. Status and prestige problems of agriculture. Particularly in West African yam cultures, one produces for ostentation, the large yam crib or yam house bringing status and position; and reciprocity in foodstuffs is most important.

6. The system of extended families. While this system provides social security and often can be useful in the early stages of development for mobilizing resources, its very distributive nature discourages innovations and accumulation for productive activity (not necessarily legal or political activity).

7. The problem of the division of labor between sexes, as discussed earlier. The implications for both the food crop and the cash crop economies are diverse.

Anthropologists are quick to point out, however, that the dynamics of rural change are already present, very strongly in some areas. Uchendu divides Africa into two societies and three economies, thus being rather more generous with alternatives than economists, who tend to stick to two-sector models. Each of these five, in Uchendu's opinion, requires separate attention for development. His two societies are the small percentage, mainly in urban areas, that are fairly well off and that live on salaries and wages, and "the larger society of the poor, deriving their meagre money income from cash cropping and petty trading, often supplemented with migrant labor activities."[27] He thus uses locational and institutional criteria as well as average income levels to distinguish between the societies.

The three economies he posits are different, in his mind, mainly because of ecological limitations on the extension of cash cropping. There is, first, the small industrial and commercial sector, often an enclave economy dominated by large agricultural estates or mining activities. The second is the monetized agriculture of smallholders. They grow the export crops (tea, coffee, cacao, and so on) as well as the bulk of their own food supplies. The third is the "purely or predominantly subsistence economy where ecology is a major barrier to cash cropping and in which cash income is derived from the export of labor to the first two economies. If this implies a degree

[27] Ibid., p. 28.

of economic interpenetration, the disparity in rural welfare which it manifests must also be appreciated."[28]

I disagree partly with this classification and will take up the reasons at the end of this chapter, where I discuss "subsistence" economies. But the dynamics of African economies arise from changing incentives in those communities that are ecologically capable of expanding output. Cultural factors and political and social organization will affect the rate of change, but growth comes from a gradually more acquisitive population's taking up changing economic opportunities and incentives. The population must also be increasingly involved in the various economic decision-making processes and institutions. New technology, including new institutional forms, is adopted when it is proved effective and financially rewarding.

The whole issue of incentives must be seen through the eyes of the farmer or herder himself. We do not try this enough, and the motivated and enterprising farmers do not write books and journal articles. All too often the planner, researcher, and extension officer designs activities and projects to solve problems *they* have identified in ways *they* would find economically justifiable.

But the farmer does not view his problems in the same way as the planner, researcher, or extension officer. As I have said elsewhere: "Most efforts at agricultural development have experienced highly limited, or very slow, success, or failed entirely, because the farmer and his family could not relate the effort to their own aspirations, their own farm's resources, or their own sense of economic viability. We need to devise farm systems which are economically attractive, which are capable of being learned fairly easily, which do not conflict with the farmer's other economic and social obligations and objectives, which are not incompatible or inconsistent with his own resources (particularly labor and cash), and which have sufficient properly trained staff to support them."[29]

INCENTIVES AND THE "FRUSTRATION GAP"

There is also a policy dimension to the whole issue of incentives. For many reasons, some farmers and communities are riper for de-

[28] *Ibid.*, pp. 28–29.
[29] "Increasing Agricultural Output to Help with the Population 'Problem' " (paper prepared for a meeting of the International Geographical Union, Pennsylvania State University, September, 1967) to appear in *Geography and a Crowding World: Essays on Population Pressure upon Resources*, ed. R. M. Prothero, L. Kosinski, and W. Zelinsky. Most of this discussion on incentives and the listing of income needs and income sources are in that paper.

velopment than others. As indicated earlier, the typical African nation does not have the resources of skilled manpower, finance, or research to develop all areas simultaneously. What criteria does one use to identify and select such areas?

Other things being equal, resources should be directed, I believe, to those communities, villages, and farms that are the most ready to use them and will combine them with their own resources to get the most substantial and rapid increases in output. Rapid survey techniques that will identify the farmers or villages best prepared to innovate and change are badly needed. Very little work of this kind has been done for Africa, at least in a manner that can be used by those responsible for allocating developmental resources. A number of researchers, however, are now working on this problem. True readiness must be distinguished clearly from lip service to the idea of development.[30] People often express an interest in a proposed change, but when they have to perform, they may refuse.

Such surveys must ferret out the "frustration gap." The typical rural household at any moment feels the need for a certain level and composition of income. It obtains the income from a variety of sources. The following list covers many of the typical rural household's most important needs and resources, though there will be local variations in the relative availability and importance of each.

I. *Needs*
   A. Physical
      1. Food for the family
      2. Food for exchange and reciprocity arrangements
      3. Food to send to absent members
      4. Shelter
      5. Tools and equipment
      6. Services (fuel collection, water supply, herding, etc.)

---

[30] In particular, Elizabeth Colson and Thayer Scudder have steadily followed the Gwembe Tonga, relocated with the Kariba Dam project, since 1956. They are testing various devices that, in due course, should help to identify the innovative individual and the constraints on change and should produce other useful knowledge. Scudder has also been concerned with the need for the rapid survey techniques I am proposing here; see his "Social Anthropology and Rural Development: The Need for Rapid Survey Techniques and Systematic Long Term Studies," in *The Anthropology of Development in Africa*, ed. David Brokenshaw, (Lexington, Ky. Society for Applied Anthropology, 1969). I can find little other research on this exact subject aside from that of David Smock in the Eastern Region of Nigeria, now known as Biafra. See his chapter in the Brokenshaw volume.

B. Cash
1. Taxes
2. School fees
3. Memberships in essential economic organizations, e.g., cooperatives
4. Food not produced on own farm or received in reciprocity arrangements
5. Other necessities for living (utensils, cloth, etc.)

II. *Possible Sources of Income*
1. Food produced on own farm, including livestock products
2. Food received under reciprocity arrangements
3. Tools, equipment, shelter, services produced on own farm
4. Sale of food crops or livestock products for cash
5. Sale of crops produced expressly for markets (usually export)
6. Commodities gathered from the wild, e.g., hedge sisal, gum arabic, honey
7. Migrant farming
8. Seasonal wage labor—local
9. Seasonal wage labor—at a distance
10. Extended migration to wage labor (year or more)
11. Trading and commerce of all kinds

It is important for our discussion of motivations to see how these pieces fit together. We must visualize the *system*—in other words, identify how the food production elements integrate with the other elements and how all this relates to motivations in the short run and the long run. The system can then be related to the heart of rural development, technological change.

There is nothing difficult about these interrelationships. A family experiences a need for a particular level and composition of income and will pursue whatever combination of activities will provide it. If one activity or set of activities results in that level and composition, then other activities are minimized or foregone. Altered relationships are particularly noticeable when basic food crops fail—more stock will be sold, more men will go off to find wage employment, and more commodities will be gathered from the wild (but not all of these alternatives are always available to all families). In the Sudan, for example, the number of rainland farmers and nomads appearing for wage employment at the Gash, Tokar, and

Gezira irrigation projects is a direct function of the amount of rain at their homes.[31]

In the short run, therefore, the farmer's or herder's interest in what the government may have to offer him is very much a function of his own particular combination of needs and income possibilities and his views of them. There is always greater interest in the livestock marketing system in periods of drought than in years of good rainfall. Time and time again I have seen farmers' interest in innovation quicken when the standard means of acquiring income are less favorable than usual. And the interest often subsides when the situation returns to normal.

What about the longer pull? There is a direct relationship between population growth and the pressures toward a more favorable set of motivations regarding technological change. In the better endowed areas that are already rather densely settled, the pressure of a farm family's growth will expand minimum food and other needs in a fairly predictable manner. One may also measure this pressure at the village, regional, or national level. Family (or village or national) population about doubles in 30 years. Hence food and other basic requirements also double. The family will probably not be able to increase its food output so much, however, so that over this period it will feel a need to increase its cash earnings.

But the family (village, region) normally will want a rising standard of living, an expectation that results from exposure to advertising in the mass media, greater mobility, more people in school, and so on.

If the alternatives for earning income are available and are used, so that the family (village, region) actually acquires what it wants, then regardless of the rate of increase of felt income needs there will be no frustration gap. The rate of increase in the propensity to seek out the means to raise farm productivity tends to follow the rate of increase in felt income needs. A frustration gap arises from relatively restricted possibilities for increasing income.

If no other factors intrude, then the family or community ripest for development is the one with the largest frustration gap, regardless of the level of income at which the gap occurs. It is likely that the gap tends to be greater among those who have already experi-

---

[31] I have discussed these relationships in a number of publications. See, for example, "Using Administration Reports to Measure Rural Labour Markets: Darfur, Sudan," *Bulletin of the Inter-African Labour Institute* (January, 1963), pp. 15–27, and "Comment on Berg's 'Backward Sloping Labour Supply Functions in Dual Economies—the African Case,'" *Quarterly Journal of Economics*, 76 (November, 1962), 660–62.

enced some degree of development. Should that gap get too large for enough people, frustration, political unrest, and other social problems will of course arise. The Kikuyu in Kenya are one of the best examples of this situation.

If the gap is very small, on the other hand, as it still is in many communities, then no amount of persuasion or pressure will induce a family or group to adopt new production systems, even if they are technically and economically suitable. Many livestock societies tend to fall in this category. Development policy for them should thus emphasize raising their aspirations as well as offering them effective production systems.

It must be remembered that the typical rural householder (and more certainly his son) prefers nonfarming alternatives for increasing his income to his farming. As long as wage labor, or trading, or whatever is available, he will usually prefer them to going through all the strain of learning and adopting a more intensive agricultural system. One of the increasingly important pressures for improved farming in many parts of the world is the relative decline in wage labor and other income earning opportunities.

This is a highly oversimplified portrayal of a terribly complicated process involving all aspects of a family's and a community's culture. But there are numerous instances where rising motivations alone have made some farmers eager for technological change, for an improved production system. And one can often help them if they have enough good land, if the appropriate institutions exist, and so on.

DEVELOPMENT POLICY AND THE "FRUSTRATION GAP"

Many of the basic problems hindering agricultural development, however, may only be met on a communitywide, not an individual, basis. This includes such items as land reorganization and the establishment of suitable economic infrastructure, such as cooperatives for marketing, credit, and supply. The community must often feel pushed to conceive an interest in agricultural improvement. The push comes from the combination of forces that threatens to reduce production and consumption per person or family, including population increases, declining yields, smaller farms or grazing space per family, and so on. Under such pressures, group after group has improved its own farming systems, intensifying to the best of its ability. It is this intensification that has permitted Africa roughly to double its food output over the last 50 or 60 years without doubling its farmland.

But the typical community reaches the limit of its ability to modify and improve its own system. It is at this point that it comes to view technological, including institutional, change with more favor. When the pressures combine with a closing of other income earning opportunities, then there are people prepared to accept innovations to maintain or increase their per capita output and consumption of basic food. As extension officers will affirm, in place after place farmers are now asking for the very technology they previously refused. The improved technology has not changed; the farmer has.

A THEORY OF CHANGE, TECHNOLOGY, AND THE CONCEPT OF "SUBSISTENCE"

What is needed is a system of principles that will help the agent of agricultural development identify the barriers, constraints, and bottlenecks of his area regardless of source and identify the resources, especially human, at his disposal. Such a system should also be capable of helping him predict the effects of given changes on the society and economy he is dealing with.

While virtually everyone acknowledges that technological change is the heart of agricultural development, no one seems to be devising a theory of rural change with the technology issue as the core of the development theory. The balance of this chapter, therefore, will discuss technological change in its theoretical relationship to the whole concept of subsistence and subsistence agriculture and to the dynamics of change.

The idea of subsistence permeates the theoretical discussions of economists and anthropologists (such as the Uchendu models discussed earlier). Virtually all of the writing concerning change and movement of these rural societies deals with dynamics in terms of movement away from subsistence toward a market-oriented and monetized economy.[32]

---

[32] Two of the most important discussions of the functions of the anthropologist with respect to African rural development and the dynamics of change are David Brokenshaw, *Applied Anthropology in English-Speaking Africa*, Society for Applied Anthropology, Monograph No. 8 (Ithaca, N.Y.: 1966), and Brokenshaw, *Anthropology of Development in Africa*.

"Subsistence" is an awkward term that has been subjected to varying degrees of use, abuse, redefinition, and classification.[33] It has been worked and reworked for two reasons. One is the need to simplify and generalize for theorizing. The other is to establish some benchmark against which to measure a rural household or community as it changes over time.

The economist interested in the rural economic development of low-output nations must center his attention on the basic issue of production. Agricultural development is the movement of a farmer or a herder, or a community, or a society from a lower level of productivity to a higher (and usually more secure) level. Certainly in the numerous projects in which I have been involved in South America, the Middle East, and Africa, the core issue is indisputably the movement from a less efficient to a more efficient production technology.

Numerous other conditions are, of course, usually necessary to assist an improved technology of production, including roads, credit, marketing, and farmer training. But the goal underlying these activities is an enhanced or more varied output. To cite an earlier statement of mine on this theme, the core of development "is *not* the transfer from no money to money, no exchange to exchange, no market to market, though these institutional mechanics may attend the process."[34]

An improved production system is the central developmental issue regardless of the sector being examined—manufacturing or transport as well as agriculture. In any country in every line of economic activity, there is a spectrum with the least efficient at the one end (the clerk who adds columns of figures by hand, the porter who carries goods on his back, the farmhand who carries water to the fields), and the most efficient at the other (the clerk at a calculating machine, the driver of a five-ton truck, the farmer irrigating with a diesel pump). Those at the more informed and skilled

---

[33] See, for example, Mellor's book cited in note 14 and the Wharton book at note 5. Another highly useful volume is Bruce F. Johnston and Herman M. Southworth, eds., *Agricultural Development and Economic Growth* (Ithaca, N.Y.: Cornell University Press, 1967). The first two chapters, by the editors and Mellor, are particularly good for agricultural development problems and theories. See also Marvin P. Miracle, "'Subsistence Agriculture': Analytical Problems and Alternative Concepts," *American Journal of Agricultural Economics*, 50, no. 2 (1968), 292–310. Many of my own thoughts in the balance of this chapter were stimulated by Miracle's article and were contained in a reply to it in the November, 1969, issue of that journal.

[34] "The Economist and African Economic Development," *Revista di Politica Economica*, 5 (May, 1964), 9.

end of the spectrum are interested in and capable of using more advanced technology.[35]

The normal fabric of Western economic theorizing regarding development is geared to the use of particular aspects of these institutional mechanics. Our development models in the social sciences, for whole economies as well as for the agricultural sector (but apparently not for other sectors), divide their subjects into several pieces in terms of these institutional mechanics (dual-economy development theory, for example). The no money–money dichotomy, the noninvestment–investment dichotomy, the rural–urban dichotomy, the no market–market dichotomy, the nonindustrial–industrial dichotomy: all these are ways of looking at and attempting to formulate the development issue. Development is seen as the movement from one pole to the other. Uchendu has done this, for example, as we saw earlier. The trouble is that such models are terribly nonexclusive and nonscientific. Most importantly, however, they do not concentrate on the real sources and nature of sustained development. The heart of the matter is technological change.

The attempt to work with the concept of subsistence has been partly caught up, I think, in this general misdirection of our theorizing. We are trying gamely, as a profession interested in its theory, to work our way out of the theoretical box we find ourselves in. From collective practical experience, it is known that ongoing and continuous agricultural change comes with improved systems of production.[36] We *know* as a matter of record and experience, everywhere, that this essential improved technology requires more motivated and capable farmers.

Yet we are nervous because we also know that the theoretical tools provided by our several disciplines are inadequate to handle this basic knowledge, these fundamental *facts* of development in high-output *or* low-output agricultural communities.

The literature brings out clearly that there are several general meanings of the word subsistence, including particularly the level of consumption of the farming or herding family, the proportion of

---

[35] For further discussion see my "Technological Change, 'Dual Economy' Theory, and the Problem of Development," *Zeitschrift für Nationalökonomie*, 26, no. 4 (1966), 473–79, and "The Need for a 'Full Employment' Assumption in African Development Theorizing," *ibid.*, 22, no. 4 (1962), 361–67.

[36] This is not to deny that total output cannot be increased in the short run by bringing unused resources, particularly land and water where economically available, into use at constant levels of technology. But we are dealing with the longer run and with the need to double output, at least, over the next generation and quadruple it over the next 65 or 75 years.

the output that is marketed, and the percentage of total family or community income that is money. I submit that to use the term in these senses is utterly misleading, at least for theorizing. The development-policy implication of these interpretations into which our theorizing has led us is that of concentrating on monetizing these rural economies by increasing the share of output that is marketed.

The key point on which we should be concentrating—technological change—is thereby sidestepped. We are dealing with only the fringes of change and some of its qualities, not the basic causes of sustained rural development. Adam Smith enjoined us to extend the market to obtain specialization of production and increased productivity. That is fine, but you have to have something to market, and that comes from constantly improving production systems.

Certainly where I have been involved with rural development projects or conducted research, I have encountered many situations in which the percentage being marketed is going up while productivity and the standard of living are going down. Conversely, one continually finds cases where the standards of real per capita output and consumption are rising but the percentage of production that is marketed is going down.

I have studied and worked with examples of the former in central Sudan, the Khuzestan (Iran), in Colombia north of Bogotá in a number of Indian communities, in Kenya and Malawi, in Tanzania and Uganda, in Eastern Nigeria, and in the Ivory Coast. The usual pattern results from a falling total output per capita caused by such factors as declining soil fertility, smaller farm size, and erosion. The cash needs for nonfood items as well as for food in some cases require the sale of a roughly constant or even rising absolute volume of output. This is a progressively larger *share* of a falling total output, and per capita food supplies fall, often rather quickly where population growth is rapid. Crop mortgaging and credit systems worsen the problem; the farmer gets stuck in an insecure poverty groove for his lifetime. This process can be a vicious business, and it often leads to wage labor or even emigration, at least for some. Livestock societies in the Middle East and Africa experience a similar process, and it appears to be common elsewhere. Thus a generally accepted meaning of "subsistence" becomes rather the opposite of what it is supposed to be.

Conversely, there are numerous examples of improvements in the system of husbandry and the technology of food crop production leading to striking changes in the volume and diversity of food crops. Certainly more is often sold. But often the producing family consumes an even larger portion of the increase. Frequently the rate of change of improvements in food crop technology and output is greater than that for cash crops. This is particularly true in those many instances where change occurs *after* the cash crop systems are well established. At a higher overall level of farm output and living standards—with greater development, in other words—such a society, by the standard definition, has "regressed" to more of a "subsistence" level, for the proportion of output being used effectively to improve food crop consumption has increased. Here, too, one of the more normal meanings of "subsistence" turns out to be misleading.

In view of these problems of definition, should the word "subsistence" be used at all in our theorizing? The word could possibly be used in two cases. One is for some physiologically determined level and composition of consumption that barely sustains an average lifetime of x years. This could be a basic benchmark from which to measure development. But even the benchmark, whatever it is, would probably embrace some marketing and monetization. Secondly, the word could be used in a relative sense to describe the poorest farmers or herders in a region or nation, those with the lowest level of output or consumption or perhaps with the shortest life span. Such a level could be higher or lower than the equivalent in some other place.

But whatever is done with the word, the theoretical problem remains. A theoretical structure is still required that concentrates on a technological spectrum, not a money and market spectrum. Money and markets are meat, technology is the bone.

"Subsistence" will no doubt continue to be used by those who accept the idea that monetization and marketing are the guts of the development process. If they are not, then the usefulness of the concept is emasculated for theoretical purposes. This is not to deny that improved marketing facilities and the like are not critically important parts of an overall package of inducements to change. Like roads and all the other items on our lists, they permit. But what do they permit? Sustained growth of production, which is what development specialists are after.

Theoreticians should therefore be developing a theoretical structure that concentrates on the technology-of-production spectrum instead of spectra in such areas as marketing and monetization, which are related but tangential to the basic issue. If we accept this as a reasonable task, however, we must of course be ready to cope with the consequences for our entire theoretical structure. This writer certainly has not thought it all out yet. But if it is true that we really should be formulating development theories geared to a technological spectrum, what does this mean for all of our macro-level and sectorial development models based on these tangential factors? Our models, as indicated earlier, are based on two-sector dichotomies that are not only nonexclusive but are beside the point. Do we throw them out, or is our professional stake in them too great to permit this rejection?

SUMMARY

In summary, it seems to me that African rural development theories might concentrate on the following issues:

1. *We need to know more about the nature of technological change* and concentrate on theories and procedures to induce it. A number of geographers are doing some interesting work in this area.[37] We should develop theories not only consistent with the realities of the resources and proclivities of change agents but also compatible with the world view and resources of the farmer and herder.

2. *An inventory should be made of all the material available that could be used by theoreticians.* A foundation or some international agency could sponsor this effort. At the moment, as in other fields, each scholar attempting theoretical work has his own field locale, his own accumulation of material, his own set of colleagues on whom to try out ideas. The cumulative and increasing volume of material means that each of us, with the best will in the world, has only a small "piece of the elephant" that is getting proportionately smaller. Is there some way of centralizing pertinent data and studies?

3. I think Africanists also need some kind of *inventory of what is available in the way of general theory developed on a world basis or at least for other "third world" regions.* A fraction of it has been

---

[37] See, for example, Peter R. Gould, "Problems of Structuring and Measuring Spatial Changes in the Modernization Process: Tanzania 1920–1963" (paper prepared for the annual meeting of the American Political Science Association, Washington, September, 1968). See also his "Research Strategies for Rural Spatial Planning," paper submitted to *Canadian Journal of African Studies*, in which he asserts that, especially for a number of areas of concern to geographers such as the theory of central places, "research in Africa must be consciously directed towards theory building and theory testing" (p. 2). I agree. Philip W. Porter has assessed the pertinent geographical literature in his "Research Directions and Needs in African Rural Geography," *Rural Africana*, no. 6 (Fall, 1968), pp. 5–14. The entire issue is worth examining.

alluded to in this chapter. Presumably each theoretician tries to keep up with developments in his own field. That is difficult enough. But we know that a theory of rural development requires inputs from virtually all disciplines. Where can a person in one discipline go economically for a briefing in another?[38]

4. *Common meanings for words must be established.* The confusion is partly due to the problem of interdisciplinary communication. There are many points of confusion, as Walter Neale has pointed out.[39] In particular, he says, there is a confusion of rationality, of maximization with greed or gain, and of maximization with rationality. Is there some organized way we can "rationalize" word meanings so that we all talk the same language?

5. We need to devise the *rapid survey techniques* such as Scudder, Smock, and others are working on so that a planner or other change agent can, with some reliability, identify the areas with characteristics he seeks.

6. We need *basic, detailed benchwork studies* that can then be followed over time to test hypotheses constantly, to identify forces for change and resistance, and so on. The cases presented in this volume could help.

7. Finally, we must investigate more precisely *how African "tribal" societies differ from the "peasant" and usually less open societies of other areas* for which theoretical materials are more plentiful. To what extent can theoretical structures for other regions be used for policy-making in Africa?

Two concluding observations. First, it is worth remarking that much of the literature cited in this chapter is relatively new and rather informal. The sources are papers for meetings and conferences, or proceedings of such, or drafts of this and that—a rather undignified assortment of bits and pieces. One hopes that more of the theoretical writing will soon find more formal and integrated channels. The need to have it easily available is urgent.

Second, without wanting to appear acrimonious or cynical, a comment is in order regarding the effectiveness of Africanists. There are several thousand Africanists, mainly in academic and related institutions. In his or her own way, each uses research, publications, theorizing, for two purposes. One is to assist, directly or indirectly,

---

[38] This undoubtedly sounds naive. But my economist's attempt in recent years to become more multidisciplinary has been continually frustrated by the sheer difficulty of finding the right people and the appropriate material.

[39] Neale, see note 21.

African welfare. The other is to assist himself professionally. The second is understandable and appropriate. The first troubles me.

In spite of thousands of articles, books, projects, committees, and meetings, we apparently have not yet come to grips with the fundamentals. We seem to be paying lip-service to African development. To the extent that some of the concepts in this book are correct, we are still in the very rudimentary stages of even conceptualizing what the African development problem is.

We are even further away, as any practioner in the field can tell us, from identifying and solving the basic problems that preclude rising levels of welfare. Many communities even now are actually experiencing a *decline* in average welfare levels. Most Africanists analyze, theorize, conduct research, and publish on matters far removed from the fundamental issue. In a cumulative manner our financial and human resources contribute to the production of materials on African politicians, African art, African music, and so on. This is all good. But where are our priorities? Can we not, somehow, collectively, begin to devote a greater share of our resources to basic issues, such as to an examination of agricultural productivity?

CHAPTER 2

SOCIAL FACTORS AND FOOD PRODUCTION IN AN EAST AFRICAN PEASANT SOCIETY: THE HAYA

Priscilla Reining

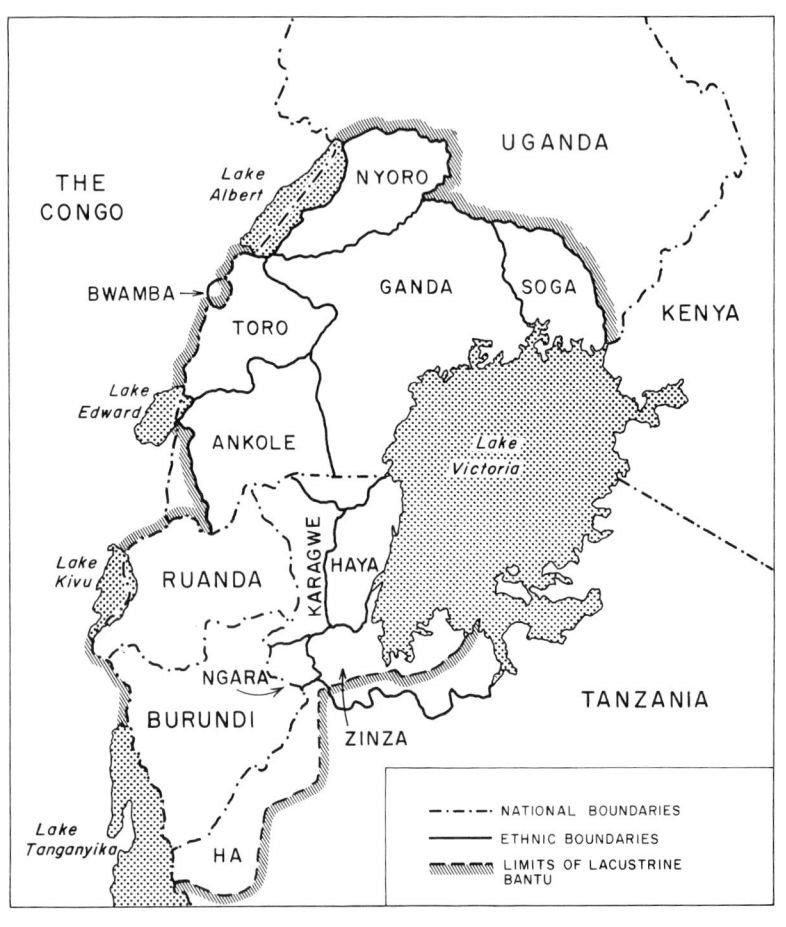

Haya Village Country in Relation to the Lacustrine Bantu.

INTRODUCTION

In attempting to apply universal standards to problems of food production in Africa, one must keep in mind that African societies are by no means all alike and that the peoples among them are not the uniform products of uniform processes. If we concentrate on the problems of the undernourished we may fail to ask whether any are well nourished and, if so, why. Here I shall examine in some detail both variations within, and the relative position of, an East African people whose intensive local food production enables them to participate in regionally organized networks of trade and specialization.

Two major regional concentrations of rural population occur in sub-Saharan Africa: the area west of the Cameroons and the region centering on the Lake Victoria basin, with an outpost in the Kenya highlands. Other isolated places of high density are found, but some are mountainous refuge areas and their isolation suggests a restriction of regional contacts uncharacteristic of the West African and Victorian regions.[1]

The Haya[2] living in Tanzania on the west coast of Lake Victoria form an example, in the statistical sense, of a concentrated rural population. We do not yet know enough about all such societies to say that the Haya are representative in a typological sense. Indeed, the political, economic, social, and religious systems of the different societies in these densely settled rural areas fall into different anthropological classifications. By these standards it is inherently impossible for Haya to be representative. A somewhat different approach, however, is to use the concept of a *peasant society,* which in my understanding imposes certain standards and ignores others.

Insofar as its agrarian regime of husbandry and tenure enables an individual to control the same piece of land through his lifetime

---

[1] Philip Porter, "East Africa—Population Distribution as of August 1962," *Annals of the Association of American Geographers,* vol. 56 (1966), Map Supplement Number 6; G. T. Trewartha and W. Zelinsky, "Population Patterns in Tropical Africa," *Annals of the Association of American Geographers,* 44 (1954), 135–62.

[2] Data on the Haya in this article were derived in 1951–53 and 1954–55 during my tenure as a Fellow of the East African Institute of Social Research and in 1967 from two Haya informants resident in Washington. Research in 1967 was undertaken with the aid of National Science Foundation grant No. GS–1421. This support is gratefully acknowledged. I am also indebted to the Joint Committee on African Studies of the American Council of Learned Societies and the Social Science Research Council for enabling me to participate in the conference on Competing Demands for the Time of Labor in Traditional African Societies before completion of this chapter.

and transmit an intact farm to someone else, Haya society is typically peasant. Based on sedentary agriculture, the peasant typology proposed by Barnes,[3] accepted by Redfield,[4] and incorporated by Wolf[5] is matched empirically by Haya data.[6] The typology includes: (1) a hierarchy of territorially based groups, consisting among the Haya of the village as a basic unit and aggregates of villages combined into several increasingly comprehensive territorial units; (2) the fields of economic specialization—trading, fishing, herding, lumbering—made possible by the nature of the agrarian system but independent of it; and (3) the countryside networks of relationships—prompted among the Haya by nonagricultural economic contacts, village exogamy, the dispersal of agnates among different villages because of tenure rules, and blood-brotherhood contracts between men of different villages.

If we typify Haya society as peasant[7] and imply that this in part results from its location in a region of concentrated rural population, the question that naturally follows is: How many societies in other, similar regions of Africa are also peasant, that is, largely self-contained but with significant economic and cultural regional contacts? In Wolf's book[8] a comprehensive answer may be found. The West African and Lake Victorian regions are among the major peasant regions of the world, the only two areas so specified in sub-Saharan Africa. The socioeconomic and demographic features coincide for what are undoubtedly self-reinforcing reasons.

In this chapter we are confined to Haya data and to contacts related to food production with others in the lake region. Domestic or household food production is supplemented in critically im-

[3] J. A. Barnes, "Class and Committees in a Norwegian Island Parish," *Human Relations*, 7 (1954), 39–58.

[4] Robert Redfield, *Peasant Society and Culture* (Chicago: University of Chicago Press, 1956), pp. 40–60.

[5] Eric Wolf, *Peasants* (Englewood Cliffs, N.J.: Prentice-Hall, Inc., 1966), pp. 41–48.

[6] Priscilla Reining, "The Haya: The Agrarian System of a Sedentary People" (Ph.D. diss., University of Chicago, 1967).

[7] In focusing on the significance of the sedentary character of residence and cultivation for a peasant society, I am ignoring for the moment the Redfield dichotomy of great tradition/little tradition applied as a standard by Fallers in his article in *Current Anthropology*, 2 (1961), 108–10. I distinguish among African cultivators and suggest that some are peasant in the Barnes typology and that others are not. Being a cultivator is not in itself a determining characteristic of peasantry. I agree with Fallers' observation that certain African societies, Ganda among them, were preconditioned or structured to embrace a greater "great tradition" when it came their way.

[8] *Peasants*, p. 2.

portant ways by the practice of occupational specialties. Fish, meat, milk, and even imported foods and spices are frequently available to supplement home output in nutritionally significant amounts.

In a Haya household, the labor contribution of members toward food production is made within the framework of domestic duties. These duties are divided along child-adult or male-female lines. But some of them must be done, and selection for such a task depends to some extent on availability. Others are optional. Haya distinguish between a duty (*mwoga*) and a job (*mulimo*), a distinction that corresponds quite closely to the division of domestic labor and the societal division of labor.

To analyze more closely the production system of the Haya, we shall proceed with a generalized estimate of the amount of time people expect to devote to cropping in a day or a year, an empirical examination of cropping in relation to the developmental phase of the family, the occupational specializations within a type village, and a more generalized summary of specialization and differentiation based on the Haya lexicon.

Haya villages are finely balanced ecosystems in an environment whose characteristics have been examined elsewhere.[9] Contiguous farms occur in areas called villages ranging from 40 to more than 1,000 acres. The remaining area consists of comparatively barren grassland used for pasturage and open-field cultivation of groundnuts and Bambara nuts. Within the villages, tree-crop cultivation dominated by bananas and coffee provides a vegetative environment for the cultivation of several minor crops, of which beans are probably the most significant. All villages are named, and historical documents dating from the early phases of European exploration make clear that Haya villages are remarkably stable in extent and site. The villages may well represent the conversion of natural patches of forest to the man-ordered "forest" of domestic tree crops. In one area of 33 villages, my field work provides an estimate of the ratio of village land to grassland of 30 to 70 percent. Aerial photographs make quite obvious the gross differences in vegetative cover between the banana villages and the grassland as well as the extensive present and previous cultivation in the grassland areas. An interim conclusion is that the cropping potential is intensively exploited in Haya country.

[9] Priscilla Reining, "Land Resources of the Haya," *Ecology and Economic Development in Tropical Africa*, ed. David Brokenshaw (Berkeley: Institute of International Studies, University of California, 1965), pp. 217–44.

DAILY AND ANNUAL SCHEDULES

Daily Schedules

Two adult Haya informants, a man and a woman, have given me generalized daily schedules. The schedules are estimates, not averages, derived from the empirical examination of a number of households. The main points accord, however, with numerous observations of Haya households in the course of field work. Each informant described the events of an ordinary day. The variations in domestic duties required for household maintenance are excluded, and the occupational specialities will be considered later.

Since the Haya live near the equator, the length of their days and nights are virtually the same throughout the year. Their clock hours conform to the day-night division so that 7:00 A.M. is "hour 1" of sunlight and 7:00 P.M. is "hour 1" of the evening, an adaptation by no means unique to the Haya. As a strictly equatorial people, the Haya convert the universal facts of sunrise and sunset into an equally reliable abstract standard of time. The readiness with which Haya have converted the anchor points of their daily routine into clock hours suggests a previously well-established schedule of activities keyed to the position of the sun and recurring at a more or less fixed time every day. The possession and frequent use of clocks and wrist watches underscores the degree to which Haya are accustomed to a regular device (formerly the sun) for timing daily activities.

Both of the adult informants had unmarried children in their households. Developmental phases in the family are discussed below.

A Man's Daily Schedule

The schedule was given to me by an informant as "A man's day in the past." To qualify and update the schedule to the time of the field work, it is presented here with my commentary.

Schedule	Commentary
He wakes about 6:30.	Because the Haya country lies between 1 and 2 degrees of the equator, hours of daylight and dark are equally divided and vary little throughout the annual cycle. Every day of the year naturally begins close to the same clock hour.
He washes his face 6:40.	

Schedule	Commentary
He visits his wife and children in his second house to see if they are well.	True polygyny is relatively rare, only 1 man in 20 having 2 wives, but where it does occur different wives and their children live on separate farms, either in the same village or in a nearby one.
He returns to house no. 1 about 7:15.	
He goes to the capital to greet his Mukama (hereditary ruler) and comes back about 9:00.	The seat of the Mukama is usually too distant for this to be feasible. But to go to greet the nearest chiefly official and to attend him is quite appropriate, especially if one is resident in that village.
He takes his two cows out of the stable and removes ticks from their skins. It is now 9:35.	One householder in 3 keeps cattle.
He takes his two cows at 9:45 and hands them over to his neighbor, who will tend the village herd for this day. It is 10:30 when he comes back.	This is about the time the herd goes to pasture, unless it is raining hard. The master herder selects who is to do the daily herding.
He eats roasted bananas brought on a tray by his wife.	The banana is a special one prepared only by roasting.
He erects his fence till 11:50, when he comes back.	
He goes to a beer party at his neighbor's and comes back at 12:30.	The principal ingredient in the beer is the beer banana, fermented with a previously prepared millet paste. To participate in neighborly activities is integral to village life. Ostracism, though rare, is real and effective.
The family has lunch at 1:00 P.M., followed by a nap.	Lunch is usually prepared from the cooked fruit of the plantain together with beans and a sauce.
At 2:30, he takes his weaned calf to a furrowed patch of land near a farm to feed, for she is not big enough to graze in a village herd.	Calving rates are low, and few householders have calves. Approximately 1 animal in 4 is immature, and they are correspondingly valued.

Schedule

At 3:15, he goes to his plantation to see if there is anything worth attention, that is, pulling unwanted suckers from plantain, transplanting young palms at a place fit for a palm, and cutting down long leaves from plantain quite close to his *mushonge* (thatch) hut, for they disturb the thatch when blown about by wind and cause leaking when the rains come.

At 4:30, he comes back a tired man. He has beer in his calabash to refresh himself and "bathes" (rub his body with a wet, fibrous, sisal-like inside stem of a banana palm).

His wife brings in the calf about 5:45; the husband while busy in the plantation has pulled some climbing grass for the calf to eat at night and the following morning.

He goes to the open land near the village, meets a village herdsman, returns, picks his two cows from the advancing herd, and returns home. It is now 6:35.

At dark, he places his door in the doorway after securing the stable.

At 6:55, his neighbor comes in. They have a men-only talk in the outer room while the children and his wife are around the fireplace, supposedly not listening in.

At 8:25 the neighbor leaves, and the man talks to his wife and dozing children, who have been listening to their mother's fairy tales and riddles.

He has his own share of roasted maize; his wife and children ate theirs while he was talking to his

Commentary

Cultivation is a continuing process.

Stall feeding of animals is an occasional alternate to open-land grazing.

Cattle are stalled within the house or immediately next to the house in a fenced enclosure.

Haya houses are large enough to be divided into 6 or 8 rooms, depending on style.

Families are small in size and many households have no young children. Most frequently a household consists of 3 persons. But a wife and other female relatives and children will sit separately and chat.

Schedule	Commentary
neighbor. It is close to 9:00. After eating, he scrubs his teeth with the cobs, one of the ways of brushing teeth.	
At 9:35 the family has its evening meal.	For this meal the main ingredient is also cooked plantain, served with a meat or fish sauce. Neighborly conviviality is confined to talk and to sharing beer. Meals are never routinely shared with neighbors.
They go to sleep about 10:00 P.M. until next morning if not disturbed by their barking dog or a neighborhood alarm to which the man must give his attention. If a journey to visit a distant relative was planned during the day, the man will awake at the second cock-crow and set out on this journey.	If a fire breaks out or a leopard is seen, response to an appeal for help is very nearly mandatory. Failure to attend may lead to an assumption of disinterest or of intent to harm by supernatural means. Those who live closest to the place where trouble occurs are under the strongest compulsion to attend. It is also important for a chiefly official to come so that he may take appropriate action and be able to report what happened.

A Woman's Daily Schedule

Schedule	Commentary
She wakes up at 6:30.	
At 6:35, she washes her face, arms, legs, and mouth. She collects twigs from coffee trees to rekindle fire.	
At 7:15, she gives children cooked plantain.	In serving the evening meal a portion of cooked plantain is saved for use the following morning. The plantain is wrapped in a piece of banana leaf used to cover the plantain during cooking, and the parcel is kept overnight beside the ashes of the fire.
At 7:30, she puts roasting banana, sweet potato, or manioc on the fire to roast. The children go to school.	
At 7:45 she is tidying the house.	

Schedule

She goes to cultivate at 8.00. If cultivating at home in the village, the children not in school play near the house or in the forecourt. If away and if she has a neighbor with children, she will leave the children with her neighbor.

She gives children a snack at 10:00 and also the husband if he is at home. If he is away, she takes cattle to the herder.

She goes to get water at 10:15.

She starts to cook lunch at 11:00.

By 11:30 she is going back and forth between house and farm.

At 12:00, she goes to peel plantain from stalk brought by husband.

At 12:15, she mixes plantain and beans or fish and covers pot.

She prepares banana juice and washes everything at 12:20.

She cuts fresh banana leaves for serving at 1.00. The children and her husband come home. The wife serves plantain and sauce, giving everybody his share.

At 1:30 she gathers banana leaves and other remains and puts them out as mulch.

At 2:00 she rests a little.

She goes to greet neighbors at 2:30 or cuts grass, washes clothes, goes shopping, or helps husband pick coffee.

She goes for water at 5:30.

At 6:00 she starts to cook.

Commentary

Women are responsible for all phases of the open-land cultivation of Bambara nuts and groundnuts; they weed in the home farm and cultivate beans and maize there as well.

If there are girls in the household, they help with water-carrying.

If beans are to be cooked, the fire is started with whole pieces of wood.

There is quite a lot of variation in the afternoon depending on the season and what the family is planning to do.

If they had beans for lunch, they will have a different kind or some

Schedule   *Commentary*

	other dish with the evening meal. If they have too much meat for the evening meal, they dry it for later. But if they had meat for lunch, they may reheat the remainder for dinner.
Around 6:30 she peels plantain, washes or bathes the children, with husband brings in anything that has been used outside or has been drying outside.	
At 7:30 they pray (if Catholic).	
They eat the evening meal at 9:00. The children are put to bed. She gathers everything.	
She goes to bed at 10:00.	The evening trash is kept in the house until morning.

My reading of these schedules, and my memory of Haya daily routine, suggest that the Haya day is composed of five blocks of time: the early and late morning, the early and later afternoon, and the evening hours until bedtime. At 10:00 A.M. and at 4:30 or 5:00 P.M. both men and women expect to shift their activity. Meals serve as other time counters to break up the day or to signal change in activity. Men and women expect to devote only one of these blocks of time to cropping activities, but some cropping or maintenance activity is seen as part of the general routine every working day in the year.

Men combine approximately two hours of time spent in cropping activity with time devoted to domestic and local affairs. The fact that most men consider their job to be something other than that of cultivator does not appear in the schedule, which is concerned only with the division of domestic labor.

Women combine work in cultivating with housework, child care and securing water. The most burdensome part of their day, or at least the one about which complaints were most often heard, is water-carrying. In the generalized schedule it is worth noting that more than an hour is spent carrying water, compared with two hours for cultivation.

Although these data are generalized, men and women expect to spend no more than two hours a day in cropping activity. It is also worth noting that men and women alternate working in the farm and perform different tasks.

Annual Labor Budget

The annual time budget follows some basic facts of Haya existence and the adaptive requirements of their cropping system. Both day-to-day and long-term scheduling are strongly influenced by their reliance on tree crops and by prevailing weather conditions—the trees because they require continuing if intermittent maintenance, and the weather because the climate is wet. Heavy and frequent rain curtails outdoor activity while ensuring the feasibility of tree crops as the main prop of their subsistence economy. The partial or total loss of more than one day in three to rain qualifies any attempt to measure the time spent on cropping. In the subcounty of Muhutwe, the number of rainy days over a ten-year period averaged 130 annually. The Haya commonly see the variation in rainfall distribution as an annual cycle of a heavy rainy season, a dry season, another short rainy season, and another dry season. The cycle moderates but does not preclude cyclical variation in some activities.

Annual cropping activities of men and of women as well as average monthly rainfall are summarized in Figure 1. It is fortunate that the detailed rainfall data available to me are from a rainfall station, Kawalinda (in the subcounty of Muhutwe), experiencing the modal annual rainfall for Haya country of 64 inches, or 1,624.4 millimeters. The western boundary of Haya country coincides with the 40-inch isohyet, and the rainiest part of the district receives 80 inches on the average.[10]

Some of the allocation of time to different activities on the part of men and women depends on the season. Figure 1 shows how the marketing of coffee coincides with the onset of dry weather. Similarly, women prepare open-field plots during the drier weather and plan to plant when the rainfall increases.

Day-to-day decision-making, however, depends on an appreciation of actual weather conditions. Each man works for himself on his own farm, unless he has a tenant (from whom he may, in fact, get some assistance, although it is no longer due a landholder) or a servant. Men manage their own plantain and expect to prune, mulch, and harvest their own coffee. Women also plant their crops

---

[10] David McMaster, "Change of Regional Balance in the Bukoba District of Tanganyika," *Geographical Review*, 50 (January, 1960), 79.

FIGURE 1
Annual cropping activities of Haya and average monthly rainfall

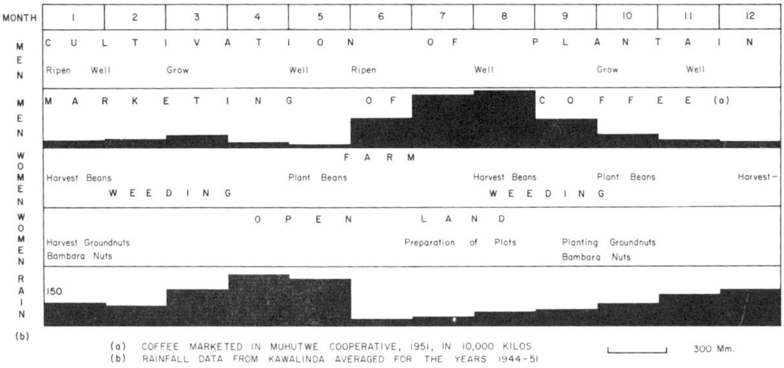

(a) COFFEE MARKETED IN MUHUTWE COOPERATIVE, 1951, IN 10,000 KILOS
(b) RAINFALL DATA FROM KAWALINDA AVERAGED FOR THE YEARS 1944-51

of beans and corn on their husband's farm (among the stalks of the plantain and coffee). Cooperative work is neither expected nor performed.

Open-land or grassland activity, however, is different. Women work side by side in preparing plots for groundnuts and Bambara nuts. Planting is also done cooperatively; the women say that this ensures each other's company at harvest time. The open land provides pasture for cattle, and the herding is done cooperatively under the village's master herder. Further cooperation is necessary to control the burning of patches of the open land. The rationale is that the cover of inedible grass and dried grass must be removed before the women plant, lest fire damage the patches of groundnuts, and before the onset of the short rains promotes the growth of new grass.

The farm and the village look much the same throughout the year, the only readily noticeable difference being the presence of beans in their time. Because the ideal Haya farm contains plantain in all stages of growth, a characteristic of plantain cultivation is that all phases are practiced simultaneously and continuously. Selecting a sucker to supplant the parent banana tree, pruning, planting new suckers, weeding, manuring, and harvesting can be performed on any single day, and some or all of these operations must be practiced at intervals through the year. The cycle inherent in the Haya observation that plantain grows well in the rainier months and ripens well in the drier months notwithstanding, rainy-season cultivation includes harvesting and dry-season cultivation includes the pruning and selection of suckers, practices crucial to Haya ideas of good management. When the bean plants are still young, considerable care must be taken not to injure them and women who have planted them enjoin everyone to be careful.

A basic substratum of the Haya cropping system is the small but continuing time necessary for the cultivation of plantain. I repeat this because the Haya see it as crucial to farm management, the value of the farm, and the significance of tenure. The usual residence on the farm gives Haya the immediate proximity that makes such cultivation relatively easy.

In view of the competition for the cropping time of the cultivator, one must assume that the basic farm is maintained with a time input of somewhere between five and ten hours a week per individual. This assumes that each active male and female adult puts in two hours each working day. Whether one wants to calculate on a five-day or a six-day working week will, of course, affect the arithmetical result. Christian Haya now certainly consider Sunday to be a day to go to church, which involves a fairly lengthy bicycle ride or walk for many, and many Haya take the time to attend the weekly market held on successive days in different subcounties. At the same time, Haya follow their own judgments about when to do farm work and can be seen doing farm work on Sunday or market day, though they may not be working on some other day of the week. Of course, non-Christians regard Sunday as they do any other day.

The remaining work hours in the week are available for seasonally oriented activities such as harvesting coffee (for men) and open field and annual crops (for women) and for other occupations.

CROPPING IN RELATION TO THE DEVELOPMENTAL PHASE OF THE FAMILY

Types of Farms

The system of husbandry among the Haya involves a number of major components. By definition, a farm in a village must have a stand of plantain, for this is basic to the usage of the word *farm*. The other components are beans, coffee trees, and cattle. They are optional and may occur singly or together in addition to the plantain. Since a full complement of crops and cattle obviously is a more ample resource base than just a stand of plantain and variation in these components is common, an attempt has been made to correlate variations with the social characteristics of farm occupants.

Haya villages come in two sizes: villages and large villages. Large villages have an expanse of 1,000 acres or more and are much less common than villages. Figure 2 represents a Haya village of 55 farming units almost exactly 100 acres with a resident population of 194. This village, which I call Kianja, is used here as a type village. As in all other Haya villages, the farms are in a cluster; each is labeled in figure 2 to indicate the person exercising the primary right to control each farm at the time of the study. In general, Haya farms are occupied by one small household, and the customary arrangement is for each small farm to have a residence.

With beans, coffee, and cattle as the main variable components on farms where plantain is the basic food crop, farms may be readily classified in relation to the presence or absence of the variable components. Five categories emerged: farms with plantain only, farms with other food crops of which beans are considered the most significant, farms with coffee trees, farms with coffee and beans, and farms with all components. Using this classification, the farms of Kianja showed the following distribution. Five farms were under minimal cultivation with plantain only. Seven farms grew no coffee and kept no cattle, although some few food crops were cultivated. Five other farms had a few coffee trees, though the production was on the low end of the range, and no food crops. Of the remaining farms, 21 fulfilled what the Haya normally think of as the usual complement of coffee, plantain, and intermixed food crops, and 17 had a maximum resource base with the addition of cattle. There are 57 separate farms; however, taxpayers number 7 and number 23 each have two farms within the village. Hence the number of farming units is 55, the number of farms, 57.

The last two groups represented most of the village in acreage and in population. Figure 2 illustrates in variable shading the distribution of farms in each category.

I am describing the distribution of types of husbandry in one cropping year. Theoretically, any farm could be in any condition of cultivation depending on its owners' resources and plans. However, this statement can be made only in the context of a Haya permanent holding or a farm which already displays a minimum vegetative condition and carries the potential for more intensive cropping. The classification can be examined for the degree of correspondence implicit in the customary allocation between adult men and women of the right to grow certain crops and the presence of men and women in the several domestic groups. A clear-cut dichotomy exists in the domestic division of labor between men, who are responsible for and have the right to the tree crops, and women, whose gardening activities center on the annual crops grown on the farms and on the open land.

Family Phase and Type of Farm

In the abstract, every human family carries the potential of a developmental career beginning with the marriage and concluding with the death of the partners. Fortes has formulated a descriptive classification of the several phases of family development. Because the position of the minor heir is prominent in Haya society, I have added a premarriage phase to those suggested by him.[11] Thus the phases I use are: premarriage, that is, the potential family of the heir of minor age; early marriage and expansion; dispersion, as children marry; and replacement, as the heir's family replaces that of his parents during their lifetime. Nearly all households in Kianja may be classified as to the familial status of its members, though some households did not form families and for these a residual category is necessary.

In a society where residency, in the sense of household composition, is oriented to the single, adult male, Haya expect the ratio to be: a farm: a house: a household: a family. It is also assumed that the man will be of taxpaying age. In fact, in Kianja village, the 59 taxpayers, 57 farms, 54 houses, 53 households, and members of 71 different families achieved the anticipated ratio in 22 instances only. An analysis of the Haya data suggests that the number of social or resource units depends to a considerable extent on what one selects to count—farm or house, household or family. The problems the analyst encounters in finding one standard for enumeration, reflected here precisely in the data for Kianja, may in fact be resolved because they reflect the principles appropriate to the operation of farms as cropping units, the use of farms as house sites, the variable character of households as domiciliary units, and finally the developmental character of the families as social groups.

Among Kianja villagers, the family phase of development in relation to husbandry components may be found in Table 1. The family phase of the 54 persons in charge of farms, whether present or absent, was surveyed. The status of his dependents determines the phase of development, and since a Haya woman can never be the head of a family, those who are in charge of farms in this village are in the category "other." I wish to bypass the problem of tenure through use of the phrase "person in charge." The enumeration was complicated by the presence in the village of one complex where

[11] Meyer Fortes, "Introduction," in *The Developmental Cycle in Domestic Groups*, ed. Jack Goody (Cambridge: At the University Press, 1962), pp. 4–6.

A Haya family.

Harvesting and winnowing Bambara nuts.

Washing and hulling coffee cherries.

House builders.

TABLE 1

Phase of Family Development in Relation to Major Components of Husbandry

Components of Husbandry	Number in Each Phase				
	Pre-marriage	Marriage Expansion	Dispersion	Replacement	Other
Plantain only	3			1	1
Plantain and beans		5		1	1
Plantain and coffee	1	2	1		1
Plantain, beans, and coffee	3	13	3		2
All components		8	3	3	3

three farms, four taxpayers, four families, and three households in no instance coincided in farm, house, household, or family—and yet where all lived, cultivated, and cohabited, following ways Haya consider proper.

If we take the potential family as being in the first phase of development of a domestic group, the unoccupied farms D, E, and G were in this group in Kianja.[12] In most families, young men pass through this phase while their father is still alive. A separate phase or category enables us to distinguish between replacement and the special position of the primary heir who has yet to come of age. The farms lacked houses and were under minimal cultivation. Caretaker cultivation was done by relatives, friends, or even the young man himself. In two other farms, A and 51, the owners were also immature, but the farms were inhabited; relatives cared for both the children and the farms as the children grew. The relatives were not construed as family heads but rather as caretakers for the child and his heritage. For example, the farm belonging to A, a ten-year-old boy living with his mother's mother, had beans and other crops planted by the grandmother, and a few coffee trees remained as well. On Farm 51, a young girl whose parents had died lived with her father's mother's sister, while on Farm B an unmarried tenant had been installed to care for a farm inherited by a minor. These adults were all cultivating a fuller complement of crops than was done on the occupied farms. Finally, Farm 42, belonging to a young man yet to be married, had some coffee trees on it.

[12] Portions of the following presentation on phases of the family developmental cycle have previously appeared in Reining, "Land Resources."

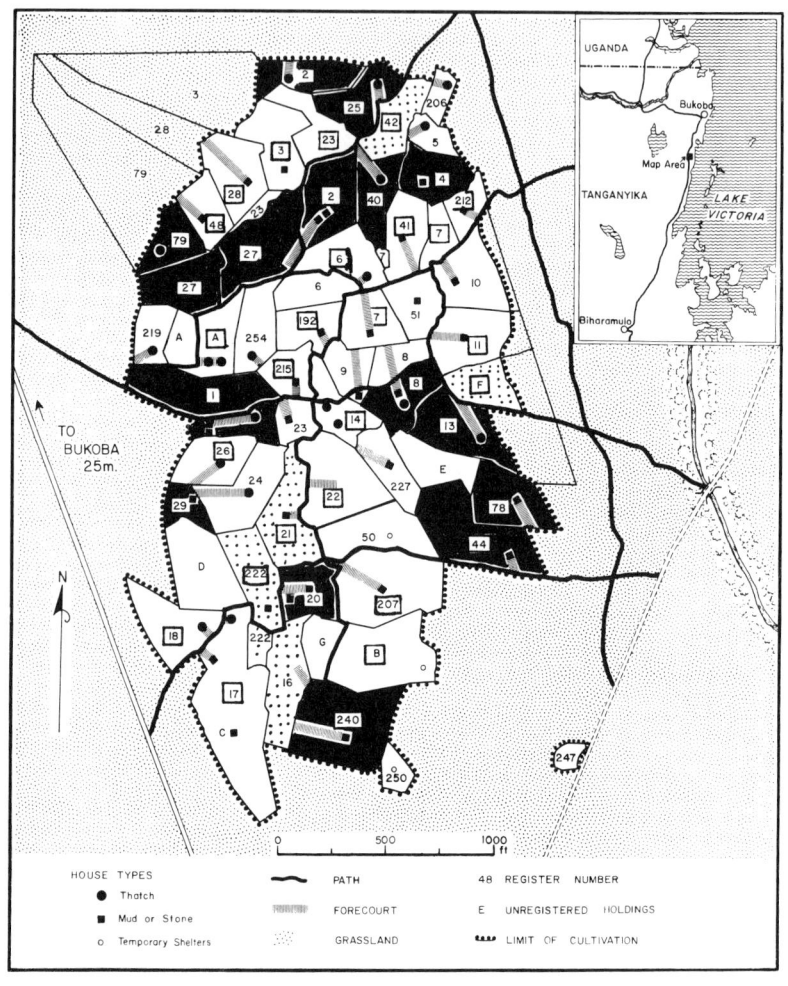

FIGURE 2
Variation in the components of husbandry in Kianja village

Figure 2. Variation in the components of husbandry in Kianja village

The unoccupied farms are both a test of the system of husbandry—for they were under caretaker cultivation for as much as ten years without occupancy—and an indicator of the viability of concepts of tenure, for even in a situation of land scarcity the rights of the minor primary heir were respected.

In this society, a first marriage takes place for a man when he is in his twenties, and for most young women in their late teens, and children are few. Twenty-five years or more may elapse following marriage before a couple has a son of marriageable age. For this reason the period of early marriage and expansion in the developmental cycle is a broad category, and most of the families in this village (and others) were found in this category. A bride is secluded in her husband's parents' house for several months after the wedding, and during this period she does not perform household chores but rather receives domestic services and depends, with her husband, on others. No houses, or at best temporary shelters, are found on their farms. Subsistence comes from the family of the groom's parents, supplemented by food gifts to the bride from visitors. The symbol of each gift is the banana-leaf ring, used for the headload, left on a stake outside the house where the bride is living. The accumulated rings, which number as many as 200, give an immediate index not only of the status of the bride but of the subsistence goods it takes to maintain such a new household. The young families in Kianja where the bride was still in seclusion were those who lived on farms F, 222, 250, and 231 (who lived with 17 and is counted there). Their farms had plantain, few or no coffee trees, and no additional food crops. The very small farm numbered 247 belonged to a man whose young wife had left, an action perhaps indicative of the status of his attempt to bring into cultivation a plot near the edge of the village. A newly married woman does not take up normal tasks of household duty and cultivation until after she formally comes out of seclusion and until after the birth of her first child if she has been fortunate enough (in the eyes of Haya) to become pregnant while still a secluded bride.

In reporting the belief that if a mature coffee tree dies the owner of the farm would have a similar fate, Rehse suggested that it led to some reluctance on the part of young men to grow coffee.[13] At the time of my field work this belief did not figure as an explicit reason for not growing coffee. Coffee was grown much less frequently among the young, however, and was uniformly grown by

[13] Herman Rehse, *Kiziba Island und Leute* (Stuttgart: Verlag von Strecker & Schröder, 1910), p. 59.

older men occupying their own farms. Farms 219, 250, 254, and C, where food crops were grown but no coffee, were all occupied by tenants whose marital condition placed them in the early-marriage phase of the developmental cycle. Their wives cultivated the annual food crops. The lack of coffee was a matter of arrangement between landholder and tenant. Farm 50 was held by a woman tenant who grew beans and other crops such as sweet potatoes but no coffee.

Families with growing but still unmarried children are properly in the expansion phase of development, and more farms in this village were occupied by families of this type than of any other. All of the families in this phase were cultivating beans and other food crops in addition to plantain, and most were growing coffee as well, as may be seen in Table 1. Although the prevailing marital pattern among the families in this phase is monogamy, a number of men had tried to keep two wives on a single farm. In this circumstance, however, the polygynous household does not have much continuity. Two of the men in this phase of familial development, who also grew coffee, were partners to polygynous marriage. The man with register number 23 was building a second house for his wife and children on the northern farm, while his more recent second wife was to live in the central one. The owner of Farm 207 had one wife residing on that farm and a second wife in a neighboring village. Finally, a number of men who were married but whose children were as yet unmarried were making maximum use of their cropping units by keeping cattle as well. All of these men were monogamous, and each wife was living with her husband on his farm.

By definition, the man whose children are of marriageable age is himself mature. The parish chief, who lived in this village of his parish and was a partner to a polygynous marriage, was in this phase of development. The few other men who were in this phase of development were similar in having monogamous marriages, sons living in the village, and farms cultivated with coffee and food crops. Several had cattle as well. Their farms were relatively large. Only one man was an exception, and of him it was said he was "bounded on all sides by sadness"—that is, a social outcast. He was later accused of witchcraft. Not surprisingly, his farm, which he was forced to abandon, was in very poor condition with no additional food crops. Even though he returned from time to time, he had very low returns on his remaining coffee trees.

Very few men are in the replacement phase of the development cycle, for, by definition, no children (or at most one) remain in the household as minors. The average age of men in this group was seventy-four. One of them was an elderly widower, and his farm had only plantain on it. Such a person is called by a term meaning "lonely," since he has no one with him in his old age. Because he had a son, he was not without an heir, but the condition of his farm reflected the lack of the crops usually grown by a woman. The other members of this group were still complete families, with adult women. The farms were fully cultivated, and the men kept cattle as well.

Older single persons of either sex and adult women who have minor children in their care do not form families, in Haya eyes, even though they maintain a household. One older woman had recently married for the second time and was the wife of a wealthy man whose principal domicile was with another wife in a different village. The variation in the components of husbandry found in these households was as disparate as the household arrangements—from minimal to maximal.

The domestic unit composed of a mature man with one wife is best suited to maximum cultivation of a farm under Haya techniques of husbandry and division of domestic labor. No entire society consists solely of persons who are physically and socially mature, and the Haya are no exception.

OTHER FACTORS AFFECTING CROPPING PATTERNS

In addition to the developmental phase of the family, at least two other factors may be examined to determine whether variation in cropping-unit components can be related to known social factors: size of farms and traditional restrictions on cattle ownership.

Size of Farm

The size of farms with plantain only varied considerably in Kianja village. The unoccupied farms were somewhat below average in size at 1.4 acres, when the average size is taken at 1.9 rounded off to 2.0 acres. Occupied farms were numbers 10 and 247, the first very close to the average size, the last the smallest farm of all at 0.3 acre. Farms with beans and plantain were above average in size at 2.2 acres, although at least one, number 206, was very small at 0.5 acre. Farms with coffee but no beans were only slightly below average size at 1.8 acres, and none of these were especially small. The remaining farms varied in size from 0.7 to 4.8 acres, the latter being the largest in the village. These data suggest that, above a certain point, size is probably not a very decisive factor in vegetative components, though the very smallest farms were probably below the minimal size for a successful cropping unit. The point of viability appears to be one acre. When negotiations are under way for a marriage, the prospective bride's parents must be satisfied in person or by the go-between that the would-be bridegroom's farm is large enough to support a family.

Cattle and Haya Society

As will be seen below, the presence of cattle apparently affects farm productivity, and social factors influencing the keeping of cattle are thus very relevant to our subject. Among the Haya in the 1950's, cattle were prized for their manure and milk products, and the indigenous herds were kept for these purposes. The demand for meat was met through slaughter cattle imported from Sukuma country, south of the lake. Local animals were not sold to commercial butchers at auction, as the Sukuma cattle were. The latter were never incorporated into village herds, for the Sukuma cattle were bound to die from trypanosomiasis infection acquired during the journey, and the Haya for this reason were unable to replenish their meager herds. Furthermore, Haya cattle were Sanga in type, with large horns and no hump, while Sukuma cattle were Zebu, with small horns and a distinct hump. The Haya readily sort animals according to such types. Although cattle trading existed before the arrival of Europeans, the Sukumaland slaughter-cattle trade is a post-European development.[14]

Stanley's observation in 1875 of many cattle in the vicinity of the villages supports Haya tradition of many more animals in pre-European and early European times before rinderpest reduced the herds, although favorable market conditions after the turn of the century may have induced Haya to sell a disproportionately large share of cattle.[15]

The phrase "Hamitic hypothesis" is used by anthropologists to subsume references to a relationship between cattle proprietorship and political domination and between both and the formation of the state. A version of the Hamitic hypothesis is found in the early

[14] V. C. R. Ford, *The Trade of Lake Victoria* (Kampala, Uganda: East African Institute of Social Research, 1955), p. 17.
[15] Henry Stanley, *Through the Dark Continent* (London: Sampson Low, Marston, Searle & Rivington, Ltd., 1890), pp. 143, 21; Ford, *Trade of Lake Victoria*, p. 21.

literature of the Haya. Traditionally, Haya society had consisted of a ruling dynasty and three other groups: (1) herders known as *Hima*; (2) clans that had daughters married to reigning members of the ruling dynasty, which required elevation of the clan's status to what was called *Nfura*; and (3) the remainder of the population born to *Bairu* clans. *Bairu,* colloquially translated as "cultivators" or "peasants," can also be translated as "slaves" or "menials" and tends now to be a term of oppobrium. The Hima herders had a legendary attachment to cattle and were responsible for animals belonging to members of the ruling dynasty, who themselves did no herding; Rehse believed the association between Hima and cattle dated from ancient times.[16] In the 1950's, Hima were not found in Haya village country except very occasionally; the ruling dynasty continued, with curtailed powers under the directives of the colonial administration, though membership in the ruling dynasty continued to carry meaning vis-à-vis the nonruling groups; and the distinction between Nfura and Bairu seemed to have small day-to-day significance.

The conventional view presumed by the Hamitic hypothesis of Haya being segregated according to occupational category—ruler, herder, cultivator—finds little support from an empirical investigation of cattle keeping in the village country. Although rulers (*Bakama*) maintained "capitals," cultivators and herders were indistinguishable as such, for men were cultivators with cattle and cultivators without cattle. Each cattle-keeper (the word is used here broadly to mean the person having day-to-day jurisdiction over the animal, and the question of formal ownership is bypassed) provides shelter for his animals during the night and in rainy weather, usually in a room of his house or occasionally in an enclosure next to it. The separation of the animals from the villages of their owners does not now figure as part of Haya animal husbandry.

All the animals kept in any one village more or less automatically make up the village herd. The herding is under the management of the master herder, who decides each day who is to do the work. As may be seen in the daily schedule, grazing and watering are accomplished during the eight hours between midmorning and dusk, and pasturage may be supplemented with some stall feeding. Manure is, of course, available for use on the farm, and some Haya say they keep cattle for the manure, relegating other aspects of ownership to insignificance.

[16] *Kiziba,* Foreword.

Any thorough consideration of the Haya village as an ecosystem should include an appreciation of the role of cattle manure in the maintenance of crop trees and the role of dairy products in the people's nutrition. Because animals are pastured outside the villages and quartered inside, they enrich the village without relying on village sources for sustenance.

In Kianja, data are available on cattle keeping and membership in the traditional social divisions. Five of the sixteen men keeping cattle belonged to the Hinda ruling dynasty (as it was in the 1950's) and the remainder were non-Hinda and also non-Hima. However, four other Hinda in the village had no cattle, and neither did other men who belonged to non-Hinda descent groups. The lack of any very clear relationship between cattle keeping and membership in the ruling dynasty corresponds to findings from other villages and to the readily available opinion that anyone can own or keep an animal.

In Table 1, where the developmental phases of families are analyzed we see that no young men had cattle while at least half of the older men in the village did. Like the other components of husbandry, cattle keeping appears to relate to family style.

Relation of Family and Farm

The match between state of cultivation and developmental type of family is close to the essence of what the anthropologist means by *subsistence economy* in that the state of the subsistence unit is adaptive to the requirements of the social unit. The match is more sharply apparent where the cropping unit has a continuity greater than the life and family cycle of an individual than it is, where the nucleus of a herd is maintained elsewhere or where uncultivated land is held awaiting a young man's marriage.

It should also be noted that a cropping unit may be brought up to full cultivation or down to a lower level in the course of a season or two and is not bound to a person's line of development. The Haya data also suggest that occupational differentiation and the utilization of cash cropping do not necessarily disturb the match between the subsistence unit and the social unit. The analysis does suggest, however, that there is a point above which sedentary residence and relatively high density of population allow differentiation to proceed much more readily than under shifting residence and low population density.

The reverse of the proposition that the cropping unit is adaptive to the state of the social unit is that the availability of a cropping unit affects the nature or composition of the family unit. The specifics of family composition relate to the specifics of the cropping unit, as we have seen, and the more general characteristics of Haya families relate to farm availability. In the Haya system, a man may not contract a second marriage unless he has a second farm. Thus, most Haya men are monogamous, although when they own another farm they frequently take another wife.

PRODUCTIVITY

In commercial farm production, the cropping unit is thought to bear a predictable relationship to inputs per acre—labor, fertilizer, and seed—irrespective of the cultivator's developmental phase. But in the Haya form of mixed subsistence and commercial cropping, the farm unit as analyzed here does bear a predictable relationship to the nature of the cultivator's household. It also appears that the nature of the domestic group influences the commercial production as well.

The nutrient requirements of the Haya system's major crop components are complementary. Rather than depleting the soil, the mixture of crops helps keep it fertile. In particular the beans are an asset, since under the Haya cropping system they supply at least some of the nitrogen required by the plantain.[17]

Beck did an economic study of Chagga farms on the slopes of Mt. Kilimanjaro where plantain and coffee were the principal crops but where soils were volcanic in origin and beans were planted elsewhere. He compared the farms where coffee and plantain were interplanted with those where they were cultivated separately. While the yields per acre of plantain and coffee were higher when separate, the interplanted crops had a higher combined value per acre, suggesting that the coffee and plantain have complementary nutrient requirements.[18]

A reliable estimate of productivity is hard to obtain, since it depends on quantitative measurements largely beyond the capacity of the investigator. But the map of the type village does provide reliable measurements of farm acreage that may be used for an assessment of productivity. The only crop production figures obtainable

---

[17] William O. Jones, *Manioc in Africa* (Stanford, Calif.: Stanford University Press, 1959), p. 18.
[18] Roy Beck, *An Economic Study of Coffee-Banana Farms in the Machama Central Area Kilimanjaro District, 1961* (Dar es Salaam: USAID, 1963), pp. 53–54.

were those of the coffee marketing cooperative, and so overall food production can only be estimated from coffee output.

Three questions were posed: Where beans were planted by the wife of a household, could a relationship be established with coffee production? If men were more apt to nurture coffee trees in their mature years, and if older men lived on farms with a full complement of crops, did this affect coffee production? Did the availability of manure affect productivity?

The returns from the cooperative were used to calculate productivity per acre, and the results were these: Where no beans were grown, the yield per acre was 10.6 kilograms; where beans were grown, the coffee output was 75.6 kilograms. Where cattle were kept as well, the yields averaged 95.3 kilograms an acre; where no cattle were kept, the yields were 45.8 kilograms. The difference is striking. The men in the dispersion and replacement phases of the developmental cycle who belonged to the cooperative produced an average of 95.2 kilograms of coffee, while the younger men averaged 42.8 kilograms.

In the Nyakato villages, a further check was made on the effect of the presence or absence of cattle. An assessment of farms was based largely on the condition of the stand of plantain; the rating was done by Haya on a 1–4 scale, with 1 being excellent and 4 being poor to the point of neglect. Comparison of the presence of cattle on the farms judged excellent (27 out of 224) with those judged poor (13), using the phi (ϕ) coefficient, yielded a positive correlation of .64. On this basis, the keeping of cattle relates positively to the condition of the farms.

The data from the type village suggest that an intimate, regular, and comprehensible relationship exists between the nature and state of the cropping unit and the nature and state of the social unit. They suggest that the more *intensively* a cropping unit is used, the higher its productivity is likely to be.

The farms in a Haya village and the crops of which they are composed meet most of the nutritive requirements of the inhabitants, family by family. The vegetative continuity of the village is not, however, impaired by supplying the bulk of the dietary requirements. The nutrients derived from the village for the support of its human community are surplus to those required to ensure the vegetative continuity of the village as an ecological community. The long-term vegetative continuity of the village enables the human community to meet its annual or immediate dietary requirements on a long-term basis, and thus gives the Haya their resource base. They daily use the increment from it.

DIVISION OF LABOR ON FARM AND SOCIETY

As we have seen, the conventional view of Haya society assumed a basic division between cultivator and herder and between ruler and subject and assumed that a child held an all-pervasive membership in his father's group. The composition of Haya society thus postulated contained the kernel of basic differences, but as I have attempted to show it proposed an unreal separation between cattle keeping and cultivation. I shall now attempt to show that it also assumed too simple and rigid a view of occupational differentiation.

Models of Societies

It has long been observed and argued that in primitive, remote, or simple societies there is no division of labor save that owing to differences of age and sex. Allowances are usually made for the appearance of a ritual specialist, and in careful accounts of hunting societies where we expect and find this type of organization, variations in demonstrated ability are still subsumed under what is possible within the boundaries of an adult's role. The contrast between primitive and complex and between remote and central is always present, explicitly or implicitly.

Near the end of his life, Redfield thoughtfully published his own views, sharpened and refined through years of teaching and experience in the field. I rely largely on his summary of the theoretical developments, starting a century ago with Maine, that polarize the visible contrasts between small groups living in marginal areas and the concentrated groups living in cities into two concepts deliberately made as distinct as possible.[19] Although successive generations of social theorists have seized upon different facets of the same phenomenon, they share a common methodology: stress is placed on the maximum difference between the two systems or societies. The requirements of such a conceptual model can be defended, but the model itself has tended to capture its proponents. The conclusions drawn from the model are readily seen in much professional thinking today and are echoed among educated nonprofessionals as well.

Different major theorists concerned with many of the same problems have constructed conceptual models composed of polar opposites. The models resemble each other and can be compared. In

[19] Robert Redfield, *The Little Community* (Chicago: University of Chicago Press, 1955), pp. 132–48.

the sequence in which they were originally published, we find these concepts at one pole: *status* (Maine), *societas* (Morgan), *gemeinschaft* (Tonnies), *societies* (Durkheim), and the *folk* of Redfield, overshadowing the earlier use of that word. Sociologists today have taken over *traditional* and *nonindustrial* or *preindustrial*, where an unplanned economy of a poor country is posed in contrast to the industrial type. This is the most comprehensive formulation of current theorists.[20] A preoccupation with the legal, political, or social facets of the polar type in the nineteenth and early twentieth centuries appears to have been replaced with an emphasis on the economic, suggesting that the generations are successive, theoretical ones and not formed simply through lapse of time. The contrasting polar types are *contract* (the individual rather than the family's status providing basic orientation), *civitas* (the citizen's residence determining his affiliation rather than membership in his kindred), *gesellschaft* (the specialized individual being a participant in a civilized state rather than an undifferentiated person displaying group identity based on personal association), *organic* (the secularly oriented individual participating in a society made integral through variety and complexity rather than a person imbued with the sacred participation in a consensus society), and the *urban* (the urbanite living in a vast, complicated, and rapidly changing world rather than the country dweller living in a small, inward-facing folk society).[21]

All these polarized models share one feature: They stress differences, the distance between the poles. Even astute scholars sometimes succumb to the logical and also rather attractive necessity of accepting the difference between the primitive and the modern. Still following Redfield, I refer to Maine's dictum:

Nor is it difficult to see what is the tie between man which replaces by degrees those forms of reciprocity in rights and duties which have their origin in the Family. It is Contract. Starting, as from one terminus of history, from a condition of society in which all the relations of Persons are summed up in the relations of Family, we seem to have moved steadily towards a phase of social order in which *all* these relations arise from the free agreement of Individuals. In Western Europe the progress achieved in this direction has been considerable.[22] (Italics mine.)

[20] John Kenneth Galbraith, *The New Industrial State* (Boston: Houghton Mifflin Co., 1967), pp. 44, 52.
[21] Robert Redfield, "The Folk Society," *American Journal of Sociology*, 52 (January, 1947), 306.
[22] Henry Maine, *Ancient Law* (London: John Murray, 1906), pp. 172–73.

The logical opposite of "kin" is "nonkin" and of "family" is "nonfamily." What is logical leads the observer to look for and find what may not be evident in fact. The logical is made explicit in a polar construct, which then becomes the model or standard. The lead paragraph in the Schneider and Homans article on American kinship reiterates a position stemming from Maine and his theoretical successors:

The American kinship system is marked by bilateral descent, and the nuclear family and the kindred are the basic kin groups. Marriage is monogamous, residence neolocal, and inheritance by testamentary disposition. Succession is absent; a man gets no political or other office simply through kinship ties. The range of kinship is narrow, and kinship tends to be sharply divorced from other institutions such as the occupational system, the effect being to make kinship appear small beside such complex ramifying institutions as economics and technology. The American kinship system appears to be "pushed to the wall" by other institutions, and much of its coloring derives from this.[23]

Twelve years later a similar sentiment was expressed in a proposal forwarded on behalf of the American Anthropological Association: "... the importance of family groups is decreasing for the transmission of values, knowledge, and skills, and the exercise of authority over its members' time and motivation has drastically declined. Formal educational systems have in large measure replaced the critical importance of kin groups."[24]

The assumption that if the family is not everything it is nothing or is in a condition of constantly diminishing importance and effectiveness has been questioned because it leads both professionals and nonprofessionals to ignore for certain purposes what we cannot and do not ignore for other purposes. The bulk of the population in this country is in fact domiciled in and attached to families, and the overall character of the family is a very strong determinant of the actual and potential life style of its members.

What is demonstrably the case at one end of the polar construct has been pursued to show that the model tends to lead us to make observations and judgments that are only a partial view of the total reality. Part of the development of the theoretical contrast between the primitive non-Western society and the industrialized Western

[23] David Schneider and George Homans, "Kinship Terminology and the American Kinship System," *American Anthropologist*, 57 (December, 1955), 1194.
[24] From American Anthropological Association, "Proposal for a Center for Anthropology and Education," mimeographed (Washington, 1967), pp. 3–10.

society has been devoted specifically to the nature of the division of labor, and that in turn to the distinction between labor for food production and for other goods and services. Because historically the development of the Western industrial state depended in part on the physical and social separation of the people devoted not only to producing food for themselves but to producing a surplus adequate for the entire population, such a separation has come to be a measure of the degree of progress achieved between the primitive and the complex, the preindustrial and the industrial.

Model Based on Haya Society

The model for the temperate-climate industrialized societies is established, but it may not necessarily be adequate to the understanding or analysis of tropical Africa. The model I am proposing is derived from an empirical examination of the Haya, and for them it explains what the model derived from the polar construct failed to explain. Although I believe the model is valuable for the Haya alone, it may also be useful in analyzing most of the major peasant regions in tropical Africa.

In outline, the model is simple. Instead of presuming the divorce of food production, residence, and non-food-producing specialization, it assumes that these three basic items go together and complement each other in regions with a high concentration of population. It also assumes that a high concentration of population cannot occur unless the other factors are also present. In this model, food production techniques are such that subsistence requires much less than a full working day every day from men or women. Residences or residential areas are situated so that persons with occupational specialities can make contact with whatever other persons they must and obtain the "factors of production" they require on a daily or weekly or even monthly basis. The proximity may be achieved through transportation or through sheer density of population.

The model I am proposing erases the dichotomy between rural and urban in those parts of tropical East and West Africa where most of the major cities are. Interposed between rural and urban is the concept of *peasant*, resulting in a tripartite division of rural or tribal, peasant or semiurban, and urban or city. In Africa the classification of some peoples as truly tribal is not likely to be questioned as readily as the proposition that some rural or country people are not tribal but peasant. But the concept is not put forward to replace the concept of tribe but is an addition made necessary by an empirical examination of one people, the Haya. One basic datum derives from the observation that Haya villages have supplied basic subsistence and residence for at least 100 years in areas where the density of population is 1,200 to the square mile.

At the same time, these 1,200-to-the-square-mile villages are not self-contained but have routine supplements from commercial transactions in a trading network, some local, some regional, and some international. To relate this observation to societies elsewhere in Africa or the world is made much easier by the conceptual apparatus attached to the idea of a *part-society* developed in conjunction with the concept of peasant. In this respect I am where Redfield was in the 1920's but have the advantage of his summation in the 1950's.[25]

Redfield's primacy, intellectual and temporal, is acknowledged with the recognition that his own ideas expressed in the 1930's and culminating in 1941[26] were considerably modified and enlarged by 1956.[27] The model I am presenting is unorthodox relative to Redfield's folk/urban continuum but is congenial with and supports the last of Redfield's statements, especially his recognition of Barnes. Wolf's survey of the literature provides a comparative framework for the rural aspects of wider societies; my own study of the Haya could be considered a case study of peasant people in Wolf's terms.[28]

Because the concept of *peasant* has had hard going among theorists working with African data, it seems necessary to defend the utility of the concept and give the evidence justifying its use. A critical feature of the concept of *peasant* vis-à-vis *tribe* is that the peasant society is a part-society integrally and routinely linked to a society more extensive physically and/or more complex socially. The part-society shows an economic dependence on regionally defined arrangements; socially the part-society is differentiated so that the rural cultivator is distinguished from an elite having some dominance over the cultivator, whether expressed primarily in terms of formal learning or in control over resources. Redfield used the term *gentry* to specify the person of elite status and, in his concern with the humanistic aspect, the literate teacher or formally certified man of religion. Although the major world religions and traditions came more readily to his mind, Redfield did not so restrict his

[25] Fay-Cooper Cole and Fred Eggan, "Robert Redfield," *American Anthropologist*, 61 (August, 1959), 655.
[26] Robert Redfield, *The Folk Culture of Yucatan* (Chicago: University of Chicago Press, 1941).
[27] Redfield, *Peasant Society*.
[28] *Peasants*.

definition that it could not subsume a sacred tradition transmitted among specialists in a nonliterate society. With Dahomey and Dogon in mind, Redfield concludes:

> These instances suggest the separation of the two traditions in societies that do not represent the great world civilizations. The content of knowledge comes to be double, one content for the layman, another for the hierarchy. The activities and place of residence of the carriers of the great tradition may remain close to those of the laymen, or the priests and primitive philosophers may come to reside and to work apart from the common people.[29]

With the other characteristics cited at the beginning of this paper—an attachment to and control of a *piece* of land, a hierarchy of territorial groups, independent fields of economic activity, and countrywide networks of relationships—a boundary distinguishing a dominant elite from the bulk of the population is also necessary. And the dominant elite must in some way be more civilized.

An ideological commitment to peasant values completes the summary of characteristics. Redfield's perception of their good life includes industrious work and a reverent attitude toward the land, but this has been modified by Foster's more recent evaluation.[30] What peasants value highly (land, health, a mother's love for her children) is perceived as being limited in quantity, finite and therefore always subject to relentless competition. Mere human effort and aspiration cannot increase what is highly valued. By now the concept of peasant, more widely and frequently used by scholars than ever before, is also less readily defined by a simple list of characteristics.[31]

The peasant-society model can be used to distinguish high-population-density East Africa in general and Haya in particular from both low-density regions and from the cities proper. The urban portion of the part-society can be touched on only in passing. However, it is notable that the cities and towns in East Africa[32] (Nairobi, Kampala, Mwanza, Kisumu, Arusha, Dar es Salaam, and Mombasa) have grown up precisely where the indigenous population was already concentrated and have contributed to the further

---

[29] Redfield, *Peasant Society*, p. 74.

[30] George M. Foster, "Peasant Society and the Image of Limited Good," *American Anthropologist*, 67 (April, 1965), 293–315.

[31] Robert Anderson, "Studies in Peasant Life," *Biennial Review of Anthropology 1965*, ed. Bernard J. Siegel (Stanford, Calif.: Stanford University Press, 1965), pp. 176–78.

[32] Porter, "East Africa Population," Map 6.

concentration of that population. For example, a reading of the memoir by J. R. L. MacDonald, the Royal Engineer entrusted with the choice of route to be followed by a proposed railroad between Mombasa and Lake Victoria, makes clear that he followed the existing trail between the port city and Kikuyu country for a number of reasons. The human and food resources of the country were just as desirable a goal for the railroad and just as necessary for its construction as they were for the support of the porters whom the railroad was to supplant.[33] Moreover, the gradient was feasible. Nairobi grew up physically new, but it is on the general site of the traditional terminus of the caravan route where there was also a native market. Kikuyu country, MacDonald said, "will, on the advent of the railway, prove a rich and valuable possession." [34]

Epstein's very useful summary of the literature of urbanization makes it unnecessary to discuss the character of African cities, which is only partly relevant here. But his use of the urban-rural dichotomy creates an analytical situation where the differences he notes between West Africa and the new industrial complexes of the Copperbelt are difficult to resolve.[35] The regional differences between high-density East and West Africa on the one hand and the Rhodesias on the other would make the resolution of the different indices on urbanization easier, as Bruner also suggests.[36]

What to call the zone or region between the city and the true hinterland is something of a problem. A tendency exists to equate *village* and *tribal* in Epstein and elsewhere, although Dalton has initiated the use of the term *village* in contrast with *tribal*.[37] *Peasant* is probably the most widely used term to typify this intermediate zone and is almost always used in contradistinction to *tribal*.

The particular model I am fashioning is unorthodox in two respects. First, I am willing to leave in abeyance the question of a sacred tradition of learning until the type and strength of oral tradition in the capitals of the *Bakama* can be evaluated by an expert scholar.[38] In East Africa, the dominant elite present in the

[33] *Soldiering and Surveying in British East Africa 1891–1894* (London: Edward Arnold, 1897), pp. 9, 49–57.
[34] *Ibid.*, p. 126.
[35] A. L. Epstein, "Urbanization and Social Change in Africa," *Current Anthropology*, 8 (October, 1967), 275–84.
[36] Edward M. Bruner, "Comment on Epstein's 'Urbanization and Social Change in Africa,'" *Current Anthropology*, 8 (October, 1967), 284–85.
[37] Epstein, "Urbanization in Africa," pp. 280–81; George Dalton, "Community Development as a Field of Social Science" (paper read before the meeting of the American Anthropological Association, Washington, Dec. 2, 1967).
[38] "Conference on Oral History in Tanzania," *Africa*, 37 (April, 1967), 222.

Lacustrine Bantu ruling dynasties proved fragile after European entry and we do not know, I believe, how authentic were elite-peasant relationships. Remnant sentiments made known to me when I was doing my field work suggest quite strongly a sense of real social distance between members of the ruling dynasty and the remainder of the population, a distance supported by real power over the allocation of farms and produce.

Much more important, my model is unorthodox in suggesting that the peasants in East Africa do not simply present a way station between tribal and urban life where all cultivate and a few are specialists, but rather present an unusual combination where all cultivate and *where all also* engage in specialization. My italics are used to emphasize the general statement. The peasant in East Africa lives in a kind of tropical megalopolis that has yet to be celebrated by the visiting scholar.

Men may undoubtedly be found among the Haya who claim no other occupation than that of cultivator or who are completely alienated from the land. Individual arrangements in combining an occupational specialty with cultivation and residence in a village show very wide variation. Proposed for the model is the practice of some specialty along with cultivation and consistent with village residence for all or much of the year. Exceptions must be considered or accounted for or acknowledged.

Even more unfortunate are men who lack land and the capacity or training to engage in a specialty as well. Interpretation of the position of landless men, who may also be poor, is basically different if they are accepted as a normal concomitant of the type of peasant society exemplified by the Haya, where tenure is held individually. Land transmitted under rules of inheritance goes to one primary heir, and unless a father is able to acquire additional farms for all other sons they are without land. As Wolf also notes, one result of this type of inheritance is the division into those with land and those without.[39]

At least three kinds of groups are posited by the model I am developing: landless persons, who may also be poor, at the bottom of the social scale; a very broad group of persons having effective control of land and with some additional specialty; and a small group of persons—professionally trained, competent by modern standards, and employed—who themselves do no cultivation whatsoever but who may well invest in land and resort to a country home. In Luhaya, the language of the Haya, there are a number of

---

[39] *Peasants*, p. 76.

words describing poor, landless, or unfortunate persons, others appropriate to the majority of the population, and others descriptive of prosperous persons.

If we were to assume that Haya society was composed solely of cultivators and that each man with his dependents was nearly self-sufficient in providing food and services for themselves, our comprehension of Haya society would be much reduced. But if we assume that Haya is the kind of composite society now most commonly subsumed under the term *peasant,* then evidence based on observation, stated occupations in known villages, diet items, lexical items, and sample time and consumption budgets are all comprehensible. These differing, though internally consistent, types of evidence all point to a similar conclusion—that Haya society is economically and socially complex.

Occupational Specialties

Haya distinguish between chores or duties or work (the exact English translation is not so easy) and a job or occupational specialty. Domestic duties are among the obligations of any person living on a farm in Haya country. Most of the activities listed in Table 2 have already figured in the expectations adult men and women have for their daily and annual schedules. Adult members of the household have primary responsibility for the execution of these tasks, but they expect assistance from younger members when they are available. The duties fall to individual men and women primarily as members of a household, but because most household members are also related to the head of the household, the duties are part of the expectations of behavior between kin. And those kin are most commonly within the boundary of the group Haya recognize as the family. The line in Haya kin ideology is, I think, fairly clear. As long as a woman is a member of her husband's household, she will do and he will expect her to do certain domestic tasks, and she will have similar expectations about her husband's duties. But they may be performed by someone else, and if a man lacks a wife, a widowed mother may well do them. A widowed and elderly woman can also expect a son to perform the domestic duties formerly undertaken by her husband. Because Haya society has been and is differentiated with regard to wealth and status, however, domestic chores—carrying water, cooking, weeding, harvesting—are all basic domestic-subsistence activities that once could have been performed by menials and now could be performed by servants. To confine to kinsmen in the household the normal expectations adults have about the performance of domestic duties could easily be misleading.

Analysis of Haya Lexicon

In Table 2 may be seen domestic tasks falling within the category of chore. One task, the harvesting and marketing of coffee, is the

TABLE 2
Division of Labor within Domestic Group Expressed in Haya Verbs

Men	Either men or women, but one in preference to the other (△ for men, ○ for women)	Women
Daily		
Take cattle to herder	Dress child (○)	Give cooked plantain to child
Cultivate plantain	Aid in taking down or putting up a headload, especially water (○)	Collect twigs for fire
Cut plantain		Make fire
Fetch firewood		Roast plantain
Have cattle for manure	Greet neighbors (△)	Cook milk
Bring cattle back from grazing	Cultivate in general (both)	Prepare banana juice
Milk a cow	Instruct that food be cooked (△)	Cut banana leaves for serving
Pray (if Catholic)	Weed (○)	Tidy house
	Cook (○) in general	Fetch water
	Peel plantain (○)	Mix foods when cooking
	Go shopping (both)	Cook beans
	Harvest (both)	Gather things around house
	Put things inside the house (△)	Clear after meal
	Undress child (○)	Bathe children
		Make beds
		Put children in bed
Seasonal or Intermittent		
Make a fence		Cut grass
Order a fence made		Leave children in the care of others
Build a house		Cut sod for Bambara nut
Have someone do the milking		Plant Bambara nut
Look after cattle		Harvest Bambara nut
		Plant, harvest beans
		Wash clothes
		Plant and harvest eleusine

NOTE: Only translations of Haya verbs are given here; a different verb occurs for each activity. Items of personal routine are not included.

prerogative of the man of the house and does not come under the rubric of domestic chore but is, instead, a job.

Lexical items in the societal division of labor, seen in Table 3, are based on the straightforward assumption that such items are indicators of Haya usage. If there are words for occupational specialties and if a person may be identified by it, then the word and the person are evidence together of the cultural items and the social reality. The terms are rendered in English; a fuller publication covering similar ground will contain the Luhaya language as well as English.

In a lexicon of this type, the inclusion of one item and the exclusion of another invokes a wealth of sociological theory. Here occupational specialities available to men and women are defined as broadly as possible as long as they come under a rubric of being practiced for economic gain and/or those which place or affect a man's occupation. Thus the word for *slave* is included but not the word for *sorcerer*. Of primary interest here are the terms that illustrate Barnes's typological category, the more or less independent economic fields of activity for which Haya occupational specialties qualify. Words descriptive of the relative status of persons are not included: *wealthy, poor, normal*. Excluded are terms for kinsmen and descent affiliation. Also excluded are all the terms referring to the administration of the hierarchically arranged territorial groups: titles of office, including the nuclear officials proper but also the many traditional specialists attached to the capitals of the top-level rulers. Similarly excluded are the items appropriate to Barnes's third typological category—the networks of kinsmen, blood brothers, dance groups, and friends other than village neighbors.

With the exception of the words for prostitute (*malaya*), priestess (*mbandwa*), and mechanic (*makanika*), the words are all prefixed with the standard form *mu-*, indicative of person. The basketmakers share a common designation with the type of basket produced; the canoe maker and the carpenter similarly share a common word— the canoe maker is a "carpenter" of canoes, or perhaps they are both woodworkers. With these exceptions, each word is different. Three words are loan-words from Kiswahili (craftsman, prostitute, cook for expatriates) and three are loan-words from English (mechanic, driver [*mudereva*], and servant "boy" [*muboi*]). Items in Table 3 otherwise label indigenous specialties or, in a few cases, adapt indigenous vocabulary items to new specialties (doctor, teacher, overseer).

The overall significance or frequency in the practice of all the occupational specialties can only be touched on briefly. Some of the

TABLE 3
Societal Division of Labor Expressed in Lexical Items of Job Specialty

	Male Specialties	
Fishing	Net fisherman Hook fisherman Helmsman	Canoe maker Weir maker
Cattle keeping	Master herder Herder of a large herd Herder	Person with special knowledge of cattle Milker
Metalwork	Blacksmith Blacksmith's helper Blacksmith's assistant	Lampmaker
House and furniture construction	House builder Sawyer Building-cane cutter	Carpenter Mason
Traditional crafts	Drum maker Bark-cloth maker Potter	
Fibers	Calabash netmaker Basketmaker Sieve maker Tray maker	
Traditional skills	Beekeeper Dog breeder Tree climber Hunter	Beer banana treader Coffee picker
Merchandising	Storekeeper Trader Treasurer (keeper of accounts) Creditor	Debtor Usurer Butcher
Recent skills	Preacher Soldier Pastor Doctor Teacher	Mechanic Truck driver Priest
Social specialties	Estate guardian Marriage counselor Go-between Escort	
Recent crafts	Craftsman (a Kiswahili word) Tailor	

TABLE 3—Continued

	Male Specialties
General terms	Cook for expatriates Servant for expatriates Watchman for expatriates Director Foreman Forest watchman Worker Overseer Servant (agricultural) Servant (for a woman) Slave Slave or bought person Laborer Messenger Porter
Traditional religious- medical specialties	Doctor Curer Diviner Diviner's assistant

	Female Specialties
Traditional crafts	Basketmaker Beaded-armband maker Ornamental-basket maker Matmaker
Traditional skills	Midwife Nurse Priestess
Recent skills	Nun
General term	Slave Prostitute

traders, butchers, bicycle mechanics, and carpenters, and at least one drum maker had thriving businesses at the time of the field work. To my certain knowledge, at the time of writing, dozens of Haya held university degrees (and retain an interest in and an attachment to the farm held by their families); they are at the top of a much larger group with varying amounts of education.

The practice of a specialty provides, in varying and undetermined degrees, a money income in addition to that produced by coffee. Three of the specialties—fishing, the set comprising cattle herding and trading, and storekeeping—are regional in operation. Cattle are traded from Sukuma country, fishing on Lake Victoria includes the offshore islands in a trading-fishing network. In combination they alter significantly the picture of Haya food production and consumption. Money and the frequent availability of fish and meat transform the domestic economy of the Haya.

Diet and Occupation

A sample survey of diets of 27 families undertaken by the East African Medical Survey in two different villages at two different seasons showed an average intake of 2,252 calories per person and a protein intake at 66.5 grams, above average by Platt's recommended standard.[40] By this standard, the Haya come into the same nutritional category as Mediterranean Europe and the Balkan countries, according to Wolf.[41] A marked characteristic of the small group surveyed by the EAMS, however, was the high degree of variability among different families: 10 averaged 2,755 calories, the other 17 just under 2,000. A further group of 4 families was also surveyed, chosen—so far as can be ascertained by the results—to show 1 with high-calorie intake (2,862), 2 with low-calorie diets (1,694 and 1,480), and 1 with a starvation diet.

Within the limits of this survey, variability in nutrition appears to be strongly influenced by two factors: occupation and family size. All men had farms, but they were also a tailor with a household of 3 (2,862 calories per person), a mason with a household of 12 (1,480), a headman with a household of 3 (1,694), and a man with no additional occupation with a family of 6 (816). The preliminary finding based on this small study is of moderate but reliable average nutrition but with wide variations from household to household. Little difference could be attributed to seasonal variation.

Occupations in Type Village

Table 3 does no more than list occupational specialties among the Haya. In the type village illustrated in Figure 2, the frequency

[40] W. Laurie and H. Trant, *A Health Survey of Bukoba District, Tanganyika*, East African Medical Survey Monograph no. 2 (Nairobi: Government Printer, 1954), pp. 14–20.

Platt is cited by Laurie and Trant (p. 15) with the following standard:
Calories	Proteins	Fats	Cho.	Calcium	Iron	Vit. A.	Thiamine
2,500	60	50	472	800	20	5,000	1.5
Riboflavin	Niacin	Ascorbic Acid					
1.8	12.0	30–70					

[41] *Peasants*, p. 5.

of different specialized occupations was also known. Although not all occupations were found in this one village, the residents showed some differentiation by occupation.

Six sawyers lived in a row of adjacent farms next to two builders and a carpenter. Two fishermen and a canoe builder also lived at the northern end of the village. A storekeeper, a trader, and a foreman lived where the paths cross near the center of the village, all of them adjacent to the farm of the parish chief.

In the area of ritual specialties, some were openly acknowledged while others depend on the point of view. One woman who had much the character of a recluse identified her occupation as that of an *mbandwa* priestess. But a man thought to be a practicing sorcerer by many of the villagers did not agree with their assessment, though he left the village when his house was burned.

A pot maker, a barkcloth maker, several other traders, two teachers, a master herder, and a former policeman (*askari*) were also in this village. Only one man considered himself simply a cultivator, though several other men did not declare any specialization. Most women declared themselves as handicraft makers of mats, baskets, and sweaters. Some of these items are sold at the local subcounty weekly market. Where farms are held until the owner attains his majority, the owners are too young to have obtained occupations, or are still in training.

Occupation and Farm Productivity

With these data for societally organized occupations in view, the data on coffee productivity and the occurrence of the components of husbandry may be examined further. It will be recalled that picking and marketing coffee is considered a job and not part of the subsistence round of activities. In Table 4 may be seen coffee productivity for men (and one woman) in the village who belonged to the cooperative and for whom marketing returns were available. In Table 5 may be seen the components of husbandry for those men who were not marketing the coffee they grew through the cooperative as well as for those who were not marketing coffee at all. What seems striking is that the men who were established in trade and house construction were also the men who were marketing relatively large amounts of coffee and whose farms showed high concentrations of husbandry components. Additional specialization and diversification on the part of the farm owner is consistent with intensive use and high productivity of the farm, not a detracting

TABLE 4
Coffee Productivity per Acre and Occupation of Cultivator

Register Number	Kilos per Acre	Stated Occupation
20	201	—
29	155	—
4	120	Builder
17	113	Builder
9	107.7	—
2	100.8	Sawyer
14	99.4	Storekeeper
18	93.5	Former parish chief
26	84.6	Builder
27	61.6	Trader
8	53.1	(Woman, wife of a trader)
1	52.3	Parish chief
240	43	Teacher
40	40.6	Sawyer
B	31.1	(Minor heir)
215	20	Foreman for a road gang
28	16.5	Sawyer
16	15	(Absent from village)
222	13.6	Builder
6	13.6	Builder
23	11.5	Sawyer
21	7.5	—

factor. For some occupations, such as fishing, one suspects that the village farm was primarily a residential site and the occupation a primary source of income. The men who owned the tiny farms at the south of the village were, out of what must be strict necessity, at work as laborer and foreman.

CONCLUSION

Among the Haya, a people who are probably better characterized by the term *peasant* than *tribe,* agricultural production for food and cash is augmented by nonagricultural food production through cattle herding and fishing, and both of these involve regional trade. In addition to the specialization inherent in food producing activities, Haya practice a wide variety of occupations that result in diversified goods and services.

Basic to an understanding of Haya society and its role in the wider regional setting that merits its identification as peasant is the

TABLE 5
Components of Husbandry and Occupation of Cultivator

Register Number	Components	Occupation
13	Plantain, beans, coffee, and cattle	(Woman)
25		Traymaker
44		Driver
78		Master herder
79		Policeman
3	Plantain, beans, and coffee	Sawyer
5		Fisherman
7		Tailor
11		—
22		Barkcloth maker
41		—
48		Sawyer
51		(Woman)
192		Carpenter
207		Cultivator
212		Fisherman
A		—
F	Plantain and coffee	(Teacher—farm unoccupied)
42		—
24	Plantain and food crops	(Mbandwa priestess)
50		(Woman)
206		Canoe maker
219		(Family from Burundi)
250		Laborer
254		Basketmaker
C		—
10	Plantain	Potmaker
247		Foreman
D		(Minor heir)
E		(Minor heir)
G		(Minor heir)

village, where a group of people resides on and cultivates a cluster of contiguous small farms. The farms are intensively cultivated under a stable regime of tree crops enhanced by stalled cattle and semiannual cover crops of beans. The village is a finely balanced ecosystem that appears to require relatively small amounts of cultivating time throughout the year. This type of cultivation is pos-

87

sible under the climatic conditions where seasonal contrast is damped by two rainy and two dry seasons rather than one of each. Seasonal activity is not precluded, however, and coffee marketing in particular appears to be coordinated with the one period in the year when conditions are comparatively dry.

Each farm is under the effective control of one individual who is the head (or the potential head) of a household that may or may not conform precisely to the simple group the Haya call a family. Households and families are small, averaging little more than three persons. Variation in the distribution of the major components of husbandry among the households is strongly influenced by the developmental phase of the family living on the farm. A full complement of husbandry components characterizes the well-established family consisting of a husband and wife with nearly mature or married children.

Although agricultural production, and implicitly what may be available to the resident domestic group's own subsistence consumption, may be accounted for in terms of the family's developmental phase, variation in the money income derived from the job of the male head of the household or family also influences consumption. Data derived from a diet survey suggest that the level of money income and the variations in the size of the domestic group together influence the consumption of food, as they do elsewhere.

The relative position of men and women with respect to domestic and societal divisions of labor, is, I think, more or less self-evident in the data presented. Men have the primary right to, and responsibility for, the major tree crops and a few other domestic necessities; women do all of the subsidiary annual cultivating and perform housekeeping and child-care chores. Nearly all of the specialties are slated for men and a few heterogeneous specialties are reserved for or are open to women.

One further conclusion suggested by the analysis here is of substantial and significant differences among the Haya. The more fortunate or wealthier Haya have farms, jobs, adequate and even ample diets, and good health. But Haya without farms or without jobs are frequently poor, in Haya terms, and have inadequate diets. Under this analysis the term *Haya* is nearly meaningless, for it glosses over important differences and assumes a homogeneity that the society has not had for perhaps several centuries. Only the role of cultivator of subsistence crops is common to them; from other viewpoints there is heterogeneity, and the homogeneity of cultivation combining with the heterogeneity of the occupation gives the more balanced picture. What proportions of the population are wealthy and poor by Haya standards, and why, become the relevant questions to ask.

POSTSCRIPT

A supplementary visit, just long enough to tour familiar countryside and revisit villages formerly known well, enables me to reaffirm and qualify my earlier observations based on much more extensive work.[42] From the air it is quite apparent that Haya villages retain their character; on the ground it is equally apparent that Haya continue to be sedentary residents of named villages. There are, however, three observations, none of which could be given the exploration they require in the short time available.

First, cropping has moved out onto the formerly open grasslands. A major breakthrough in Haya cropping potential has come from utilization of a commercial fertilizer now available as a by-product of the manufacture of instant coffee. Cultivation of plantain and tea in what was formerly open land alters the previous boundary between land under tree-crop cultivation and comparatively barren grassland. Incorporation of new land in tree-crop and vegetable-crop husbandry has many ramifications which should be traced in future work.

Second, herds of 50 to 100 cattle of the Zebu type are to be seen on the roads and at pasture in the grassland, a visible indication of new breeding stock and the results of a ranching scheme.

Third, as noticed through conversation as well as observation, the apparent standard of living is more diverse than formerly. Thoughtful Haya are concerned about distribution of cattle and commercial fertilizers.

In sum, the questions asked on the basis of earlier data, what proportions of the population are wealthy and poor by Haya standards, and why, *are* relevant questions.

---

[42] In September, 1968, an international trip on behalf of the Smithsonian Institution made a revisit to Bukoba feasible as part of the continuing study of the Haya under the auspices of Catholic University and with the aid of NIMH Grant MH—16132–01. Acknowledgment is gladly given to all who made this visit possible.

CHAPTER 3

THE FOOD PRODUCTION SYSTEM OF A SEMI-NOMADIC SOCIETY: THE KARIMOJONG, UGANDA

Rada and Neville Dyson-Hudson

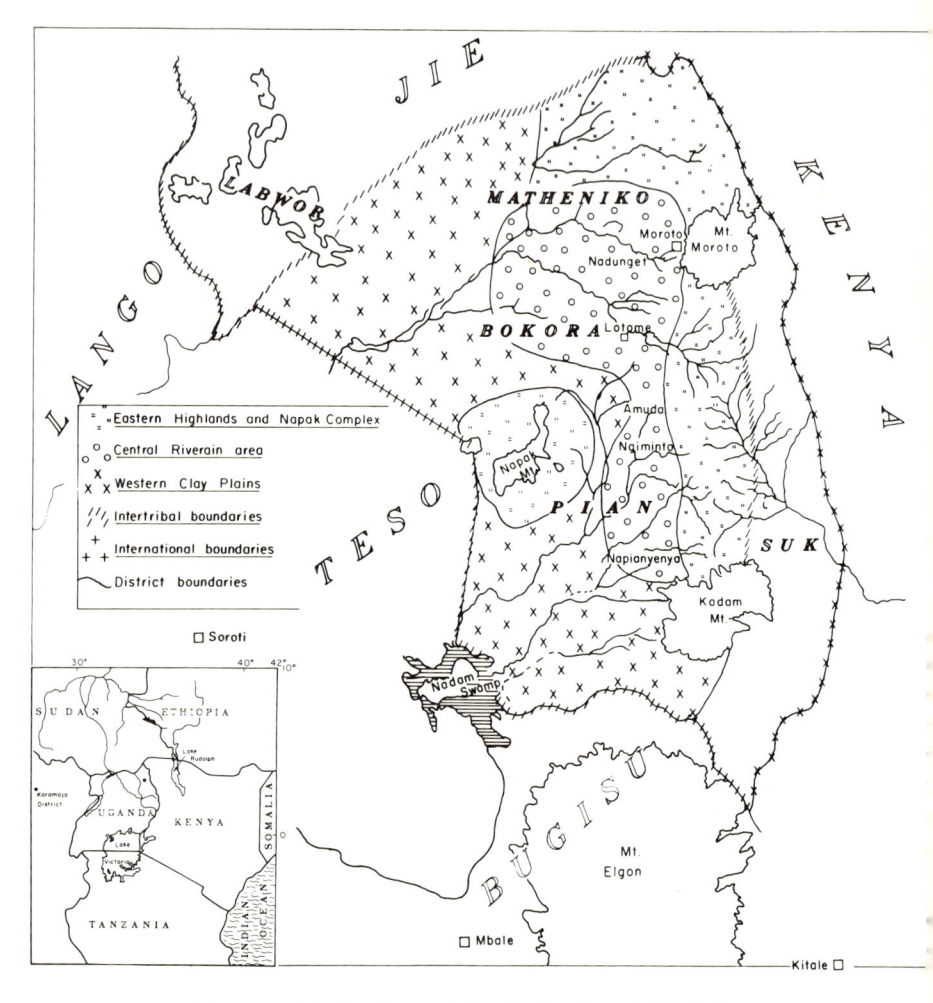

Topographic Regions of the Karimojong Tribal Area.

INTRODUCTION

A society is made up of people; the behavior of men is purposive; and food is essential for man's survival. Thus the quest for food is a continuing and conscious concern in any society and exhibits the same features of purposive, institutionalized, and interconnected activities as any other area of social behavior. It is therefore legitimate to speak of the food production system in any society. The concept is particularly useful in a society that has a subsistence economy, however, since virtually the total economic system is subsumed under it and this simplifies the analysis.

As with any other system of human activity, to understand the food production system one must ask what its component elements are and what relation it bears to the other systems of behavior in the society such as the kinship system, the political system, and the religious system. One must also be aware of the larger setting in which the society itself is situated—the ecosystem of plants and animals as well as other human populations also seeking survival.

The food production system is the result of various factors, some biological, some social. There are environmental factors, the most important of which are temperature, rainfall and availability of surface water, and soil types. Obviously slash-and-burn agriculture is not possible if the rainfall is 15 inches and the soil is shifting sand dunes, nor can people living in an area with 100 inches of annual rainfall successfully become camel-keeping nomads. The indigenous fauna and flora, including disease-producing parasites, and the availability of introduced crops and livestock help to determine the food production system. Important considerations in relation to plant and animal resources are the numbers of plants and animals or the area of production, the capacity of each individual organism to produce, and the periodicity or frequency of production. These three factors determine the amount of food produced by each type of organism.

The demography of the human population—the number of hands to work and mouths to feed—is also an important factor in determining the food production system. A system suitable for a relatively stable population would no longer be adequate if the infant mortality sharply dropped and the population increased. On the other hand, a food production system dependent on a large amount of child labor would no longer be suitable if the birth rate dropped.

Cultural factors also affect the food production system, in particular technology and cosmology. A human population with an advanced technology can overcome the environmental constraints on its food production system. The tractor and plow can vastly increase the extent of crop production; irrigation can turn deserts into agricultural areas; and with drainage, swamps can produce crops.

On the other hand, the values of a society limit the food sources that are exploited. Animals considered sacred (such as the cow in India) or unclean (such as the lion in much of Africa) may not be eaten. And a society that will not allow its women out of their houses (such as the Muslim Beja nomads in the Sudan) may not exploit all of the food resources available to it because of a labor shortage.

To summarize, environmental factors such as temperature, soil, rainfall, and water supplies set fairly narrow limits on the means of food production available to the people living within a particular environment. The numbers and productivity of indigenous and introduced plants and animals determine the amount of food available to the human population. Improved technology may modify the environmental limits of the food-production system. A society's values can set other limits that appear to have no biological basis. All these factors, taken together, determine the food production system of a particular society.

In this essay we will consider the food production system of the Karimojong [1] (see map insert), who subsist by a combination of animal husbandry, agriculture, and food gathering, supplemented by a very small amount of imported food purchased in the stores. This complex system is an adaptation to the important environmental variables of rainfall and habitat (topography, soil, and vegetation) and secondarily to water supplies inasmuch as they affect the movements of the cattle and the people. To understand the food production system it is first necessary to describe the environment of the Karimojong. Then each of the three means of exploiting the environment to provide food will be discussed. We shall show how the diversified methods of providing food, together

[1] The three-year field study (1954–58) in Karamoja, Uganda, on which this chapter is based was made possible by a Fulbright post-doctoral Research Fellowship, and by fellowships and grants-in-aid from the Guggenheim Foundation, the American Philosophical Society (Penrose Fund), the Society of Sigma Xi, the American Academy of Arts and Sciences (Permanent Science Fund), and the Wenner-Gren Foundation. Research grants to assist the analysis of data were provided by the American Philosophical Society, the American Association of University Women, the Society of Sigma Xi, the Kendall Fund, the National Science Foundation, and the Wenner-Gren Foundation. In this short chapter we can only present the conclusions from the data we have collected. The detailed presentation will be published as a book by The Johns Hopkins Press.

with cultural exchanges of trade, begging, bridewealth, and herd-splitting, provide insurance against the hazards of the environment, most particularly drought, but also against livestock diseases and cattle theft by enemy tribes.

Because of the limitations of length, our primary concern here will be with explaining the components of the Karimojong food production system, touching only briefly on its relation to other behavior systems in the society and to the total environment.

ENVIRONMENT

General

The Karimojong are a tribe of some 60,000 people who live in the southern part of Karamoja District in northeast Uganda, which borders on the Sudan to the north and Kenya to the west.[2] The people occupy a plateau of some 4,000 square miles ranging in elevation from 3,500 to 4,500 feet. Rising to about 10,000 feet above the plains are three major peaks—remnants of old volcanoes—which strongly influence rainfall patterns within the area. The vegetation is savannah grassland. Though the region is only 4 to 6 degrees north of the equator, the climate is relatively mild because of the elevation. Shade temperatures in the district occasionally go as high as 96 degrees Fahrenheit during the dry season, and a maximum of over 90 degrees in the shade is frequent during the months of January, February, and March. The temperatures in the rainy season do not often exceed 85 degrees in the shade. Temperatures at night often fall below 60 degrees.

Rainfall

On the plains, the rainfall ranges from 17.82 to 55.86 inches per year[3] and is higher near the mountains, often exceeding 50 inches. The Karimojong consider the year to have two main seasons. There is the rainy season (*akiporo*), which starts in March or April and continues through September, and the dry season (*akamu*), which begins in September or October and continues through March. There are also two transitional seasons, which roughly translate as "spring" (*atepunet*, beginning of the rains) and "fall" (*ayet*, drying of the grass). These come at the beginning and the end of the rainy season.

[2] This account refers to the Karimojong during the period 1954–58.
[3] Lotome 1952; Napianyenya 1952.

Karimojong, like farmers and ranchers the world over, are pessimistic when they discuss the weather. They have better reason than most, however, as is shown by the rainfall probability figures listed in Table 1, which illustrate how wide the range of probable rainfall is—even at the 80 percent confidence level—making it impossible for the Karimojong to count on agriculture as their sole means of subsistence. The rainfall probability shows that in Moroto, for example, a farmer could in the last ten days of April predict with 80 percent certainty a rainfall of between 17.9 and 205.8 mms. a range from far too low for germination of seeds through excellent conditions for planting and growth of crops. And this enormous range of rainfall probability continues throughout the rainy season. Even in the dry season there is considerable probability for rainstorms. The dry season storms do not help agriculture but are important for livestock, since they cause the perennial grasses to grow and replenish dwindling water supplies.

A fact that is not shown by Table 1 is the unpredictability of the spatial as well as temporal distribution of rainfall. Storms are often very localized. One locality may receive a storm during a dry period in the rainy season which just saves the crops from being drought-damaged, while another locality ten miles away just misses it, and its crops will be stunted or killed. Or, during the dry season, "grass rains" may fall very locally, bringing grass and water for the cattle only in a particular spot and leaving much of the dry weather grazing areas parched. The only predictable thing about Karamoja rainfall is that it will be higher on and near the mountains and highlands than on the plains.

Habitat (Water Supplies, Soil, Vegetation, Land Use)

The Karimojong tribal area may be divided into four topographic regions (see map). These are the eastern highlands, the central riverine areas, the western plains, and the mountain areas.

Cutting across the topographic regions are the five major rivers, which flow from east to west. They run for short periods following rainstorms (from a few hours to several days, depending on the amount of rainfall), rising rapidly, flowing with tremendous force, and then subsiding to leave the sandy riverbed dry.

Eastern Highlands and the Napak Mountain Complex

The rivers originate in the rocky highlands and are confined to the sandy or rocky beds. Springs flow to the surface in the eastern highlands and the Napak Mountain complex (and also in the moun-

TABLE 1
Range of Probable Rainfall at Moroto, Karamoja District (in millimeters)

Standard Period (10 day intervals)	80 Percent Confidence Interval Limits for Rainfall	
	Lower Limit	Upper Limit
Jan. 01	0	30.1
02	0	11.7
03	0	17.4
Feb. 04	0	42.5
05	0	50.4
06	0	51.6
Mar. 07	0	90.9
08	0	121.9
09	1.5	119.4
Apr. 10	0	133.0
11	10.7	146.4
12	17.9	205.8
May 13	24.9	221.8
14	29.1	172.1
15	4.7	179.0
June 16	3.4	164.1
17	0	119.2
18	12.5	122.0
July 19	19.8	154.1
20	13.9	154.5
21	26.1	180.7
Aug. 22	24.9	171.1
23	18.4	147.4
24	9.7	160.6
Sept. 25	0.4	123.7
26	1.7	84.9
27	0	81.1
Oct. 28	0	72.0
29	0	73.5
30	0	69.1
Nov. 31	0	82.5
32	0	92.4
33	0	75.0
Dec. 34	0	72.5
35	0	53.8
36	0	42.8

NOTE: The data were collected by the East African Meteorological Department; the computer program was developed by H. L. Manning (1956) and computed by International Computers and Tabulators (East Africa) Ltd.

SOURCE: H. L. Manning, "The Statistical Assessment of Rainfall Probability and Its Application in Uganda Agriculture," *Proceedings of the Royal Society Series B*, 144 (1956), 460–80.

tain areas), and water is also caught in the riverbeds in pools of varying permanence. Though there is relatively little permanent water in these areas, the higher rainfall means that only in very dry years is water in critically short supply, though it may be locally unavailable at times during the dry season.

The rocky highlands have shallow, rocky, well-drained soil that is unsuitable for agriculture. The vegetation is a mixed deciduous orchard-type vegetation (*Grewia bicolor, Carissa edulis, Harrisonia abyssinica, Combretum ternifoium, C. molle, C. gueinzii, Teclea nobilis, Terminalia brownii*, and others); many of the trees have edible fruit. The ground cover is mixed perennial grass species (*Themeda triandra, Hyparrhenia dissoluta*, and others), many of which are excellent feed for cattle, and these regions are grazed (primarily by cattle) throughout the year.

Central Riverine Area

In the central area, the riverbeds become wide, sandy stretches, often with low banks. The alluvial plains adjacent to the rivers are choice sites for agriculture. Clear water can always be found by digging wells at certain places in the riverbeds, and these sources supply the permanent settlements of the Karimojong.

This region has varied soils—river alluvium, sandy loams, clay loams, and gray clays.

The vegetation of the central riverine area is destroyed bush-thicket type, the most abundant trees being *Acacia* ssp. and *Lannea* ssp. The ground cover is primarily herbs, annual grasses, and annuals, which sprout after rain storms but quickly die back if there is a dry period. Along the rivers are a variety of tree species (*Ficus sycamorus, F. platyphyla, Croton zambesicus, Carissa edulis, Acacia albida, A. seyal*, and others), many of which bear edible fruit.

The central riverine area is the only part of Karimojong country used for agriculture. The river alluvium is excellent for crops because the soil is rich in minerals (being fertilized each year by alluvium brought down by the rivers) and holds the water well. The gray clays become waterlogged, and thus less suitable for agriculture. The red sandy soils, called "hot soils" by the Karimojong, dry out quickly if rainfall is sparse and grow crops only in a year of abundant and well-distributed rainfall.

This region provides grazing for cattle only when there is ample rain. The herbs and annual grasses come up quickly after rainstorms but die back quickly if there is a dry period. Since the ground cover is sparse and the grazing heavy during the rains, residual dried herbs or grasses do not remain to feed the livestock after growth has stopped, although goats do browse on the trees.

Western Plains

In the western plains, the rivers spread out into seasonal swamps and finally, as underground water courses, seep into the Teso swamp at the western border of Karamoja. These drainage courses show clearly on aerial photographs because of a pattern of more dense vegetation, but they are difficult to follow on the ground. The dry season water in the western plains is very scarce. It is found in some large ponds that dry up only after six or more weeks without rain; in temporary pans full only a short time after storms; in the permanent swamp, Nanam, which is also used by the enemy tribe, the Teso; and, more recently, in government-built dams, only some of which hold water throughout the dry season.

This region has alternating ridges of red, sandy soil and valleys of heavy, dark gray clay. The vegetation is much more open than in the other regions. In the valleys are sparse stands of *Acacia drepanolobium*, a spindly tree, while the ridges are almost treeless. The perennial grasses of this region include *Themeda triandra, Hyparrhenia rufa, H. dissoluta, Heteropogon contortus, Sehima nervosum, Cymbopogon excavatus*, and others.

The area is not used for agriculture and is used for livestock only during the dry season. The heavy clays make travel difficult or impossible during the rains. If sudden heavy storms come when the cattle, particularly young and old stock, are weakened by a long dry season, some may die of exhaustion after bogging down in the waterlogged soil (as happened at the beginning of the 1954 rainy season). The grass grows very tall and in many areas quickly becomes too tough for the stock to eat. The dense stands of tall perennial grasses provide cover for marauding lions—dangerous to both livestock and herdsmen. For all these reasons, the western plains are not used for grazing livestock during the rains. In the dry season, on the other hand, problems of travel do not exist. The dry perennial grasses provide abundant feed for cattle when water is also locally available. Many of the grasses are nutritionally deficient, however, and the cattle gradually lose condition when fed on this alone. In an effort to overcome this problem, herdsmen burn off parts of this vast grassland, and if there are dry season storms the growth from the roots of the burned grasses provides excellent forage to supplement the dry grass.

The Mountain Areas

The mountains of Kadam, Moroto, and Napak are forest covered. They are occupied by a distinct tribe, the Tepeth, and are not used by Karimojong herdsmen. Therefore the soil, vegetation, and land use of this region will not be discussed.

Pattern of Exploitation

The distinct ecological regions of the district are exploited in different ways. In the central riverine areas, there are permanent settlements which we shall refer to as *homesteads*. They are near permanent clean water and have areas suitable for agriculture. These homesteads are built by the women, who live in them throughout the year. The grain is cultivated in nearby fields and stored in granaries within the stockaded homesteads. The women subsist mainly on grain foods, with milk to supplement their diet when grazing for cows and small stock is available nearby.

The homesteads have corrals for the cattle and a pen for the goats and sheep. But the herds graze near the homesteads only when the rainfall is abundant and the herbs and annual grasses of the area can provide enough grazing. The men have an area in the homestead, near the stock corral, that is theirs; a man may enter the yard of a woman, even his own wife, only with her permission.

The western plains and eastern highlands are exploited from temporary stock camps built by the men, particularly the young men, who live with the stock throughout the year. While staying at the stock camps the men live almost exclusively on blood and milk from the cattle, supplemented by grain food—usually in the form of beer—which the women may bring with them when they visit from the permanent settlements, and, particularly in the eastern highlands, by fruit and berries from the bush.

There is visiting back and forth between the homesteads and the stock camps. After the harvest is finished, women go to the camps to see their husbands or men friends and to drink milk. And if there is another responsible herdsman in the stock camp, a husband can leave for a short period to visit his family.

PLANT AND ANIMAL RESOURCES

Livestock

General

The Karimojong have large herds of cattle, sheep, and goats for food. They also keep donkeys for carrying loads but not for riding

In the settlements the women milk each cow every morning and evening; a child holds the calf nearby so the cow will release her milk.

Every evening the herd boys collect blood from the jugular vein of an animal and share it between the herdsmen.

FOOD PRODUCTION SYSTEM OF THE KARIMOJONG

Most cattle are slaughtered at public ceremonies. The men eat most of the meat.

About one year in five a bumper crop of sorghum is harvested—and then follows a time of plenty.

Sorghum is ground and cooked into porridge.

Kodet drinking beer. Sorghum beer is an important Karimojong food, particularly during the dry season when no milk is available to improve the flavor of sorghum porridge. Hot water is repeatedly added to the fermented brew to keep the pot full.

(see Table 2).[4] Livestock are an important food source for the Karimojong. Many of the young men and boys live almost exclusively on blood and milk, and milk and meat are important supplements to the diet of all the Karimojong.

Techniques of livestock management

Livestock may graze all over Karimojong tribal land except in the fenced fields of grain during the growing season. During the day they graze freely, guarded by a herd boy; at night they are kept in thorn-fenced corrals to protect them from hyenas, lions, leopards, and enemy tribesmen. The livestock's only food is the grass they can eat or the leaves they can browse. They are fed neither grain nor hay.

When possible, the stock are driven to water once a day. They either drink directly from an available pool of water or, if the source is a well, from a large, carved wooden tub into which the water is poured and from which each animal is allowed to drink in turn. During the dry season there is neither sufficient time nor water for cattle to drink all they want. Particularly in the western plains, where water sources are few and far between, dry season grazing near the water holes often becomes exhausted. The stock camps are then built between the water source and the grazing, and the herds are driven to graze one day and to water the next. Goats and sheep must drink every day.

Extensive labor is needed for herding. Herd boys are needed to guard the cattle and calves of both the village and camp herds (calves are kept separately from their mothers) and also for guarding the goats and sheep, which may be divided into several herds. A grown son or age-mate must be available to take charge when the herd owner visits his family. A moderately prosperous herd owner with, say, 100 to 150 cattle, 100 sheep and goats, and a few donkeys needs about 6 herd boys ranging from six to twenty-five years of age to maintain a herd by himself. A man with many cattle but few sons must herd together, and share the yield of his stock, with a man who has few cattle and many sons. These are relatively permanent herding associations, and the livestock will be handled as a single herd.

The aim of the Karimojong herd owner in organizing his herd is twofold. He wants to provide food for his family in the homestead;

[4] For a more complete account of the Karimojong rationale see Rada and Neville Dyson-Hudson, "Subsistence Herding in Uganda," *Scientific American*, 220, no. 2 (1969), 76–89.

TABLE 2
Livestock and Human Population, Karamoja, Uganda

	1922	1926	1934	1949	1953–55 (approx.)
Cattle	100,000	116,081	241,275	309,742	470,000
Donkeys	11,000	13,000	23,806	36,217	20,000
Sheep	400,000	520,834	489,353	376,943	400,000
Goats	80,000	53,355	281,227	252,927	300,000
Taxpayers	10,793	13,558		23,282[a]	25,150[b] 26,327[c]
Estimated Population	53,965	67,790		116,410[a]	125,750[b] 131,635[c]
Cattle/Taxpayer Ratio	9.265	8.561		13.304	18.261[e]
Cattle/Population Ratio[d]	1.853	1.712		2.661	3.652[e]

SOURCE: Karamoja District Records, Moroto.
[a] 1948.
[b] 1952.
[c] 1956.

[d] Based on an estimate of a ratio of 1/5 for taxpayer/population. The ratio was 1/4.1 in 1931 and 1/5.4 in 1948.
[e] Based on the average of the number of taxpayers in 1952 and 1956.

he also wants to keep his animals in the best possible condition. These two aims are often incompatible, however, since the best grazing, particularly in the dry season, is in the eastern highlands and the western plains, while the homestead containing his family is in the central riverine area. Therefore, a man with reasonable cattle resources (100 to 150 head or more) will usually divide his animals into two or more herds. One herd is kept in the homestead as long as grazing is available nearby. When grazing becomes scarce in the central area, this herd is either moved away as a unit or a few beasts at a time are sent to join the camp herd. Cattle from the homestead herd are kept as near to the permanent settlement as grazing conditions will permit so that the women and children can visit the camps to drink milk.

The camp herd may separate from the homestead herd only during the rainy season, when the homestead herd moves to the permanent settlement while the camp herd stays in the peripheral grazing area. This would appear to be the pattern followed when the herdsmen are older married men who want to remain near their families and when they are young boys who cannot supervise the herds alone.

In other cases the camp herd will go in an entirely separate orbit from the homestead herd, sometimes grazing up to fifty miles from the permanent settlement and never staying in the same camp with the homestead herd. This herd would be supervised by a group of young unmarried men with no family ties, while the homestead herd would be supervised by the older herdsmen.

Goats browse in preference to grazing and so can stay near the permanent settlements throughout the dry season, eating the leaves of the scrub vegetation and providing a little milk for the children.

Herd movements depend on each individual owner's assessment of the present and potential herding conditions and on the manpower available. A herd may stay in one area for an entire year, moving only short distances as its camp becomes too fly infested, or it may move every two or three weeks during the dry season, ranging from the west of the tribal area to the east. A Karimojong can, by tribal custom, graze anywhere in Karimojong country. An individual may tend to herd in the same area year after year because he comes to know the situation in that area as regards grazing, water, and enemies and because he can claim priority at regularly used waterholes when water is in short supply. But a detailed study of the moves of seven herds over a two-year period showed remarkably little pattern to the cattle movements.

In contrast to the permanent herding association based on shared food and labor, there are temporary herding associations. For security and sociability, Karimojong herd owners build stock camps together. Each herd owner then has his own corrals within a common stockade. Because of the individualistic nature of herd movements, such herding associations are frequently changed as one herd owner moves on to another location and another moves in.

The Karimojong live on the yield of their herds—milk from the cows and blood tapped from the jugular vein of all cattle except stud bulls and pregnant or lactating cows. In the morning and evening, the calves are allowed to suckle briefly to bring down the milk. Then the mother is milked and the calf suckles again. All the milk that is collected is available for human consumption. The men and boys in the camps drink milk fresh, mixed with blood. The women in the homesteads put the milk in gourds to curdle, churn the milk to remove the butter (which is boiled and stored as ghee), and mix the buttermilk with sorghum porridge.

Blood is usually tapped every evening in the stock camp to mix with the milk. The amount and frequency of bleeding varies with the size and condition of the animal and with the grazing conditions. Four to eight pints of blood taken every three months is typical, though a second bleeding may not take place for five months if the dry season is severe.

Though the Karimojong live primarily from the daily yields of their herds, any animal that dies is eaten. Animals that die of disease or accident are divided by the owner among his family and friends.

Cattle slaughter occurs only as part of a religious ceremony. However, the sacrificial aspects of slaughter must not be allowed to obscure the fact that meat is available to supplement the diet in times of food shortage. To pray to God for better times, large religious ceremonies—with the resultant slaughter of large numbers of cattle, particularly oxen—are frequent during times of famine. Then too, an owner may kill an animal to give meat to his family, providing he invites the local elders and prays to God.

Goats and sheep are slaughtered in a more casual manner than cattle, for instance if relatives or friends come to visit, but only as authorized by the herd owner. Though a woman may be given a goat as a gift if she has a beer party for the neighborhood, she may kill it only with her husband's permission.

Productivity of herds

As we have seen, the Karimojong have large herds of livestock, and the yields provide an important part of the food eaten by the Karimojong. During an adequate dry season, only the men and boys subsist on blood and milk. Ideally, however, a man's herd must be large enough not only to feed the herdsmen and boys adequately during a normal dry season but to act as a food reserve in years of crop failure, for when grain is not available in the permanent settlements, almost the entire population goes to the camps.

In 1953-54 the Karamoja Veterinary Department estimated the cattle numbers of the Pian section of the Karimojong (with whom we mainly worked) to be 40,593, and the 1948 human census estimated the human population of Pian to be 18,227. This gives a ratio of 2.23 cattle per person in the area of Karamoja where we worked (as compared with 0.54 head per person in the United States).[5]

However, yields of the cattle, not just the number, are important in evaluating cattle as a source of food, since basically the Karimojong subsist on the yield of the livestock, not the meat.

Data from a census of eleven cattle herds, shown in Table 3, indicate that some 60 percent of the adults in the herd are females. Since Karimojong cows do not have their first calves until they are 3½ to 4 years old, this would mean that less than half of the total number of cattle would be potential milch cows. The average calving interval is about 443 days, while the lactation period is about 230 days.[6] Therefore, only about half of the potential milch cows would actually be giving milk at any one time. Thus only about 25 percent of the total Karimojong cattle holdings would actually be giving milk at any one time. This would mean fewer than one milch cow per person (0.557). Data collected on a herd of native cattle indicate, in fact, that this figure might be much lower. Out of a herd of 110 animals, there were 27 cows with calves. Thus, close to 25 percent of the herd was giving milk. But only 13 cows, or

[5] Statistical Abstracts of the United States, published by the United States Department of Commerce (U.S. Government Printing Office, 1969), gives the total number of cattle in the United States as 109,661,000. *The World Almanac* (New York: Doubleday and Company, Inc., 1969) gives the human population of the United States as 201,750,000.

[6] The first figure is based on 175 observations of Karimojong cattle kept in the Moroto dairy herd. The actual average was 442.7 with 95 percent confidence interval of ± 18.5.

111

TABLE 3

Composition of Eleven Herds of Karimojong Cattle

Herd	Bulls Mature	Bulls Young	Oxen Mature	Oxen Young	Cows	Heifers	Calves[a]	Total	Percentage Females (Adult Stock Only)
1. (C)	10	15	222	18	30	17	—	112	54.2
(M)	—	—	—	—	30	—	24	54 166	
2. (C)	1	15	14	2	17	21	—	70	58.6
(M)	5	5	10	1	37	—	44	102 172	
3. (C)	1	19	11	2	24	16	—	73	52.6
(M)	1	2	—	—	19	—	13	35 108	
4. (C)	4	26	29	3	36	40	—	138	60.3
(M)	—	0	0	0	18	—	18	36 174	
5. (C)	9	38	32	15	50	34	—	173	60.7
(M)	5	5	8	—	86	3	53	160 338	
6. (C)	—	8	—	—	25	13	—	46	84.5
(M)	1	—	2	1	22	—	18	43 89	
7. (C)	3	8	6	1	38	20	—	76	71.4
(M)	1	3	4	2	12	—	3	25 101	
8. (C)	5	30	8	8	31	24	—	106	60.1
(M)	4	—	—	—	28	—	25	57 163	
9. (C)	3	18	7	5	29	27	—	89	65.6
(M)	1	6	4	—	22	6	14	53 142	
10. (C)	6	25	13	6	51	23	—	124	58.3
(M)	6	24	16	5	54	13	39	157 281	
11. (C)	3	22	20	26	29	30	—	130	48.9
(M)	1	—	—	—	10	—	7	18 148	

SOURCE: Karamoja District Records, Moroto. Information collected by the District Veterinary Office who counted the cattle in eleven camp herds (C), then returned to the settlements to count the cattle in the eleven settlement herds (M) of the same owners. The herds were of the NgiBokora section.

[a] The calves of the camp herds were obviously not counted. These are kept in a separate herd near the camp and were missed.

11.8 percent of the total herd, were giving milk beyond the need of their calves. If only 12 percent of the cattle give extra milk at any one time, the number of milk cows per head of population in Pian could be estimated at 0.267.

Table 4 gives data on the amount of extra milk produced by cows in a native herd. It shows a maximum of almost 5 pints a day in September, the end of the rains, and a minimum of slightly more than 2 pints daily in May, just after the beginning of the rainy season. The dry season when this study was made (1957-58) was not particularly severe, and other measurements indicate that in a harsh dry season the cows give less than 1.5 pints of extra milk per day. The milk from the cattle camp is supplemented by a small amount of blood daily, which is undoubtedly important in providing nutritional elements not available in milk alone.

TABLE 4

Milk Production of Karimojong Cows
(Average Daily Yield per Cow Available for Human Use)

Month	Pints
July	2.31
August	3.49
September	4.78
October	3.58
November	2.64
December	3.05
January	3.51
February	2.94
March	2.62
April	2.79
May	2.13
June	3.47
July	3.46

NOTE: Based on data collected one day each month from a native herd in 1957-58.

These data indicate that even in the rainy season milk is not abundant, and during a severe dry season the yield of the cattle is not enough to support the human population of Pian.[7] Clearly an additional source of food is necessary.

[7] This was supported by our experience that even during the rainy season we received very little milk from our neighbors. They obviously felt badly about not giving us more.

Agriculture

Crops

Farming is primarily the work of the women, though more and more men are helping in the fields as larger areas are being planted and as cattle are being used to plow the fields.

Sorghum is the main crop planted by the Karimojong. They plant numerous varieties of the tall sorghums, each of which has particular merits for porridge, beer, or storage. The short varieties are not used, since they do not have the drought resistance of the tall varieties, do not yield as well except under very special conditions of rainfall that rarely occur in Karamoja, and do not make good beer.

Cucurbits (pumpkins, squashes, cucumbers, and gourds) planted between the sorghum and along the stockades of the settlements are the second most important agricultural food group but rank far below sorghum in importance.

Finger millet, planted in the swamps, is raised as a specialty crop and is prized for its sweet flavor. It needs more water than sorghum, however, so probably does not make a significant contribution to the food of the Karimojong. It succeeds only in years when sorghum is abundant.

Maize was introduced in 1923, and the people like it. It is planted only in small patches near the homestead, however, and produces only in years when sorghum gives a bumper crop.

Tobacco is grown by specialists—usually men who have few livestock—on the rich soil at the sites of old homesteads. Its producer sells it for money or trades it for food directly.

Technology

Though the total rainfall in Karamoja would appear to be adequate to raise sorghum successfully almost every year, the fact that the rainy season is spread over six months (rather than concentrated in three) makes agriculture very risky. A period of rain is often followed by three or more weeks of drought; if this occurs at critical periods during sorghum growth, the plants will die or be severely stunted and yield poorly.

Sorghum is planted when the rains begin, and takes three to four months to ripen. Since it is difficult to know when the rains have begun, the first plantings often fail, and the fields are replanted as many as four or five times—until early June. On the other hand, in other years only the early sowings succeed. A study of the agricultural history of the district makes it clear that no rule can be made about planting dates. But some of the older women are obviously particularly skillful at agriculture, and they succeed each year in harvesting much more than their younger co-wives.

The method of cultivation varies through the rainy season. In January, February, and March, the women begin to cut the trees from the garden areas and repair the fences. Then they cultivate the ground with a short-handled hoe and may plant some seeds if the rain seems imminent. On the whole, however, they wait until after a major rainstorm to hoe and plant the sorghum. As the ground becomes soft from the rain, the ox-drawn plow is used, and large areas can be cultivated if the rain continues. Weeding begins about a month after the initial successful planting and is carried out with the short-handled hoe. As the grain heads begin to form, a dawn to dusk watch is kept over the fields, to chase the birds from the crops.

The grain is harvested by cutting off the heads of grain with a knife and carrying them to the homestead in large wooden tubs. The drying grain is stored in special storehouses and is threshed with a flat wooden paddle. The threshed grain is kept in large woven granaries, and is ground as needed. Sorghum porridge is the major food in the permanent settlement, and beer is also considered to be a food, not simply a drink.

The pumpkins and squashes are harvested and eaten fresh through December, and they are also dried and stored in the granaries to be cooked with the sorghum porridge.

Thus the technology of agriculture, like that of herding, is relatively simple.

Productivity

Sorghum is the most drought-resistant grain and will often give an adequate crop once a year during the rainy season. In years of good rainfall, sorghum will produce a yield estimated at 1,000 pounds per acre. The area under cultivation in Karamoja has been estimated at 53,519 acres,[8] but only a very few areas (mainly in southern Karamoja and in the Labwor Hills) would produce grain at this high level and then only during years of well-distributed and abundant rainfall.

[8] Karamoja District Records, Moroto ecologist's report, 1954.

In many areas of Karamoja the soil is depleted by repeated cultivation, so even in a year with adequate rainfall a scanty crop is harvested. Thus it is impossible to get a reliable estimate of the amount of grain produced in Karamoja in any one year. The unreliability of the rainfall (already discussed with Table 1) means that partial or total crop failures are frequent.

Table 5 illustrates the unreliability of the harvest in Karamoja during the period 1917–57. In the 39 years for which records were available, there were 4 total crop failures, 8 years of poor crops, 12 years with average harvests or harvests that were good in some areas and poor in others, 9 years with fairly good crops or excellent

TABLE 5
Harvests in Karamoja District
1917–57

Year	Quality of Harvest	Year	Quality of Harvest
1917	3	1937	3
1918	0	1938	3
1919	2	1941	3
1920	2	1942	1
1921	1	1943	2
1922	1	1944	0
1923	3	1945	2
1924	0	1946	4
1925	4	1947	1
1926	3	1948	2
1927	0	1949	2
1928	3	1950	1
1929	3	1951	2
1930	1	1952	1
1931	4	1953	1
1932	2	1954	4
1933	2	1955	2
1934	4	1956	3
1935	4	1957	2
1936	2		

Numbers are symbols on a four-point scale, as follows:
4. Bumper crop (total—six years).
3. Fairly good, or excellent in some areas, failures in a few (total—nine years).
2. Harvest average, or failures in some areas, good in others (total—twelve years).
1. Crop poor, or partial, though not complete, failure (total—eight years).
0. Total failure (total—four years).
SOURCE: Karamoja District Records, Moroto. There was no information available for the years 1939 and 1940.

harvest in some areas and poor in a few, and 6 years of bumper harvest. In general, in southern Pian (an area only recently settled) the crops seem to be adequate for the minimum needs of the people (realizing that a person may lose 10 pounds of weight or more by the end of the dry season) and in some years suffice for trading and for large celebrations and feasts. In northern Pian and Matheniko (except in areas along the Omanimani River, where flooding renews the soil) the crop is barely enough to provide food for more than a few months in the dry season. Though agriculture is an important food source, clearly the people cannot depend on it.

Bush Foods

There are a large number of animals found in the bush that are eaten by the Karimojong. These range from elephant, giraffe, zebra, and the more than a dozen species of antelope found in Karamoja (eland, kongoni, bush buck, roan antelope, dikdik, duiker, topi, oribi, klip-springer, water buck, kob, Grant's gazelle, oryx, lesser kudu, greater kudu) to various species of rodent, such as field rats and cane rats, and other small mammals, rock hyraxes and hares, for example.

Many plants or their fruits also are eaten. A complete list would not be possible in this chapter, but we can give a few examples. The fruit of the tamarind tree (*Tamarindis indica*) is gathered and stored to flavor porridge during the dry season when no milk is available in the permanent settlements. Groups of people go to the eastern highlands in the late dry season to gather the fruit of *Ximenia caffra* (*ngalam*) in large wooden tubs. The fruit is eaten, and the kernels are cracked and the fatty nut used to tan the skins for the women's skirts. Some herbs (for example, *Justicia exigua* and *Cleome monophylla*) which sprout after the dry-season rainstorms are gathered and cooked as spinach (*ediya*). Certain roots (such as *Coleus edulus* and *Lannea humilis*) are dug up and eaten. Also the seeds of grasses, particularly *Dactylocetenium aegyticum*, can be gathered in times of famine and ground to make a millet-like porridge.

At present, the Karimojong do not go out of their way to hunt, though they will kill game if it is easy to get. The children will gather small rodents, cook them directly on the fire, and eat them. Aside from a few fruits that are systematically collected, most of the food gathering is casual. For example, a boy will gather fruit and berries while he herds the cattle in the eastern highlands, where bush food is abundant. Or a woman, going to visit a friend, will see evidences of edible roots and dig them up to eat along the way.

In the late 1800's rinderpest decimated the herds and smallpox reduced the human population. Many of the people in Karamoja then had to support themselves by hunting and gathering food in the bush. Early accounts described the Karimojong at the turn of the century as hunters and food gatherers, but the careful questioning by Turpin [9] made it clear that this was a result of the epidemics.

The Karimojong traded ivory for cattle which gradually rebuilt their herds, and the population has increased steadily over the last sixty years. Though there is still a very high human and livestock mortality, the large-scale epidemics have been controlled by medical and veterinary measures. Thus the "bush food" could no longer support the human population in times of famine. But, bush foods, particularly fruits and berries, undoubtedly do provide an important dietary supplement during the dry season when fresh foods are rare.

FOOD DISTRIBUTION

The cattle products, blood and milk, cannot be kept for more than a few hours. Only the ghee, made by boiling the butter, can be stored. But by the end of the rainy season a woman would have only a few quarts of this reserve food in her storehouse. Meat is eaten fresh or can be kept for several months by sun-drying, but only a few pounds of meat would usually be available as reserve dry-season food.

Sorghum is the main source of food during the dry season when the cattle are away at the camps, but it cannot be kept successfully for more than a year. The Karimojong have a system whereby excess food can be distributed to areas where crops have been less successful. This is based on three different social phenomena—ceremonies, begging, and trading.

Huge public beer drinks occur after a bumper harvest. Many young men will also be initiated after a good sorghum crop, after which there are feasts in the villages. In this way, large quantities of grain are consumed and shared. The hosts at the beer drink are given goats in exchange for their hospitality.

The Karimojong learn from childhood to beg, and it is a perfectly acceptable pattern of behavior. You beg from relatives and

[9] E. A. Turpin, "The Occupation of the Turkwel River Area by the Karimojong Tribe," *Uganda Journal*, 12 (1948), 161–65.

friends who have more than you do, and if later you have more than they do, they will beg from you. In this way, surpluses are redistributed among neighborhoods and kin groups.

By trading, people from drought-stricken areas can get grain to survive the dry season. The standard exchange is a goat or a sheep for a skin sack of grain. During bad years, donkey-loads of grain are "bought" from Southern Karamoja and from the tribes living to the west, both areas where rainfall is usually higher.

In 1941, government cattle-buying was initiated. This provides money so that when food is short the people can buy cornmeal in the shops. Though the Karimojong do not casually sell an ox to buy cornmeal, they do sell livestock in famine years. Thus in the famine years 1944 and 1945, 17,000 and 10,000 cattle were sold to the government cattle buyer. This is in contrast to 1946 and 1947, both years with good harvests, when only 4,158 and 5,500 cattle were sold. Trade in small stock (with which the Karimojong would more readily part) is conducted mostly by local Somali shopkeepers. There is therefore no record of the numbers of goats and sheep sold.

SUMMARY

Thus livestock yields and agricultural produce provide the basic foods of the Karimojong, supplemented by food gathered in the bush. Crops, cattle produce, and bush foods are all dependent on rainfall, but on rainfall in different seasons.

The crop yields depend on a concentrated three-month period of rain sometime between April and September to enable the sorghum to germinate, grow, and ripen. An intense three-week drought period will seriously affect the harvest. Though local crop failures are frequent, there are methods of distributing surpluses to less fortunate areas.

Fruit depends more on the overall amount of rainfall during the six months between flowering and fruiting. The crop is less sensitive to short drought periods, though a long drought would reduce yields.

The grass growth for livestock benefits from any period of rain, and the dry-season storms are particularly important in maintaining the condition of the cattle. Periods of rain followed by three weeks of drought—a pattern disastrous to agriculture—do not seriously affect the growth of perennial grasses.

Conditions leading to a high mortality of cattle have occurred six times in the past thirty years. But, it is rare indeed for crops to fail totally in a year when the grazing conditions are so bad during the dry season that the cattle would yield no milk. And should such a dry year occur, the full effects of livestock mortality would not be felt until later, since the animals that die from lack of grazing and water provide meat to keep the people going until the next rainy season.

Thus, by using three alternative sources of food in their food production system, the Karimojong are able to survive in their uncertain environment.

PROBLEMS, AND PROSPECTS FOR DEVELOPMENT

The Karimojong method of exploiting the environment supports only a limited number of people. And it is likely that, since epidemics have been reduced, this limit has been reached in Karamoja and that entirely new methods will have to be developed.

There are three alternatives for development in Karamoja—improving agriculture, improving animal husbandry, or developing new sources of income.

Before examining these alternatives, it is important to note that Karamoja is the least developed district in Uganda. There are no paved roads and only a few miles of bush tracks in the entire district. Though there are roads to Mbale and Soroti in Uganda and to Kitale in Kenya, these cross unbridged rivers and swamps, are extremely rough and difficult to drive on, and are subject to rainy season washouts. In the past the government of Uganda apparently has been unwilling to invest money in Karamoja, and there is no indication that they will do so in the near future.

The main problem in Karamoja is not total rainfall but the three-to-four-week droughts, accompanied by hot dry winds, during the rainy season. Any improvement in agriculture should thus be aimed at enabling crops to survive these periods. Sorghum is the crop most suited for growing in semi-arid environments, so it is unlikely that a better basic grain crop could be introduced. Different varieties of sorghum have been tried. On the whole, the short-term sorghums yield less than the local strains, do not store as well (they are prone to weevil infestation), and produce poor beer. (These varieties are suitable for areas like the Sudan, where rain is concentrated in a short period.) Drought resistance is the quality necessary, and the local Karamoja strains are already highly selected for this characteristic. So without careful and extensive breeding in the area (or one similar) it is unlikely that an introduced strain will improve on them.

The introduction of mechanization in agriculture could increase the acreage under cultivation. By their present methods, however, the Karimojong are able to produce ample food in a year of abundant rainfall. Machine cultivation of marginal lands would reduce the area available for grazing and simultaneously increase the problems of erosion.

Irrigation could be used to provide water during dry periods. There are problems, however, in damming the rivers for irrigation. The large rivers come down with such force that it is almost impossible to harness them. A mission and government irrigation scheme on the Omanimani River was completely destroyed in its first month of operation when the river came down in flood and cut away the bank on which it was built. There are only a few small rivers such as Amuda, Ngimin'to, and Nadunget that could be easily controlled and used for irrigation. But they would provide water for only a small area.

Perhaps one good way to aid agriculture would be long-range weather forecasting. This would help the people to know when the rains have really begun and to predict if the season will have enough rainfall to raise crops. If the prospects were for a good year, a large acreage could be planted. If the prospects were poor, planting would be restricted to the swamps, river terraces, and areas near the mountains. It would then be necessary either to sell surplus food grown in good years and buy during bad years or to have a means of storing grain for more than one year.

Animal husbandry methods could be changed to get better yields from fewer cattle. Limiting the size of herds and upgrading the quality of the cattle are obvious areas of improvement. Karimojong cattle are already among the finest in East Africa, however, and if they were bred for higher milk yield and bigger size they might not be able to stand the periods of deprivation they must endure.

There is also a social factor that inhibits the culling of stock. Marriage involves the giving of cattle to all the relatives of the bride. And a man wants to marry a girl with as many kinsmen as he can afford so that he will have as large a family as possible. Since there is no effective government protection of the individual, the only satisfaction a man can get if his property is stolen or if his rights are abused is to get his kinsmen to back him up. During times of shortage, or if his herds are decimated by enemy raiding or disease, he can also beg from his kinsmen. The more kinsmen a man has, the more secure his position. A man therefore keeps all his animals, even culls, because he wants large numbers to give in marriage, rather than limiting his herd to good milking animals. Thus culling of herds and improving livestock would be precluded indirectly by the lack of effective and honest local government.

The willingness of the men to endure great physical hardship to take their livestock where the grass is abundant means that all of the Karamoja grazing land is exploited. The eastern highlands are at present very efficiently grazed from the stock camps both in the dry season and during the rains. The government tries to keep the people from this area because of tribal warfare, but they should be encouraging the people to utilize the excellent grazing available.

The western plains are only used during the dry season, and a great deal of grass is not utilized. A portion is burned over each year and some is simply left standing. But there are great difficulties in utilizing the grass in this area because of the lack of water, the nutritional deficiency of the grass, and the nature of the soil.

An alternative to the nomadic method of exploitation would be to settle the people and bring the food to the cattle. But this would be extremely difficult because of the lack of roads and because of the nature of the land. The eastern highlands are rough and rocky, and hay could not be harvested by machinery. Though the land is flat on the western plains, it would be almost impossible to cut and bale hay when the grass was ripe but before it was dry. Heavy machinery cannot operate in the area until the heavy clay soil is completely dry. The grass when dry is not good cattle fodder, however, and must be supplemented by green grass or the cattle lose condition.

The periodic burning may also be important for bush control and for sweetening the acid soil. And if cutting were substituted for burning it might well be necessary to add lime and fertilizer as well, which would be expensive.

There is often more milk at the camps than there are people to consume it, and it is simply fed to the dogs. To collect the milk and redistribute it in the area of permanent settlements, however, would be enormously expensive and would require roads.

The base of Kadam Mountain, one of the finest areas for grazing and agriculture, is not being used to the extent it might be because of the presence of east coast fever, a tick-borne cattle disease.[10] This

[10] V. R. Dyson-Hudson, "East Coast Fever In Karamoja," *Uganda Journal*, 24 (1960), 253–59.

could be controlled by installing cattle dips, and the area could once again be fully utilized.

Sources of income other than agriculture and animal husbandry, particularly mineral deposits, have been studied. Mineral deposits, principally copper and radioactive materials, do exist in Karamoja, but in no case are they of economic significance, given the enormous problems of transportation and exploitation.

Any attempts to develop Karamoja can only succeed if the indigenous system is thoroughly understood and the enormous environmental problems in Karamoja fully appreciated. Development would require a large, imaginative, and sustained investment of money and manpower by the government. Given the other claims on government resources, it will no doubt be a long time before Karamoja's food problems receive appropriate attention.

CHAPTER 4

ZANDE SUBSISTENCE AND FOOD PRODUCTION

CONRAD C. REINING

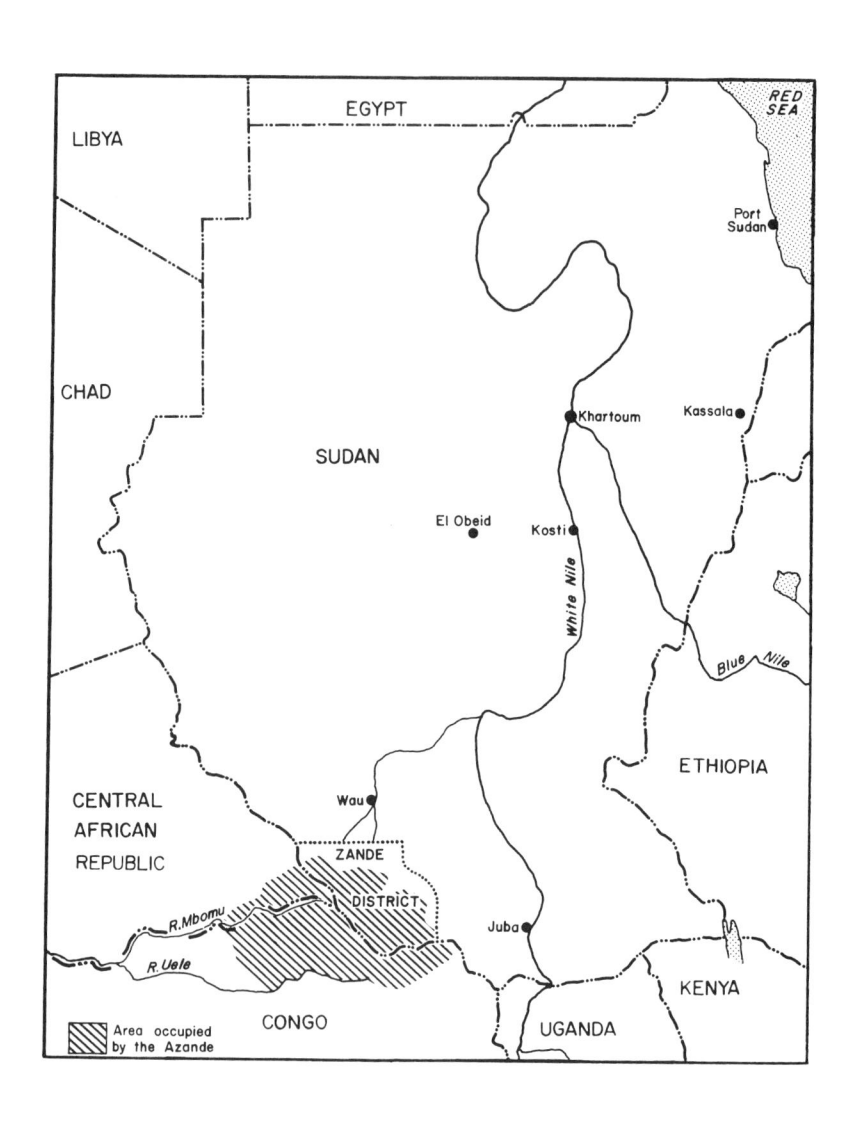

This essay summarizes the agricultural system of the Azande and some of the changes they have experienced to illustrate problems of food production in a modern, tropical situation where shifting cultivation is practiced. These problems are widely found, and their solution and prevention are the responsibility of a variety of experts. An anthropological analysis is not attempted here, and I allow the reader to draw his own geographical, technical and cultural implications. To this end, I try to distinguish between Zande notions and those of the non-Zande administration, which often vitally affected the agricultural practices, and I further attempt to keep these distinct from my views as an observer of the situation.

Severe political upheavals have influenced most of the Zande population since the time of my study (August, 1952, to August, 1955), and unsettled and (to me) unknown conditions prevail to this day. Although some of the subsistence patterns probably remain, the total situation has changed so markedly that it might well be misleading to use the present tense—as is the tendency—for the time of my observations there. I therefore use the past tense for all but the most obviously replicable of natural phenomena and for analytical points.

The Azande (plural; singular is Zande) live in the center of Africa where the Congo (Kinshasa), the Sudan, and the Central African Republic meet. At the time of my research, about 400,000 Azande were reported to be living in what was then the Belgian Congo, 175,000 in the Sudan, and about 30,000 in what was then called French Equatorial Africa. They were unevenly distributed throughout an area of about 60,000 square miles. Zande country lies along the Nile-Congo watershed at between 1,800 and 3,000 feet of altitude. The area is well watered, with about 40 to 60 inches of rainfall annually and with many springs, particularly along the divide. These give rise to the numerous streams that have shaped the countryside to its gently rolling pattern. The climate is moderate for an area only 4 to 6 degrees north of the equator, and it is a green and pleasant place in contrast to the hotter and drier areas to the east and north. The greater part of the country is covered by scrub forest, with tall grass filling the spaces not dominated by trees and rocks. On the higher ground, the rigors of the dry season and bush fires favor hardy types of vegetation. But a variant, similar to the equatorial rain forest to the southwest in the Congo basin, occurs along many of the streams and in depressions where the water table is relatively close to the surface the year round. The Azande were expert at exploiting the different sets of flora and fauna found in their country—and suffered from the equally wide variety of pests, parasites, and diseases to be found there.

The area comprised the remotest parts of three colonial territories, each oriented to its capital and seaports. Communication and transport were slow and costly. The remoteness of the region, along with its lack of valuable natural resources, had kept it undeveloped, even by African standards. The main concern of the European administrations was to keep law and order, with development of minimal commercial activity based on the sale of forest produce. To combat sleeping sickness and for administrative purposes, the Zande populations of all three countries were moved early in the colonial period from their habitat along the streams to the roads, which followed higher ground.

In the early 1920's the Belgians introduced cotton as a cash crop among the Azande and other tribes in the northern Congo. The other two countries did not follow this example immediately, and in the Sudan, where I made most of my observations, the southern provinces were kept deliberately isolated to protect the population from commercial exploitation. But changes in policies brought pressures to develop the southern Sudan after World War II, and Zande District of the Sudan was selected as a pilot area. The ensuing development scheme, based on cultivation of cotton, produced many changes which were the focus of my research. They have been reported in my book and need not be detailed here.[1]

The activities within the Zande subsistence economy could be divided into four major categories: construction and maintenance of the homestead, agriculture, hunting and gathering, and handicrafts. Of these, agriculture was undoubtedly the most important and the most time-consuming, but some of the other activities were necessary for subsistence. The construction and maintenance of the homestead was, of course, indispensable and had to proceed with all other activity. Hunting had special interest to the Azande in its sport and excitement as well as in producing most of their meat. The activities falling into hunting and gathering, however, were probably the most likely to be affected in the event of conflict with other work. The subsistence activities varied in relative importance according to the seasons. Agricultural work was most intense during the rains, when hunting was difficult because of the high grass, while hunting and construction were favored activities during the dry season, when agriculture could not be practiced.

[1] Conrad C. Reining, *The Zande Scheme* (Evanston, Ill.: Northwestern University Press, 1966).

ZANDE CROPS

Although a good deal had been written about Zande agriculture and diet,[2] it was necessary for me to investigate the entire range of food products and the mode of cultivating them. To understand the domestic economy of such a people, an investigator must be fluent in the agricultural processes and the characteristics of the various food plants. The knowledge of these things is comparable to a knowledge of the language; it may be considered a logical extension of the learning of the language. An investigator must also be conversant with the processing and the uses of food crops, for the process from the clearing of a field to the eating of the produce is a continuous one.

The agricultural system had been altered under European administration because of conservation measures and the resettlement of the population to the roads in the 1920's and 1930's. Far greater were the effects of the Zande Development Scheme, with its resettlement plan, in Zande District of the Sudan. I did not try to reconstruct the pre-European agricultural system but did attempt to find out what the Zande regarded as their most effective system as it had been adapted to the changing situations. Comparison with Azande in French and Belgian territories, where the people lived along the roads but were still quite free in choosing their cultivation sites, aided considerably in assessing the Sudan situation, which the Azande claimed had been seriously distorted by the imposition of resettlement and a cash crop.

The Azande grew a relatively wide variety of crops that can be assigned to the following categories: cereals, roots and tubers, oilseeds, vegetables, leafy foods, and fruits. Zande usage brought out another distinction: that of garden crops, grown in and around the courtyard, as opposed to field crops. Most of the cereals and oilseeds were grown as field crops, while the vegetables and fruits were usually garden crops; roots and tubers were both garden and field crops.

The Courtyard and Garden Crops

When a Zande used the term *kporo*, "homestead or home," he included, in a general way, his cultivations as well as his buildings

---

[2] G. M. Culwick, *A Dietary Survey among the Zande of the Southwestern Sudan* (Khartoum: Ministry of Agriculture, 1950); A. G. McCall, *A Note on the Agriculture of the Azande*, Ministry of Agriculture Bulletin, no. 2 (Khartoum, 1950); Pierre de Schlippe, *Shifting Cultivation in Africa* (London: Routledge and Kegan Paul, 1956).

A newly established homestead.

Weeding with a hoe.

Planting peanuts.

Straining beeswax.

and courtyard. It was natural to make all cultivations near the courtyard at first and then go farther and farther away for field cultivations. The most usual pattern was for the courtyard to have a belt of cultivation around it, in the nature of a kitchen garden. Sweet potatoes were generally dominant here, for they are perennial and an excellent cover crop; their vines discourage the growth of most other plants not aided by cultivation. This made for a weedless belt around the well-established courtyard. As time passed, the area covered by the garden in a newly established home expanded and became more uniform. Beyond the garden belt there was usually a tangle of fallow bush, or, if the homestead was new, there might be some cultivated fields.

The crops that were grown in the courtyard or in the garden around it may be roughly described as the perennials and the miscellaneous, and they may be distinguished from the field crops, which were mostly annuals and which furnished the bulk of the food supply. The Azande regarded the garden as a place to get a bit of food for immediate preparation, whereas the field crops usually required large-scale harvesting, processing, and storage.

Cultivated Trees and Fruit Crops

In the courtyard and the garden around it were found most of the cultivated trees and other perennial plants. Some cultivated trees were merely ornamental, but most of them yielded useful products. The most common trees were oil palms (*Elaeis guineensis*); mangoes (*Manifera indica*); bark cloth trees (*Ficus platyphylla*); and banana (*Musa* spp.). Of these, the banana was undoubtedly the most important because it produced large amounts of food, especially in the well-established homesteads. The Azande ate bananas of all varieties, ripe and uncooked. Only in the southern reaches of their area in the Congo, I was told, did Azande cook bananas into a porridge. Another important fruit, grown by most Azande, was the pineapple (*Ananas cosmosus*). The bark cloth tree, a fig, was grown only for its bark. These trees could be seen on the sites of old homesteads in great numbers and were still being planted by the Azande, although bark cloth had been largely superseded by imported cloth. Other trees of lesser importance included papaya (*Carica papaya*); citrus of several kinds *(Citrus* spp.); mulberry (*Morus* spp.); and guava (*Psidium guayava*). It will be noted that many of these were relatively recently introduced trees. The Azande were quick to appreciate new additions to their perennial plants.

The mango deserves special mention as the most successful of all newly arrived plants. It was within the British administration that the first seeds had been brought from the Belgian Congo, where the tree had been introduced from East Africa and India. The first seeds were planted in the Sudan about 1918, and within thirty years mango trees had become an outstanding feature of the countryside in Zande District. All buildings, whether Zande or official, had mangoes planted about them, and the large trees gave enormous quantities of fruit. Because the fruit ripened at the end of the dry season, when food tended to be scarce and fresh food was very rare, the harvest of mangoes was welcome and an excellent addition to the diet of the Azande. Large quantities were consumed, some individuals and even families virtually living on them for days at a time. A particularly cynical Zande observed to me that the introduction of the mango trees had been the most important contribution of the Europeans to Zande welfare. In some areas there were more than could be consumed. The resettlement program of 1946–50 removed the population from the old stands of mangoes along the roads, but the Azande were quick to plant trees in their new homesteads. These were useful as guides to the age of homesteads. The mangoes were seeding themselves and were being spread by the monkeys, elephants, and other animals that ate the fruit.

Leaf-yielding Plants

The most important plants yielding leaves used for food were sweet potatoes (*Ipomea batatas*); cassava (*Manihot esculenta*); pumpkin (*Cucurbita maxima*); amaranth (*Amaranthus* spp. and *Celosia argentea*); mock tomato (*Solanum aethiopicum*); and jew's mallow (*Corchorus olitorius*). The first three of these also yielded other food. A variety of other leaves of both cultivated and uncultivated plants was also eaten; the Azande ate a relatively large quantity and wide range of leafy food.

Vegetables and Miscellaneous Plants

The principal plants yielding other vegetable foods were okra (*Hibiscus esculentus*); cucumber (*Cucumis* spp.); pumpkin (*Cucurbita maxima*); red sorrel (*Hibiscus sabdariffa*); and gourd (*Lagenaria siceraria*). Some varieties of cucumbers, gourds, and pumpkins were eaten as vegetables when immature; they could be allowed to mature for other uses, including the use of the seeds as food. An inedible watermelon (*Citrullus* spp.) was also grown by the Azande for its seeds, which were shelled and ground into an oily paste, as were pumpkin and gourd seeds.

Of the other crops grown in or around the homestead, the yam (*Dioscorea* spp.) was once a much more important food crop but had been largely supplanted by sweet potatoes and cassava. Yams in my time were grown only as occasional plants. Other miscellaneous plants included aerial yam (*Dioscorea bulbifera*); taro or cocoyam (*Xanthosoma sagittifolium*); green gram (*Phaseolus mungo*); cowpea (*Vigna unguicanlata*); tobacco (*Nicotiana tabacum*); and Deccan hemp (*Hibiscus cannabinus*). This hemp was the only plant grown by the Azande, other than the bark cloth tree, especially for fiber. In some parts its leaves were used for food. Still other crops were to be found in and around the courtyards, but those listed were the most common. Although only a few of these were also grown as field crops, small plantings of the field crops discussed below were found in most of the courtyards and gardens observed. If not much seed was available for a field crop, it might be planted close at hand, or some particularly early stand of field crop could be planted close to the courtyard. This was often the case with maize, which was the earliest of the food crops to mature after the beginning of the rains; when it was still too early to plant a large quantity, a few seeds might be planted near the courtyard on the chance that they would sprout and produce an early yield. Cassava was found everywhere: in the gardens, courtyards, and fields. The bushes often were planted as hedges and bordering plants.

Field Crops

Field crops are those that the Azande regarded as their staples and planted in quantity wherever good land could be found. The most important were: cassava or manioc (*Manihot esculenta*); eleusine (*Eleusine coracana*); maize (*Zea mays*); and groundnuts (*Arachis hypogaea*). Others, of lesser importance, were: sorghums (*Sorghum* spp.); upland rice (*Oryza* spp.); Bambara nuts (*Voandzeia subterranea*); bulrush millet (*Pennisetum typhoideum*); sesame (*Sesamum orientalé*); hyptis (*Hyptis spicigera*); gourds (*Langenaria siceraria*); and melons (*Citrullus* spp.). The last two have already been mentioned as garden crops.

These were by no means all the crops grown in Zande fields, but they were the most commonly found. There were various varieties and subspecies within the categories of crops listed above. De Schlippe gives partial lists of the varieties within the various species.[3] There was some variation within Zande country, particularly as to the relative importance of the staple grains, but in general the types listed were found within most normal homesteads. There was a remarkable uniformity in the types of crops grown in all homesteads. Because each homestead was regarded as a self-sufficient unit, at least as far as food was concerned, each grew all of the common crops. Some of the less generally grown types not mentioned above are described by Culwick. Her excellent lists do not, unfortunately, indicate the relative importance among crops.[4]

Relative Importance of Crops

The trees, garden crops, and field crops listed furnished all but a small portion of the food of the Azande. Approximately thirty different plants were usually found in most homesteads. It is difficult to assign relative importance to them, but cassava, eleusine, groundnuts, maize, bananas, and sweet potatoes undoubtedly formed the largest part of Zande diet.

Eleusine had the reputation, backed by the accounts of earlier observers, of having been the staple crop in earlier times. It was still the most important grain and the favored ingredient in porridge and beer at the time of my research, but it had been displaced in greatly varying amounts according to locality and stability of population by cassava.

Cassava had taken the position as the most important food, in terms of calories, among the Azande because of its ease in cultivation and processing into food. It is not critical of soil and is highly resistant to drought and insects. It requires little care aside from rough weeding and keeps well in the ground. It is an almost perfect famine reserve crop and had been encouraged as such in Zande country, though the danger of famine was not as great there as in other parts of Africa. The processing of cassava into flour was done in two stages: the tubers were fermented in a pool or stream for three to five days, and the resulting lumps were then dried, pounded, and sifted. This is much less work than the flailing, winnowing, and grinding required of eleusine. But the nutritional value of cassava flour is low compared with flour prepared from eleusine or other grains. Mrs. Culwick, in her nutritional survey, concluded: "Cassava had a valuable role to play as a supplementary food and famine reserve, but it has encroached beyond those limits, is ousting cereals,

---
[3] *Shifting Cultivation*, pp. 48–77.
[4] *Dietary Survey*, pp. 79–91.

and unless checked, threatens to undermine the whole nutritional position. Its attraction lies as much in its low processing costs as in its ease of cultivation."[5]

Zande preferences coincided with the nutritional findings; they preferred other foods, using cassava as a substitute when they were in short supply. Cassava in the diet made a good indicator of social stability, for it was the cheapest and most available food but one of the least desirable; the proportion of it in the diet gave me a rough indication of the stress under which a household or individual was operating. Cassava was rarely eaten unmixed with other food except in what may be considered abnormal situations, such as after resettlement of the entire population of an area, in urban situations, and in homesteads lacking the services of a woman. Cassava flour was observed and reported to be an ingredient of most porridges—the main dish of the family meals—in the early 1950's. But its use as the sole ingredient in a dish was not favored by the Azande and could be taken as an indicator of an abnormal situation. Any increase in its use indicated a shortage of grain, particularly of eleusine. The "sweet" varieties of cassava, that is the varieties containing less hydrocyanic acid, could be eaten as snacks by merely peeling and roasting a piece of the tuber. Cassava flour could also be used as an ingredient in beer, though it was regarded by the Azande as an adulterant. It was an insult to refer to somebody's beer as *buda gbanda*, "beer of cassava."

Sweet potatoes were an incalculable part of the diet, since they were mostly consumed as snacks. Azande did not consider them as proper food and would sometimes fail to mention them when talking about items in their diet. The tubers kept well in the ground and were available for consumption when needed. Because they were often prepared by individuals as food aside from family meals, they seemed to occupy a more important part of the diet than the Azande realized. Sweet potatoes and cassava formed valuable reserves of food, and their supply in any stable homestead was seldom, if ever, consumed completely.

Maize was another food that probably had a greater part in the diet than was realized, because so much was eaten on the cob as individually prepared snacks. This was particularly true early in the rains, when maize was the first food crop to mature. Flour from dried maize was used both in brewing beer and in porridge, but with a good deal of variation among Zande households. Some persons

[5] *Ibid*, p. 8.

said they liked maize for porridge, while others used it only in making beer. There had probably been a great change in the use of maize, for with the prohibitions on the cultivation of the land along the streams and in the forests, the large fields called *nbaya bire*—the maize of the forest—were no longer known in my time.

Rice had been encouraged by the governments in the Zande areas of both the Belgian Congo and French Equatorial Africa as a cash crop. It was the "upland" or "dry" variety. In parts of both of these territories, rice seemed to be partly displacing eleusine as the main cereal. It was carried by Azande into the Sudan, where it had only a very minor part in the diet, though some individuals said they were acquiring a preference for it. Under favorable conditions rice can give high yields, an important feature in Zande eyes.

The storage characteristics were vital factors in the selection of food crops. Eleusine keeps well for four years or more in the store, cassava roots and sweet potatoes keep in the ground until the new rains cause them to sprout, but most other cereals are prone to insect and fungus infestation. Sorghums were grown everywhere, but only in small quantities compared with the drier areas to the north and east. This grain did not keep well in Zande country and generally had to be used quickly. Maize was stored for one dry season at most, with the husks left on ears and strung on a tree in the open. Considerable insect and fungus damage occurred, but not enough to discourage the use of dried maize. Sesame kept relatively well. There was thus an inverse correlation between the size of the grains and their keeping qualities.[6] Animal pests, such as rats and mice, had to be guarded against but were normally not a major problem when the granaries, raised on their four wooden posts, were in good order.

Peppers

The tiny, hot peppers, or "chilies" (*Capsicum minimum*), were in a separate category from the rest of their agriculture. For one thing they were semicultivated, and for another they were a major source of cash. The bushes were mostly sown by the droppings of birds, and while they were also found in the forest and bush there were concentrations of them around the courtyards and in the cultivations. Perhaps this was because birds often rested in the bare trees that had been killed in the clearing operations. The Azande

---

[6] H. S. Darling, "Insects and Grain Storage in the Sudan," *Sudan Notes and Records*, 32 (December, 1951), 137.

kept the pepper bushes clear of competing vegetation when they were in convenient places, as in sites of previous fields. This was the extent of cultivation for pepper bushes, but because they are perennial, clumps of them could be seen being cared for on the sites of fields long abandoned. Azande sometimes attempted to sow peppers, usually broadcast along with cereals, but reported that there was very little return from these efforts.

The pepper bush was evidently a recent introduction, mostly sown by birds, from the west. The arrival of the naturally sown bushes had been observed, about 1932, in the Maridi area just to the east of Zande District.[7]

The peppers were sometimes used in the food of the Azande, but the amounts were negligible compared with the supply. The peppers were gathered sporadically, whenever there were enough ripe ones on a bush or a clump of bushes. They were dried in the sun for two or three days and then stored until a trip was made to a shop where they could be sold. In a sense, this activity overlapped the gathering activities discussed below. It was an easy and important part of the money economy. The total amount paid for peppers in Zande District varied tremendously from year to year, but often the amount was comparable to that obtained in a good year for all cotton grown in the district. In the estimation of the Azande, chilies were a far better and easier way to make money than was cotton.

AGRICULTURAL METHODS

The Azande believed themselves to be good and industrious agriculturalists, able to choose the best land and knowing the requirements of various crops. They had a good reputation as cultivators with neighboring peoples. It was difficult to find any overall systems underlying their agriculture, nor did they state any large principles of agriculture.[8] They chose their fields partly by type of natural vegetation and partly by intuition, which appeared in the disagreements that arose when I asked different persons for opinions. The real test of land was to try it; only if there was a good yield would

[7] J. R. Catford, "The Introduction of Cotton as a Cash Crop in the Maridi Area of Equatoria," *Sudan Notes and Records*, 34 (December, 1953), 157.

[8] De Schlippe's *Shifting Cultivation* contains some codification of Zande agriculture. Since much of his information was gathered at second hand, he probably tended to oversystematize Zande agricultural practices. See my review of this work in *Journal of the Royal Anthropological Institute*, no. 222 (October, 1958), pp. 64–65.

the primary crops be planted a second year. It must be kept in mind that the Azande, particularly after resettlement in the Sudan, no longer had a free choice. This induced confusion and apathy in many cases for the people felt that the government was responsible for their difficulties by interfering with their agricultural practices.

Only very general rules were stated by the Azande for soil selection. The best land for groundnuts was friable, sandy soil; maize required a moist field. They knew that virgin soil was best in all cases, that rocky places were to be avoided, that the same crop would not do well twice in succession on any but the best places, and that cultivated land must be left fallow for a period long enough to allow it to regenerate the natural vegetation, as found on virgin soil. These were obvious things to them, and they were ideals. Sometimes they were forced to violate their agricultural principles, especially when the government interfered.

Clearing was hard work in the bush and forest of Zande country. It began in the dry season, usually in January or February, after the eleusine of the previous season had been harvested. The earliness of a man's start in clearing was one of the best measures of his industriousness, according to the Azande. Large trees were girdled with the ax, or they might be killed by burning brush around the bases. Smaller trees were cut down, leaving stumps about three feet high; branches and bushes were hacked into pieces; and the grass was cut. All the cut vegetation was left to dry, and only shortly before the time for sowing was it burned. The ash, the Azande believed, was necessary to give good yields. A heavy, preliminary hoeing then cleaned the fields of roots and unburned vegetation, which was either cast to the side of the clearing or heaped up to be burned again.

The tools were simple and few in number: a small ax for felling trees and lopping branches, a large knife or machete for cutting smaller bushes and grass, a straight stick to rake debris, and a round iron hoe about five inches in diameter, hafted to a short, V-shaped wooden handle, for the actual cultivation.

The Zande agricultural year usually began in March, for with the first rains a little corn and some vegetables might be planted near the courtyard. When the rains had begun properly, the sowing of groundnuts and maize began in the cleared portions of the fields. But this was not the end of the clearing operation, for it was a continuing process and, as more land was cleared, more groundnuts and maize were sown. Peanuts could usually be sown until the middle of June and maize as late as August. The first groundnuts were ready for harvesting in August and, as they were lifted, eleusine was broadcast into the same soil. This was accompanied by the sowing of the other cereals and the melons and gourds grown for their seeds. Clearing might continue even after all groundnuts were harvested for planting more eleusine. The rains usually ceased in November, and the harvest was usually at its peak in December.

If the soil proved to be good in the first year, the same primary crops, peanuts and eleusine, might be planted in the second year. It was more usual, however, for sesame, maize, melons, and gourds to be grown in second-year land, though there were great variations in this practice. Cassava could be planted at any time, but it was usually started in the year before the field was to go to fallow and harvested after one to two years, according to variety, while the field was already regenerating its natural vegetation. Then, ideally, the land was left fallow for many years.

While there was a great deal of variation and improvisation from this general procedure, certain overall characteristics can be extracted. The general pattern was one of the succession of peanuts and eleusine (in the same plot in the same season) with maize and other crops possibly being interplanted with one or both. Cassava could be started along with other crops, usually in the year before the last full use of the field, but it was not uncommon to see cassava planted twice in succession in a plot.

Another general characteristic was that more than one crop would be grown in a field, except where maize was occasionally grown alone. The number of crop combinations seemed to be limitless, and in some cases four or even five different crops were observed in the same field. In plots near the courtyard, perennials such as bananas and sweet potatoes might be started in the first or second year, along with everything else. The advantages of intercropping were enormous: one operation might serve two crops, the ground was better covered, and the need for weeding was reduced. Furthermore, intercropping served as insurance if one crop failed.

A third general characteristic of Zande agriculture was its flexibility. Individual variations and improvisations were wide. Supplies of seed or outside commitments might require novel treatment of cultivations, or there might be administrative interference with what the people considered the best practices. The absence of rigid rules allowed for considerable adaptability, as in the alteration of the usual crop succession plan in the event of unusually good or poor yields in any plot. The flexibility of the system was strained beyond its limits, however, by the attempt to stabilize the Azande upon arbitrarily designated plots of land in the resettlement that accompanied the development scheme.

ARRANGEMENT OF FIELDS BY PERSONS

The division of the courtyard into segments under the tacit control of each of the wives in the household extended outward, so that the section of the garden behind each wife's portion of the courtyard was hers. I was told that this division theoretically extended into the arable land beyond, so that each wife had an ever-widening segment of land starting from the courtyard and extending indefinitely. Ideally this system had paths, radiating from the courtyard, as boundaries between the segments of land. In checking into this, however, I could find only vague tendencies toward this sort of division. While each wife tended to cultivate the land beyond her part of the courtyard and garden, there was usually no further clear delineation of land to be cultivated by certain persons.

This brings up the basic allocation of fields among persons. Each adult ideally had his own fields of all major crops. This principle was most apparent with the women; because each woman should be nearly self-sufficient, she cultivated what she needed for her own and her dependents' needs. Each field was the primary responsibility of a certain person into whose store its products would go. The persons who regularly ate with a woman were also expected to help with her cultivations. Each man, except for young unmarried men who were still eating with their mothers, also should have had his own fields, but this was not adhered to nearly as uniformly as with women. There was considerable variation even among the heads of homesteads in this regard. Food was prepared for the head of the household by his wives in turn and, if he had only one wife, he sometimes had no fields of his own and merely helped his wife cultivate the food they both consumed. The head of a larger household usually had his own fields and his own store. This produce was used for his guests and for entertainments that were his responsibility. His stores were also the reserve food for the entire household.

This personal allocation of fields did not mean that each person did all the work on his or her fields. A woman's fields were cleared by her husband or a male relative; he also helped with the cultivation of the crops. She in turn helped him in the weeding and harvesting of his fields. The head of a monogamous household explained that he and his wife generally worked together on their fields, on one set for a few days at a time and then on the other. The work was mutual, to varying degrees, in the fields of the various persons of a homestead. When Azande spoke of an entire homestead or household, they referred to all fields as belonging to the head, in contrast with the way they referred to so-and-so's fields when they were speaking in terms of members of a household. The head of a household was ultimately responsible for its welfare, and the products of the cultivations of the household were the most important factor in that welfare. When his household was examined by outsiders, he got the credit or the blame for its total performance, for he was in the position of the director of the household.

When the Azande were free to choose the land for their cultivation, the fields of one household were usually together, I was told. My informants usually described the fields cleared for a man's wives before resettlement as being roughly circular.

PROBLEMS OF MEASUREMENT

When I began my observations of Zande agricultural methods, it seemed desirable to obtain precise calculations, such as man-hours of labor and yields an acre. Such information would obviously be of value in comparisons with other peoples and other climates as well as for the testing of new methods of agriculture among the Azande. It would also be most useful in comparing the amounts of work that went into the cultivation of cotton and subsistence crops.

The attempt to obtain precise data was largely frustrated, partly by the nature of the Zande approach to their work and partly by outside interference. It must be realized that there was no traditional system of measuring; the Azande were quite satisfied with their powers of estimation and regarded it as something of a game to judge the most advantageous containers of beer and other produce in the markets. The difficulties in making any accurate accounting can be imagined when the usual way of indicating quantity is considered. When questioned, the Azande would indicate with a casual gesture the height of a "big basket" or grasp a thigh or forearm to show the thickness of an object such as a piece of smoked meat or a tuber. I tried to check these rough indications by getting an approximation of the diameter of the basket in question or by weighing and measuring whenever possible, but I was usually left with only a vague estimate of the quantities involved.

In the course of the cultivations on my own plots, I was able to get some accurate measurements and sometimes to calculate production. But even there serious disturbances entered in, as when baboons devastated an entire field of maize during a short time while the fields were left unguarded. It was this sort of event that brought home the difficulty of trying to obtain representative figures on yields in subsistence agriculture.

Despite the most careful observations, it was virtually impossible to measure the total production of any one crop in any homestead. One reason was the tendency for a portion of the crop to be consumed during the harvesting and processing. Another was that some crops, such as sweet potatoes, yams, and cassava, were stored in the ground and taken up only as required for immediate use. Total yields could be estimated only roughly, but the Azande found such estimates adequate for their purposes.

The common complaint of the Azande that they could not cultivate as much as formerly because of the introduction of cotton and the restriction of their plots in the resettlement pattern made me curious about how the size of their fields had been affected. They insisted that they had cultivated much more grain prior to resettlement when they could freely choose land for cultivation. But they could give no definite field sizes. According to their estimates, as laid out on the ground for me, it was not unusual for a man with two or three wives to cultivate about three acres of groundnuts and eleusine. This was larger than all but a few plots that I found in the new settlements, but how much exaggeration had been brought on by nostalgia cannot be guessed.

In a study before the resettlement, an agricultural officer found it difficult to measure the area normally cultivated by a household, but he concluded that a man with one wife would, on the average, clear and cultivate about 1.5 to 2 acres of new land during a season. He estimated that about 1 acre of the previous year's land would also be used again,[9] making a total of about 1.25 to 1.5 acres per cultivating adult. In comparison, the plots I observed in the resettled plots ranged from 0.25 to almost 1.5 acres per cultivating adult, exclusive of cotton fields, cassava fallows, and courtyard gardens, with a median of 0.5 to 0.75 acres for a cultivating adult. The cotton plots added about 0.25 acres to this amount.

That my findings showed smaller fields than those estimated by McCall might be interpreted to confirm the contentions of the

[9] McCall, *Note on Agriculture*, p. 10.

Azande that they did less cultivation in the days after resettlement, but caution must be used in applying any of these figures.

G. M. Culwick, in the course of her nutritional study, was able to measure fields both in resettled areas and in one not yet resettled. Her figures lead to a conclusion opposite to what might be drawn from McCall's and mine. She found that an area in its second year of resettlement had 0.93 acres of cultivation for an active adult, exclusive of cassava fallows and cotton fields, while an area in the first year after resettlement had 0.73 acres and an area not yet resettled had only 0.63 acres per active adult.[10] So, while the fields she measured were smaller than McCall's earlier estimates, she found the fields in the resettled areas to be larger than in the area not yet resettled. Some five years later, after resettlement, I came to know very well the particular subchiefship from which Mrs. Culwick's unresettled figures were obtained and found it difficult to believe that her figure included all cultivations. The people there often told me of their extensive cultivations at considerable distances from their houses, and we must keep the reservation that the figure as obtained by Mrs. Culwick and her assistants might not have included all fields of the unresettled group.

The measurement of the area of fields was complicated by the interplanting of crops, along with double cropping in each season in part of most fields. The continuing process of clearing and sowing throughout the growing season also prevented precise measurements. By measuring fields in the dry season, the total size for the past season could be obtained, but it was not usually possible to get more than approximations about which areas had had two crops and which had had only one. Another complicating factor was the occurrence of the fields of one household in more than one place. Furthermore, it cannot be stressed too strongly that the quantitative variations of Zande agriculture were so great from individual to individual and from household to household that averages were virtually meaningless. It is therefore dangerous to assume that estimates such as the above are anything but rough. Keeping all these reservations in mind, we may use the figure of one acre of cultivation per active adult as a rough guide, close enough to the Azande approximations of what they needed for minimum food production.

The Azande had great confidence in their ability to cultivate more than enough for all needs. They attributed shortages primarily to governmental interference. They cited particularly the

[10] *Dietary Survey*, p. 122.

demands for outside labor, the disruption of their homesteads in resettlement, the extra work involved in cotton cultivation, and the restrictions and prohibitions on choice of land as the main things deterring them from cultivating effectively.

The determination of agricultural labor requirements was, if anything, more difficult. Even the observation of the clearing of a plot only a few yards from my house proved to be impracticable. Although I often went to see if the man was in his field, I missed him at work on several occasions. On discussing this problem with my Zande friends, they suggested: "Send for him and tell him to work on the field so that you can watch him." At first I rejected this solution as making the situation highly artificial, but later I decided that it would be better than nothing. When I went to see the man in question, I discovered that he had left on a long journey and that there was great doubt whether he would be back to finish the clearing of his field in time for the sowing of cotton.

The Azande had a firm grasp of what they needed to accomplish in a certain season. But they did not allocate time to each task, nor did they perform certain kinds of work at the same times each day. The nearest thing to daily regularity that I could find was a tendency to cultivate fields after the dew had dried on the grass in the morning and until the heat of the sun became oppressive. After this main period of cultivation, the women began to prepare the main meal of the day. Some people might cultivate again in the afternoon. Within this general plan there were many variations and omissions, for not even the meals were regular. Mrs. Culwick, in her dietary study of the Azande, was driven to conclude, "The most striking thing about Zande domestic arrangements is their astonishing lack of routine." She continued:

It seemed at first a mere tale to be told by men, "we don't have any usual mealtimes, we eat when our wives decide to cook," but in trying to establish the recording routine it soon became all too apparent that this was the plain truth. All that can be said is that common times of day for cooking and eating a meal are early morning or midday or evening, but in a group on any given day there will also be some eating about 10 A.M. and others about 3 P.M. and so on. Nor, in many cases, does the individual family have its own or normal routine; it varies from day to day.[11]

What seemed to the outsider to be an annoying lack of routine or planning had its basis in the Zande concept of time and its relation to the work to be done. This was very different from ours. To the Azande, a task was not to be performed at any specific time

[11] *Ibid,* pp. 50–51.

of day or month or year. A variety of tasks had to be done as the need and the occasion arose; there was a relationship of tasks to one another rather than of tasks to time. Tasks were performed in sequence, according to priorities established by circumstances, but inevitably interruptions occurred and new priorities had to be established. For the Azande, time did not regulate the flow of events; rather events, as they happened, determined the activity of the person. There was no concept of the flow of time as a material quantity, but only the occurrence of happenings such as light, darkness, rain, and drought. As light and dark determined activities, so did the occurrence or absence of rain. Such units of time as existed for the Azande were more determined by circumstances than determinants for any particular actions. For example, it was tempting to assume that the lunar months, as recognized and named by the Azande, were the guides by which they regulated their agricultural activities, for they often said that they planted particular crops in certain months. This proved to be an oversimplification, since they in fact recognized the lunar months by the natural phenomena that also influenced the agricultural work. They would not plant their groundnuts simply because the moon had come into the time called *Zerekpe*; they would wait for the rains to begin, as they usually do in *Zerekpe*, to plant groundnuts.

The Azande performed what seemed to be the most urgent work and then went on to other work. There might arise new and more urgent activities, such as those associated with the death of a relative. Then the new work would take precedence and the previous work at hand had to wait. As the grain began to mature, one noted a marked tendency to build new granaries or refurbish old ones. The leaking roof of a house had to wait until the granary was secure and the grain gathered and put away; by that time, the rains had stopped and preparations for hunting became important. The leaking roof of the house would serve until the rains were due to break again. Similarities with our way of establishing priorities of actions and putting things off with various reasons are superficial, because the Zande way of looking at the relationship between work and events did not include any inherent value of routine. The Azande judged a man by how hard he worked and how well he managed his affairs, but not by his punctuality or regularity.

Their contentment to let one task follow another did not influence the effectiveness of their work but made for difficulty in obtaining figures for the total work put into any one thing, whether it was a handicraft item or a field. Agriculture was, in the Zande view, by far the most important phase of their activities, but they did not make any fine measurements or calculations, and the many variations and exigencies did not allow for predictions. Results were what counted to the Azande; they worked and cultivated as they saw fit, in hopes of good harvests. They then made do with what they had.

The importance of agriculture in the economy of the Azande is immediately obvious when one considers that the ordinary Zande almost never bought food regularly, except perhaps for salt. He bought an occasional cup of beer, a piece of meat, or some fish, but these were in the category of luxuries. For at least 95 percent of the population, that is, for other than daily laborers, traders, teachers, and clerks, all food consumed was grown locally, usually by the household that consumed it. Assigning a monetary value to this food was impossible; it is enough to realize that by any standard that could be applied, such as the sale value, it represented a figure far greater than any ordinary person or household could have hoped to earn in money. This fact was the tacit basis for the development of Zande District. Even the permanent laborers depended heavily on the food that they and the other members of their households raised. The special cases, representing a tiny fraction of the population, of those people who had to live on what they could buy or, more usually, who supplemented their diet with purchased food had difficulties resulting in poor diet and profound dissatisfaction with their rates of pay. The best solution in such cases was to attach oneself to a homestead as a temporary or permanent member, sharing in its subsistence economy. But this could not always be done.

That the Zande system of agriculture was not dependent on calculations and that it did not permit precise measurement does not say, however, that such information would not be of interest. Especially for comparative purposes, both with other peoples and other methods, more precise information would be of value. The accurate observation of the work of cultivating and processing crops requires special techniques and more than one observer. Some such work has been done by others.[12] Such precise information is not needed here, for the relative importance of those aspects of Zande economy under discussion became quite clear as my experience increased.

[12] De Schlippe's *Shifting Cultivation* contains material gathered by as many as 20 native observers working simultaneously. Culwick used up to 8 native observers to make quite precise measurements for her *Dietary Survey*.

LACK OF LIVESTOCK

The Azande did not keep livestock and had no pastoral traditions. They kept only dogs and chickens; the chickens were consumed largely in the poison oracle,[13] and the dogs were valued as pets and for hunting. The dearth of livestock left the Azande without domestic meat supplies, and game was virtually the sole source of meat.

The presence of animal sleeping sickness has generally been given as the explanation for the lack of livestock among the Azande. This theory needs examination, for it has been shown that livestock can be kept in Zande country. The Greek and northern Sudanese merchants of my day kept flocks of goats and sheep and had done so for years. Sheep did not always prosper in the southern and more moist regions, but goats seemed to do well anywhere in Zande country. Goats were useful in clearing areas of excessive vegetation and offered no problem of destruction of vegetation through overgrazing, as can occur in areas with sparser vegetation.

Cattle had been brought in from other areas, particularly from the Dinka country to the north, for dairy and slaughter purposes. A dairy herd had been maintained at Yambio, the district headquarters, for more than twenty years before my arrival and, with the development scheme, various other stations had started dairy herds. Large numbers of slaughter animals were also brought in. At Nzara, the industrial center, a dairy and beef herd numbering in the hundreds was maintained for several years. Relatively little incidence of sleeping sickness was found; pulmonary diseases accounted for more fatalities among the cattle than trypanosomiasis. The cattle were injected with an anti-sleeping-sickness serum before beginning their journey to Zande country, for they walked through areas that were heavily infested with tsetse fly. In Zande country certain precautions were required regarding the cattle's grazing grounds and drinking places. Evidently the type of tsetse fly in this region was very limited in its flight and would not generally leave the heavily forested areas near water. If cattle were grazed and watered not closer than one hundred yards to dense forest, they seemed to be in little danger of contracting sleeping sickness. Sheep and goats appeared to be even more resistant to sleeping sickness than were cattle.

[13] E. E. Evans-Pritchard, *Witchcraft, Oracles, and Magic among the Azande* (Oxford: Clarendon Press, 1937).

I saw only one Zande family that kept any livestock. After eighteen months of visiting hundreds of Zande homesteads, I found a homestead near Yambio that had three goats. The Zande did not take up the care of cattle, despite years of examples of successful animal breeding about them. So there appeared to be factors other than the presence of sleeping sickness that kept the Azande from animal husbandry. Persons I asked about this were about evenly divided for and against the idea of trying to keep sheep or goats. Those in favor of the idea said that they would be able to arrange the care and grazing of the animals satisfactorily but that they did not know where to obtain the animals and that they did not have the money to buy them. Those against the idea pointed out that the animals might damage cultivations or might be lost to predatory animals, particularly leopards.

Despite discussions over a period of years, the administration tried no experiment to introduce goats, sheep, or cattle into the Zande subsistence economy. The usual explanation was that the Azande did not want to be prevented from traveling freely by keeping animals in the homestead. This argument did not seem valid to those Azande who wanted to have animals; they were sure they could make arrangements for someone to care for the animals at all times. Neither they nor those Europeans who commented on the theoretical value of livestock to the Azande were aware of the need for larger family groups than could be found among the Azande for successful livestock husbandry. The efficient care of cattle and even of smaller livestock requires large herds and, therefore, larger social groups than the Azande would be able to muster, as E. E. Evans-Pritchard pointed out in conversational comparison of them with pastoral peoples he knew.

HUNTING AND FISHING

Hunting and fishing ranked high among the Azande in two respects: in interest, and as the prime source of animal food products. The Azande were always classified as agriculturalists, but if one were to judge from the talk of the men one would think of them as hunters. Even the women talked more about hunting and fishing than about agricultural matters. Agriculture was undoubtedly important but was not a great topic of conversation.

Large-scale hunting was done in the dry season, when the tall grass withered and dried up or was burned over, for otherwise visibility was virtually nil. Many families trekked to uninhabited areas for weeks at a time after the harvests to lay in a store of dried meat and fish for the year. The men did the actual hunting, while women and children might act as beaters. But the latter's usual tasks were fishing and processing meat and fish. The hunting parties made camps, often including several families, consisting of temporary grass sleeping huts and smoking platforms. The men went out to hunt at some distance each day.

Hunting was done with nets, the game being driven into them and then speared by men waiting in hiding. These nets were made in various sizes, weights, and meshes for various types of game. A usual type for smaller antelope or buck, which made up a large part of the bag, would be about 7 feet wide and 50 feet long, with a mesh of 2 inches. The material was a hand-rolled twine, about one-eighth inch in diameter, made of any of several fibers. The heaviest nets, intended for buffalo, were made of cord over one-half-inch thick. The nets were erected on slender poles, cut at the site, and several nets were put end to end. They were arranged so that the animal would cause them to drop and tangle in them. Animals were driven into the nets by fire, dogs, or human trackers and beaters. A pair, male and female, of good hunting dogs was a most valued possession of the Azande.

Governmental restrictions on hunting practices were considerably greater in the Sudan than in the other two territories. The use of pit traps was forbidden, as was the use of fire for hunting. Limits were also set on the number of elephants that might be killed in each chiefship, and the use of nets was illegal from December through March to reduce the killing of pregnant and newly born animals. Firearms were carefully registered, and permits for guns were very difficult to obtain for anybody but chiefs, particularly in the Sudan. The Azande found these restrictions hard to understand, for they saw no danger of depleting the game in their country. They regarded the reserve of animals in the uninhabited areas to be limitless. This reasoning was enhanced by the very considerable trouble they had with animal predators of all kinds in their cultivations. The only time I saw Azande lose their polite demeanor with European administrators was over this matter at a chiefs' meeting. When the district commissioner was asked why the Sudan game laws were so much more restrictive than those of French and Belgian territories and he replied that these regulations were designed to prevent the depletion of animals, the assembly broke into a roar of amusement. The idea was completely strange to them.

The administration in the Sudan has always been concerned to conserve the game, but the Azande saw in this only a major nuisance and hindrance in utilizing their primary source of meat.

Two former British inspectors of agriculture in Zande District recommended in a publication that the game laws be altered to allow the Azande to cope better with animal pests.[14]

Pit traps seemed to have been discontinued, but other methods, including fire, were continued secretly. It was a considerable worry to hide these operations from the administration, but the hunting and the meat obtained from them were important enough to warrant the trouble. Hunting with fire was the most profitable method. A large area was burned over in the dry season, carefully leaving unburned a circular stand of vegetation as much as a quarter of a mile in diameter. This area then served as the refuge for game and, when partly ringed with nets and burned, could yield many animals. Nets were used throughout the year, though they could be used only in remoter parts during the prohibited period.

This summary of hunting procedures should include a mention of the minor methods. Snares of various kinds could be used the year round, usually somewhere near the courtyard. Another method used primarily during the rains was to cut a path around a circular area, called a *gbaria*. The path was regularly inspected for spoor, and when an animal was detected to be within the *gbaria* nets were set up around part of it. The animal was then tracked and beaten into the nets. This method was more restricted than the large-scale dry season hunting, for each household could have its own *gbaria*. These could be found even in the plots of the resettled areas. Generally they were near the courtyard, and they might be 50 to 120 yards in diameter. This method was of no use in the dry season because the hard earth of the surrounding path would not show the tracks of the animals crossing it.

There were two main types of fishing. The first utilized strong, conical basket traps set in rapids, particularly during the dry season when the rivers were low. This method was used by men. The other main type involved the damming of streams into a series of pools in the dry season; the water was then emptied from the pools by hand, using all sorts of vessels as dippers. This was primarily done by women, though men might have helped in the building of larger dams. As the pools were drained, all sorts of fish, snakes, and

---

[14] A. G. McCall and K. L. Lea-Wilson, *Some Notes on Zandeland*, Memoirs of Field Division, no. 6 (Khartoum: Ministry of Agriculture, 1950), p. 10.

crustaceans could be picked up. Some fishing was done with various poisons known to the Azande and with spears and nets, but these methods were of minor importance.

FOOD PROHIBITIONS

Most of the wide variety of fauna in Zande country was acceptable as a source of meat. The animals, birds, and reptiles that were not eaten constituted a very small proportion of the total variety available. The Azande had preferences in meat; the flesh of the "cane rat," *renvo,* for instance, was often acknowledged to be a particularly good dish. But meat was scarce and much desired, so almost any kind of meat was considered suitable for consumption. The major exceptions were totems of one's clan and of one's mother's clan, and leopards and lions. It was usually said that the flesh of the large cats was not good. These animals were also the totems of the ruling clan, and it was at times acknowledged that leopard or lion flesh should not be eaten since the spirit of a dead chief might have gone into that particular animal.

Vestiges of food prohibitions retained from the beliefs of tribes absorbed by the Azande were also noted. An example was the strong prohibition, persisting among the descendants of the Pambia group, against eating the flesh of chimpanzees. It seemed even stronger than the prohibitions concerning clan totems. The Pambia had the legend that they were descended from the union of a man with a female chimpanzee and that they were therefore related to these animals. In general, a person could kill and handle one's totem animal and even eat with persons who were eating its flesh as long as he did not eat the meat or other food that had been prepared with it. In the case of leopards and lions with all Azande and chimpanzees with the Pambia, the revulsion was more generalized and extended to a reluctance to touch the dead animal and to see others eating its flesh.

Other animals not eaten by the Azande, for no specified reasons, were hyenas, nightjars (a nocturnal bird), and eagles. Owls and wildcats were avoided because of their association with evil magic. Kites and some cranes were not eaten simply because their flesh was too tough. Giraffe meat was said to cause its eaters to become spotted with leprosy. Poisonous snakes were said to have poisonous flesh, but I noted that the extremely venomous puff adder was considered to be a delicacy. Python flesh was also a great delicacy; these snakes were considered to be in a category by themselves because of their great size and because they were not poisonous.

TERMITE HUNTING

Termite hunting was a source of both excitement and food. Various kinds of termites fly in large numbers at different times of the year. The Azande gave high priority to the gathering of certain kinds, such as the large variety that flies at the end of the dry season. Some termites were eaten uncooked, but the most important kinds were roasted. A fine cooking oil was extracted from some varieties; the great demand for this oil did not seem to be at all satisfied in the days while I was there. The appeal of termite hunting was so great that the administration tried to get the cotton sown early enough for its picking to be finished by the time the major flights of termites took place. Otherwise the cotton would often go unpicked. The avidity with which the people ate termites seems to be supported by the analysis of their nutritional components. Mrs. Culwick found considerable fat and protein in them. So they may be regarded as a source of animal food, though the exact nature of termite protein and fat is not known.[15]

The Azande also ate other insects and larvae, such as certain types of caterpillars that at times are found in large numbers in the forests. But nothing else of insect origin compares to the importance of termites.

GATHERING

This summary of gathering will deal primarily with noncultivated plant products. There are, of course, some things that do not fit readily into any category.

Certainly the most important item of gathered produce is the chili pepper described under the section on Zande crops. Next in importance was the beeswax and honey gathered from wild hives in the bush and forest. The Azande did not erect hives as did some of their neighbors, although they would at times prepare hollow logs and other containers for the possible use of wild bees. The gathering of honey and wax was particularly favorable in the drier regions in the north of Zande District, where the bush afforded myriad blossoms of many varieties. There were considerable variations from year to year both in the amount of honey gathered and in the prices obtained.

Little else of commercial value was gathered in Zande District. Spices and rubber could be obtained in the deep forest but were

[15] *Dietary Survey*, p. 140.

not collected in commercial quantities. By contrast, numerous natural vegetative products were gathered for domestic use. The Azande were excellent woodsmen, being familiar with a great variety of plants and depending on forest and bush for many products vital to their economy. These included fibers for construction and cordage; wood for carved articles; firewood and charcoal; materials for baskets, sieves, winnowing trays, mats, and hats; timber for all construction; thatching grass; food and seasonings; medicines and poisons; and cosmetics. What seemed at first glance to be a minor category of their life proved on deeper examination to have many facets and to be relatively important. The study of their use of natural products could easily grow into a major work, but here I can give only a glimpse of the main categories of forest produce and its significance to them.

Fibers were obtained from a variety of plants. In a short time I collected a list of thirty-four different plants that yield fibers in common use by the Azande. Of these, only five—bark cloth, sisal, Deccan hemp, banana, and pineapple—were cultivated. The fibers from wild plants were used in much greater quantity than those from cultivated plants. Fibers for construction, mainly bark as stripped from the plant, and for cordmaking constituted the largest amounts, though plaited articles such as baskets and mats also used much fiber of different types.

Even momentary consideration of the amount of timber consumed in construction and carving, as well as for fuel, gives an indication of the part it played in the life of the Azande. As most of this material was readily available, with a certain amount of effort, it was generally taken for granted by both Azande and outsiders.

Natural food products were of no great value to the Azande except in times of exceptional food shortage. They had knowledge of various things that could be found to eke out the diet, but the reserves of cassava and sweet potatoes had probably taken away most of the need for the forest food products. Oilseed-bearing trees were of the greatest regular significance. Two species of indigenous trees were outstanding: *Butyrospermum niloticum*, and *Lophira alata*. The former grows only in the northernmost regions of Zande District, being a tree of the drier regions. The oil from its seeds was expressed in considerable quantity in those regions and entered into the rest of Zande District as an item of local trade. It was important when other sources of cooking oil were short, which was quite often. The latter tree was found in much more of the district and was utilized by individual producers in greatly varying amounts. Oil from its seeds, as well as from the cultivated palm nuts, was extracted without presses and relatively inefficiently. The seeds were boiled in water until the oil could be skimmed off the top. Then the seeds were pounded and squeezed in a cloth or fiber strainer to get out more of the oil. The oil in the kernels could not be utilized.

Other natural food products included a wide variety of fungi and various fruits, none of which were collected in significant quantity or in a regular fashion. The private fungus beds referred to by previous observers seem to have lost their usefulness because of the various moves of the population. One other category of plant food product should be mentioned: many varieties of cultivated and natural plants were burned and the ashes dissolved in water, strained, and evaporated to obtain the chemical residue. It was used as a seasoning and had the same function and name (*tikpo*) for the Azande as commercial salt. Most Azande bought commercial salt, but some women still made their own to use with commercial salt or as a substitute.[16]

A wide variety of natural plant products was used for medicinal and cosmetic purposes as well as for fish, arrow, and bee poisons. These are discussed in other works[17] but have only minor significance here.

DIVISION OF LABOR BY SEX

The division of labor in Zande practice required the work of both men and women to make a complete homestead, the basic economic unit. The element of cooperation between the males and females was present at any level of observation. A functioning household was ideally the result of successful marriage, but other arrangements were possible. If the head of a household was without a wife for whatever reason—death, divorce, or separation—he would attempt to get a female relative to live at his homestead in order to preserve at least some of its normal daily procedure. The presence of considerable numbers of such households without wives and some even without women was probably a new feature of Zande

[16] See *ibid.*, p. 85, for a list of salt plants, and pp. 111–12 for the mode of preparation.
[17] A. M. de Graer, "L'Art de Guérir Chez les Azande," *Congo*, 1 (1929), 220–51, 361–408; Culwick, *Dietary Survey*, pp. 112–14, 88–91; E. E. Evans-Pritchard, "Zande Therapeutics," in *Essays Presented to C. G. Seligman* (London: Kegan Paul, Trench, Trubner, 1934), pp. 49–57.

life and evidently resulted from various disturbances in the years before my time there.

The well-being of a household could usually be gauged as soon as one entered the courtyard. If, for example, the open space was well swept, household equipment was not lying about, and the drying grain or other food was neatly arranged, one knew that there was an industrious wife or, in the case of a polygynous household, probably a senior wife who was a good manager. If the buildings were in good repair, all with sound roofs, one could assume that the head of the household was competent. In some cases the women's work might be bad and the man's good, or vice versa, but in most cases the homestead would either be a credit to both sides or there would be an obvious lack of efficiency. The latter could usually be traced to some difficulty, such as illness, or to a lack of harmony in the household relationships.

A considerable portion of the productive energy of the Azande went into the construction and maintenance of their buildings and courtyards. The forces tending to destroy the neatness and effectiveness of the homesteads were constant and vigorous. The inroads of natural vegetation and animal and insect pests, such as termites, were factors that only constant care could counteract. There were great differences in the appearances of homesteads. I learned that the Azande were very much aware of these differences and that many things were to be learned by analyzing the physical features of a courtyard. It became a game in my visits to sit down in an empty courtyard to rest with my Zande companions and, while waiting for the occupants to come in from their fields, to try to work out the composition of the family, the age of the homestead, the state of food supplies, the handicraft specialties, and the general industriousness of the male and female members. The evaluation of the homesteads and their occupants would continue after we had left. This analysis of courtyards as reflections of their inhabitants, particularly the heads of households, was not confined to other's establishments, for the Azande were acutely aware of the impressions that their own homes made on others. I had a number of apologies from heads of households for the state of their courtyards, with full explanations for the deficiencies of which they were ashamed.

There were no clear categories of activities assigned to the sexes, only tendencies for certain types of activities to be regarded as men's or women's work. And there were no specified prohibitions against a member of one sex doing anything usually considered the work of the other. But the type of work done was a primary mode of expression, along with attire, of maleness or femaleness. The total effect, in the case of any one individual, was what counted. A man might perform or assist in a woman's task, but he usually did so as a man doing something unusual. If he were to do so regularly he might lose his social identity as a man, which is to say, be considered abnormal.

The activities regarded as the province of men were those requiring greater strength, including the clearing operations in cultivation and the construction and repair of buildings. Women helped in construction only in the carrying of materials. Work with an ax was generally that of the men, although one occasionally saw a women with an ax, almost always in connection with collecting firewood, a woman's job. The construction of houses required a great deal of work with an ax, for the timber had to be felled and prepared in the forest. The clearing of fields also required much work with axes in girdling larger trees, felling smaller ones, and lopping branches. There was, however, no Zande idea of a connection between man and the ax, nor was there any prohibition of the use of an ax by a woman.

Most of the crafts were exercised exclusively by men; only pots were manufactured by members of both sexes. The playing of musical instruments, particularly the beating of drums, was much more commonly done by men. Hunting was the most clearly defined category of male activity. Women might help in beating the game, and they did certain types of fishing, but the actual tracking and killing of animals, as well as other kinds of fishing, were performed only by men. Once when I noticed a woman wearing shorts in what was then French Equatorial Africa, people explained that she was the sister of the subchief, an unusual woman who did many things that men did. The things cited as the epitome of the male activities in which she took part were drumming and hunting. She had not left her role as a woman, however, and still did many of the things required of women. I saw her at other times in completely feminine attire. She was a sort of tomboy, a woman who occasionally did things normally done by men.

Activities usually performed by women among the Azande were processing crops, preparing food, making beer, keeping house, carrying water, and collecting firewood, as well as most of the caring for children. In agriculture, women were responsible for much of the lighter work, and some special activities such as the harvesting of groundnuts were regarded as women's work. More than anything else, the grinding stones used for making flour or oilseed pastes and the mortar and pestle used for pounding food were in the province of women. Even little boys, who might help their mothers with other phases of cooking such as peeling or washing, would not grind or pound food. The brewing of beer was a most important activity done only by women. Men who were forced to live without the help of a woman usually existed on foods that did not require grinding or pounding or bought flour or other prepared foods. Very occasionally, I heard, men did prepare their own flour, but they and everyone else considered this to be a temporary and dire circumstance.

One principle emerging from the consideration of the division of labor is that the Zande woman was more nearly a self-sufficient unit than was the man. She had virtually all tools at her disposal and the widest range of activities. Furthermore, she performed the major portion of the work connected with everyday life. She could live alone more comfortably than a man could, for she needed only some of the occasional, major tasks to be done for her. If she had a house and store, she could manage by looking for fields that did not require much heavy clearing for her cultivations. A man, on the contrary, was continually discommoded if he had to live alone, since he could not arrange for the proper execution of his daily needs, particularly the preparation of food. This does not mean that women did, in fact, live alone very often nor that it was considered by them to be an agreeable thing to do. Azande of both sexes consistently referred to the ideal situation of the homestead that was the result of the cooperation of a man and his wife.

The sphere of the Zande women was largely within the home, while that of the men connected with the outside world. The work of men was largely that which occurred, or could be arranged to occur, at longer intervals than that of the women, who were largely concerned with the domestic daily routine. One effect was that the men had more free time and could leave the homestead more readily.

This arrangement did not mean that the man was free of routine work; far from it. He shared with his wife many activities, especially in the realm of agriculture. The head of the household and each of his wives had their own fields of the more important crops, but the man was expected to help his wife and she to help him in the clearing, cultivation, and harvesting of crops. There was great variation in the proportion of work done by men and women according to the nature of the homestead (principally the number of wives), the demands of the situation, and the industriousness of the heads of households. After the men had completed the clearing and, with the women, the heavy preliminary hoeing to clean the field, the remainder of agricultural work was considered to be women's work. But some men helped a great deal at all stages, which meant that the production of their homesteads was greater than where men would not or could not do much to help their women.

An industrious man would not, unless he was one of the rare ones with a large number of wives, sit back and direct activities from the shade of his granary. He had to work in the fields himself. The extent to which he applied himself to the cultivation of all the fields was usually a crucial factor in the welfare of his household. The Azande were fully aware of this and contradicted the impression of many Europeans that the women did all the cultivation. The shortage of a man's time to devote to cultivation could be seen in the households where the heads were daily laborers. These households never cultivated as much as comparable rural households. When I inquired into the reasons, the Azande made very clear that, while most of the work of cultivation was normally that of women, men in fact did a great deal of it. Administrators expected that the wages of men working regularly would replace the efforts lost to their household cultivations. But that was not always possible, and the Azande did not want to use money for buying food.

A variety of conditions—the emancipation of women, the cash value of crops, the cessation of warfare, the reduction of hunting, and the availability of tools in shops—had altered the roles of men more than those of women because the men were the links with the outside world. The work in the homestead and its cultivations had changed relatively little, but various functions of men had been eliminated or altered. Agriculture had always been the basis of the subsistence of the Azande, and they realized fully that everyone had to work at it for the household to prosper. It is doubtful that there was ever a time when ordinary men did not work hard in the agricultural activities of the household. The impression of Europeans that the men were idle and spent a great deal of their time away from home was probably based on observation of important men engaged in activities at the courts. For the men were in charge of the field of litigation, and to them fell most of the activities concerned with the commercial world or with the administration. They were the laborers and servants for the administration, traders, and missionaries. Their former function as warriors had been superseded largely by one as wage earners. This was confirmed by the designation of the men as taxpayers and as the individuals responsible for the supervised cash crops.

DEVELOPMENT

Although never made explicit, the basis for the social and economic development of the Azande was that they would continue to feed and house themselves by traditional means while raising a cash crop to provide "a modest cash income for reasonable imported amenities," in the words of an administrator who was one of the prime movers for the Zande Development Scheme of 1946–55. An important factor was that the European administrators believed the male Zande population to be virtually unoccupied and its labor available in practically unlimited amounts. The district commissioner had to take strenuous measures during the construction phase of the development scheme to overcome the tendency to use so much conscripted labor that the scheme's agricultural base was endangered.[18]

The wages for labor and prices for cash crops indicate that there was agreement—albeit for different reasons and with different expectations—between the Azande and the European administrators that money income was to be a sideline to the basic subsistence economy. The Zande economy throughout the colonial period never developed more than what might be called a pin-money economy.[19]

On the whole, the Azande still managed to carry on their traditional system of agriculture while I was there, but with difficulty. They constantly complained of interference and distractions, such as work for the government and the chiefs, the labor of constructing paths and new homes in the resettlement scheme, and the cultivation of cash crops. The planners had hoped that cotton would become absorbed into the routine Zande subsistence cultivation, but this failed to happen because the people regarded cotton as a nuisance. They resented the compulsion used for its cultivation and complained of the time required for its care and of unsatisfactory returns when it was sold. The misjudgment about the amount of free time available to the men caused hardships that were important in the failure of the development scheme.

Particularly disturbing was the resettlement program that was carried on from 1946 to 1950 as a preliminary to the development of cotton as a cash crop. The resettlement of the entire Zande population of the Sudan—about 50,000 families—from their homes along the roads onto a gridiron pattern of straight paths gave the homesteads only long, narrow plots. This pattern interfered seri-

---
[18] Reining, *Zande Scheme*, pp. 163–64.
[19] *Ibid*, pp. 91–92.

ously with the normal selection of fields for cultivation. The administrators, in failing to distinguish between shifts in residence and shifts in cultivation, assumed that courtyards were moved frequently as a result of shifting cultivation. But the Azande made an implicit distinction between residential and cultivation moves; they regarded themselves as residentially sedentary, maintaining that they were willing to go considerable distances to find land suitable for cultivation. The administration's attempt to stabilize the population by assignment to fixed plots resulted in overcultivation of portions of the plots and to restiveness because of the arbitrary and isolated locations. The resettlement—considered at first to be a necessary prerequisite for development of the Azande—came, in time, to be seen as more of an obstacle than an aid to development. Furthermore, it was clearly untenable and had begun to break down by the time of my research. The Azande were beginning to move out of their assigned places, and the administration was trying to devise some way to get them into homes of their own choosing without making it seem like yet another government ordered move. The resentful Azande had come to regard every action of the administration as something deliberately unfavorable for them. The impasse was dissolved by the uprising of 1955 against the northern Sudanese who had replaced British officials in the move to self-government for the Sudan. The Zande area in the Sudan has been disrupted since then, and in the Congo since 1960.

The Azande had been chosen for the pilot development scheme because their subsistence economy was judged to be famineproof and because they were so amenable to administrative direction. The agricultural system did prove to be resilient enough to survive the heavy demands of resettlement and the introduction of a cash crop, but serious strains developed because various ecological and social factors were not taken into account. The amenability of the Azande did indeed permit them to be moved about arbitrarily, but it was pushed beyond its limits. In time, resentment replaced the initial enthusiasm and faith. The undoubtedly sincere desire of the administration to help the people failed because of poor communication and because the way of life of the people was arbitrarily and drastically changed despite assurances that it was not to be altered any more than necessary. Necessity was judged by unrecorded and probably even unexpressed motives based on ideas arising outside the Zande culture and situation.[20]

[20] *Ibid*, pp. 127–29, 138–39.

CHAPTER 5

FOOD PRODUCTION BY THE YALUNKA HOUSEHOLD, SIERRA LEONE

LELAND DONALD

LOCATION OF YALUNKA CHIEFDOMS OF SIERRA LEONE
(YALUNKA CHIEFDOMS SHADED)

This study describes food production by the households of the Yalunka of northeastern Sierra Leone.[1] Little has been published about the Yalunka, and as background material I include a brief description of their agricultural technology before turning to household production and its problems.

The people described here are known to themselves and their neighbors as Yalunka. They speak a Mande language and like other Mande speakers are patrilineal. They inhabit three chiefdoms in the northeastern corner of Sierra Leone; there are many more Yalunka in the neighboring portions of Guinea, but as I have done no research among them this chapter is restricted to the Yalunka of Sierra Leone.

The three Yalunka chiefdoms have a total area of about 800 square miles and have a population of 28,882 in the Sierra Leone census of 1963. Of these, 19,140 were listed as Yalunka.[2] Most of the remainder were either Fula or Mandinka. My own data from a few localities indicate that the figure for the Yalunka was too low. How much larger the figure should be and whether or not the non-Yalunka portion of the three chiefdoms was also underenumerated is hard to say.

The Yalunka chiefdoms are located on the Koinadugu Plateau, a part of the Guinea Highlands. All of the area lies between 1,000 and 2,000 feet above sea level.[3] The area is hilly, but the relief is not as great as in most of the areas immediately south and west. The vegetation is mostly derived Guinea Savannah with a few isolated patches of high forest remaining.

Rainfall averages about 80 inches a year, almost all of it falling during the wet season from May to November.[4] Soils are of the types normally associated with Guinea Savannah. Low-lying areas bordering valley streams are sometimes quite fertile owing to pe-

[1] I carried out research in northeastern Sierra Leone from October, 1965, to August, 1967, under a predoctoral fellowship from the National Institute of Health and a dissertation research grant from the National Science Foundation. I would like to thank Vernon R. Dorjahn for his comments on this paper and Joseph G. Jorgensen for his advice on statistical matters. I would also like to acknowledge the assistance of John Roche, Agricultural Officer for Koinadugu District, Sierra Leone.

[2] All references to the 1963 census of Sierra Leone are based on figures found in Sierra Leone, Central Statistics Office, *1963 Population Census of Sierra Leone*, 3 vols., vol. 1 and 2 (Freetown, 1965). In vol. 1, material was drawn from pp. 3–7, 16, and 34–35. In vol. 2, material was used from pp. 13–16.

[3] John I. Clarke, ed., *Sierra Leone in Maps* (London: University of London Press, 1966), pp. 14, 26.

[4] S. Gregory, *Rainfall over Sierra Leone*, University of Liverpool, Department of Geography, Research Paper no. 2 (Liverpool, 1965), p. 17.

riodic flooding and alluvial deposition. In restricted local areas laterite is sometimes a serious problem.

Most Yalunka live in large villages of 500 or more. They are primarily subsistence agriculturalists whose staple crop is rice. Some Yalunka own cattle and most keep sheep, goats, and chickens. They practice a mixture of shifting and semipermanent cultivation. Two types of location are used for food crops: "gardens" in or very near villages and "farms" which are usually farther removed from villages.[5]

AGRICULTURAL PRACTICE

Crops

The staple crop is rice. Important subsidiary crops are funde, cassava, maize, and groundnuts. Other commonly grown food plants include sweet potatoes, cocoyam, Sierra Leone Guinea corn (durra, a variety of sorghum), and Sierra Leone bulrush millet. Minor crops include yams, okra, pepper, lima beans, melons, and beniseed. Minor tree crops include banana, orange, lime, pineapple, papaya, mango, and kola. Tobacco and cotton are also grown.

Rice seems to have been the main Yalunka staple since at least the early nineteenth century. Both the indigenous West African rice (*Oryza glaberrima*) and Asian rice (*O. sativa*) are grown. The Yalunka recognize and name several dozen varieties of rice. Varietal recognition is based on type of location for best growth, maturation time, and color and shape of the grain and grain heads. Some varieties are the improved ones introduced at various times by the Sierra Leone Department of Agriculture. Other varieties have older and unknown origins.

Funde (*Digitaria exilis*) has been an important subsidiary crop for as long as I have information on the subject (late nineteenth century), as have groundnuts. In late August and in September, before the rice is ready to harvest, funde is often the major source of food. Just before the funde is ready to cut, maize is an important stopgap food.

Cassava seems to have been introduced to the Yalunka from Guinea by the Fula after World War I. Improved varieties of cassava are more recent introductions from coastal Sierra Leone.

[5] Many Yalunka terms have no completely adequate English counterpart. This is true of such agricultural terms as those that I have glossed "farm" and "garden." Such glosses are only an approximation of the meaning of the Yalunka terms.

Guinea corn, bulrush millet, and beniseed are long-standing crops that are declining in importance. At one time bulrush millet was a very important subsidiary crop.

Banana, citrus, and pineapple are all fairly recent introductions, especially as far as significant production goes. Small-scale kola production has a long history, but the Yalunka do not grow enough kola to satisfy their own wants.

Most households grow a few yams, but they are not an important part of the Yalunka diet. Okra and pepper are garnishes for the sauces that invariably accompany rice. Most households plant a number of sweet potato and a few cocoyam hills. They are used to provide variety in the diet toward the end of the dry season.

Local varieties of tobacco are slowly being replaced by improved types that have been introduced by the Aureol Tobacco Company, Ltd., as a cash crop. Cotton was once important as the source of thread for the weaving of cloth. Now few people bother to plant it.

The Yalunka plant both single crop and mixed crop fields. "Swamp" rice (see below) is always planted alone, as is funde. A little Guinea corn (or occasionally beniseed) is often mixed with upland rice. Maize, okra, lima beans, and melons are usually planted together. Often groundnuts and cassava will be planted with them, though individual fields are also made for these two crops.

Tools

The agricultural tool kit of most Yalunka farmers is simple. It consists of a machete (and perhaps an ax) for clearing fields of trees, brush, and weeds; a hoe for breaking the soil; and a knife for harvesting. The hoe has a short two and one-half to three-foot handle.

Types of Field

A plot is called a "farm" or a "garden" on the basis of its size, its distance from the settlement, and the type and number of different crops planted in it. The distinction is not always clear-cut. Rice and funde are always grown on farms. Groundnuts and cassava are grown on both. Other crops are nearly always grown in gardens.

Gardens are always within or adjacent to settlements. They are usually small and contain a greater variety of crops. The houses in Yalunka villages are built fairly close together, but small gardens are planted beside most houses. These frequently occupy no more than one hundred or two hundred square feet. Most often they contain corn, groundnuts, cassava, okra, peppers, yams, and cocoyams. The crops are intermingled. No rows are made, nor is any other regular order introduced into the garden. In addition to houseside gardens, larger ones with many of the same crops are planted on the edges of settlements. The larger gardens may be bordered by mango or orange trees, and some contain a few banana plants. Gardens tend to be planted in the same place every year. Fertility is maintained by dumping refuse and the unused parts of food plants on the plots.

The most important source of food for the Yalunka is the rice farm. There are two kinds of rice farms—"dry land farms" and "swamp farms." The dry land farms are similar to the upland rice farms found throughout the rice-producing areas of West Africa and are made on slopes and hillsides, which sometimes have quite steep gradients. Swamp farms are not the typical wet-rice farms found in some areas (including most of the rest of Sierra Leone). They are, rather, farms made on low-lying, flat, moist, occasionally flooded alluvial areas near streams. Although these areas are not swamps in the usual sense, they are called such throughout this essay in deference to the Yalunka word applied to them.

Dry land farms are planted on sloping ground that has been fallow for at least five but preferably eight years. Occasionally rice will be planted on such a farm for two consecutive years, but this is rare and two years is the maximum. If rice is planted on a field a second year, production declines considerably. Sites are chosen on the basis of the quality and quantity of plant growth on the area. Weed and bush growth should be abundant and there should be some small trees. A few Yalunka look for particular species, but most are concerned with the overall character of the plant cover.

Swamp farms are made in valleys alongside streams. They are planted year after year. Sometimes a swamp farm will lie fallow for a year, but many of the farmers I interviewed were using swamp sites that have been continuously cultivated for more than twenty years. Occasional flooding and silt deposition seems to keep up fertility. New swamp sites are chosen by seeking flat areas near streams that flow the entire year. But almost no one I interviewed had initiated the use of his swamp farm. During the dry season the part of the field closest to the stream may be made into sweet potato heaps. Swamp farms are usually within half a mile of the settlement of the owner, while upland farms are often as much as two miles from settlements.

Funde is planted on the same type of site that is used for upland rice. Sometimes fallow bush is cut for this crop, but more often it is planted either a year or two after an upland rice crop was grown on the site or it follows groundnuts.

Besides planting some groundnuts and cassava in gardens, most households make groundnut farms and not a few also make cassava farms. These farms are fields devoted exclusively to one or the other of these crops and are a little farther from the settlements than gardens. Land is rarely newly cleared for either groundnuts or cassava. They are often planted from year to year on the same site. They may also be alternated or they may follow funde, with a fallow year appearing regularly in the cycle. Table 1 lists the crop sequences of several farmers that are typical of the rotating system.

TABLE 1
Yalunka Crop Rotation in a Single Field
(Selected Examples)

1	2	3	4	5
Upland rice	Groundnuts	Groundnuts	Groundnuts	Cassava
Funde	Funde	Funde	Funde	Funde
Fallow	Cassava	Groundnuts	Cassava	Cassava
	Fallow	Funde	Groundnuts	Fallow
		Fallow	Fallow	

The Agricultural Year

As might be expected, the Yalunka recognize two seasons, "rainy" and "dry." The rains begin in April and continue until October. Agricultural activity is keyed to rainfall. The heaviest agricultural work begins in March just before the rains and continues until the rice harvest is over in December. Some farm work goes on throughout the year.

Here I will discuss the agricultural year for each major crop individually. This is to prevent the loss in continuity that would result if the year were discussed month by month. Table 2 summarizes farming activity by the month.

General. From January to early April, fires are set to burn large areas of the bush that surrounds settlements. These are frequently set in places where people plan to make farms, but large tracts that are not used are also burned. Farm sites are selected at this time if they are not already known from the previous year. In March, after the large fires become less frequent, the men begin to cut the trees on areas where they plan to lay farms. The trees are then burned. In April, smaller trees and the undergrowth are cut and there is a second burning of the future farms. Large clumps of weeds, bushes, and the remains of trees are piled up for this burning, and the ashes are scattered later during planting.

Upland rice. By late April, rain begins to fall in significant amounts. The sites selected for upland rice farms have been cut and burned (unburned tree trunks and limbs are left lying where they fall). The cleared areas are roughly rectangular. Usually the fields are not prepared further until the day of planting.

Planting is in April or May. Most farmers try to complete the sowing of a farm in one day. To do this they usually need more workers than are present in their households. For this help they call on immediate kin, descent group members, affines, members of a "cooperative work group," or, in a few cases, hired labor. Those who agree to come assemble in the field early in the morning of the appointed day. At planting time rain is not yet a daily occurrence, so sowing is almost always done on a rain-free day. The workers are divided by sex into two major groups. The men use the short-handled hoe to dig up the field to a depth of about two inches. They generally work in a line from one side of the field to the other. This group is followed by the owner and perhaps one or two older men, who broadcast the seed over the hoed area. Following in a line behind the sowers, the women use their hoes to break up clods and cover the seeds. This is also supposed to kill the weeds that have been dug up. A large work party usually has one or two drummers who play continuously while the planting is in progress.

Until the rice is a few inches high, several people (usually small boys) are left at the farm to scare off birds. No additional work is done on the field until weeding is necessary. Weeding is done in July and early August and is predominantly women's work. The weeds are pulled by hand. Shortly after the weeding is finished, watch must be kept on the fields again to scare birds who come to eat the ripening rice. About the time of weeding some farmers build wooden fences around their fields to keep out wandering cattle.

The rice is harvested from October through December, depending on the time of planting and the variety of rice planted. All upland rice is usually cut by November. The rice is cut by both men and women. It is cut three or four stalks at a time, and when

TABLE 2
Yalunka Agricultural Activity by Crop and Month

Month	Upland Rice	Swamp Rice	Funde	Groundnuts	Maize, Cassava	Potatoes	General
January						Take out potatoes Make heaps	Big bush fires
February							Big bush fires
March							Burning of farms
April	Start planting		Start planting		Start planting maize		Second burning
May	Planting	Start planting	Planting	Start planting	Plant maize	Take out potatoes	
June		Planting	Weeding	Planting	Weed maize		
July	Weeding	Weeding	Weeding	Weeding	Weed and pick maize		
August	Weeding	Weeding	Cutting	Weeding	Pick maize		
September	Cutting	Weeding	Cutting	Harvest			
October	Cutting	Cutting		Harvest		Make heaps	
November	Cutting	Cutting			Plant cassava Harvest cassava	Make heaps	
December		Cutting			Plant cassava Harvest cassava		

a bundle six to eight inches in diameter has been gathered, it is tied with a few more stalks and piled in a central location. Rice is cut just before it is fully ripe so that the danger of the grains' shaking loose from the head is reduced. At the end of each day the harvested bundles are carried to a storage area on the farm or near the owner's house. There the rice is dried on racks for some time. Then the grain is removed from the stalks either by walking on the rice or by beating it with sticks. The rice grains are then stored in large round containers of woven split bamboo or in burlap bags until they are ready for use or sale. Upland rice is usually ready for storage by late November or early December.

Swamp rice. Preparation of fields for swamp rice begins in late April or early May. Usually the previous year's field will be replanted and there is no heavy growth to clear. The owner of the field uses a machete to cut the weeds and other growth from the area he decides to plant. He and his household use hoes to break up the soil to a depth of about two inches. The weeds may be burned, but often they are merely thrown to the side of the farm. Swamps are usually planted later than upland farms. If the two kinds of farms are side by side (people make them this way whenever possible), both are usually planted at the same time. The same kind of labor force used to plant upland rice is often called upon for swamp planting, but outside help is used with somewhat less frequency. The planting procedure is the same as for upland rice. The seed is broadcast; there is no use of seedbeds or transplanting. The ground is redug, even though it may have been broken only a few days before. The fields are guarded from birds immediately after planting. As swamp rice is sown later than upland rice, weeding is usually later too, in August and early September. Harvesting begins in late October and continues through early December. Again, the time of harvest depends on planting time and the variety of rice planted. Harvesting and storage techniques are the same as for upland rice. Swamp farms are usually fenced to keep out wandering cattle.

Funde. Funde is planted on the same type of site as upland rice. Smaller groups of people work on the planting. The work group is rarely larger than the household and perhaps a few close relatives. The ground is hoed to a depth of about two inches. Men and women break the ground together. When a significant portion of the field has been hoed, the owner broadcasts the seed over it and the soil is hoed again to cover the seed, as for upland rice. Planting is in late April and May. Less attention is given to scaring birds, and since the funde is less well guarded than rice it is more open to depredations by cattle and wild animals. Weeding, again by women, is done in June and July. The funde is cut by both men and women in August and early September. As with rice, a knife is used to cut a few stalks at a time, which are tied into bundles. Funde (except for next year's seed) is rarely stored. The last harvest's rice has usually been exhausted, and it is needed to feed the household until the new rice is ready.

Groundnuts. Groundnut farming is considered strictly women's work. Groundnuts are planted on old upland rice or funde farms or on sites that are continuously used as groundnut farms. Thus little or no heavy clearing must be done. Each woman has her own groundnut farm. Singly or in twos and threes they hoe the site and plant the seed in late May and in June. Seeds are planted singly or in pairs a few inches apart. Weeding is done in July and August. Groundnuts begin to ripen in September and are pulled from the ground in September and October. Each woman weeds and pulls them alone or with the help of her smaller children. Occasionally two friends or cowives help each other. After harvesting, the nuts are separated from the plants, which are left on the field to rot.

Cassava. Cassava is planted in either mounds or rows. (It is the only food plant the Yalunka grow in rows.) The mounds are about one and one-half feet high and three to five feet in diameter. Cassava is planted in either November or December and is harvested in the same months a year later. If it is not needed, it may be stored in the ground for some time. Planting is done by putting several cuttings of the root in each heap or by placing the cuttings about 6 inches apart in rows.

Sweet Potatoes. Sweet potatoes are an important subsidiary crop. Nearly everyone grows one crop a year, and many people grow two. Sweet potatoes are grown in "heaps." Most frequently they are planted close to streams in parts of the sites used for swamp rice. Hoes are used to make mounds of the rich black streamside earth. These mounds are about the same size as those used for cassava. About twenty eyes are planted in each mound. The mounds are made and planted in early January and the potatoes are taken out in May, just before the heaps are leveled and swamp rice is planted.

After the rice is cut in October more heaps are often made. Potatoes from the October planting are taken out in January.

Maize. Maize is nearly always planted only in gardens near houses and is mixed in with other garden crops. The ground is prepared with the hoe in the same way as for groundnuts. The maize is planted in late April and May, is weeded in June, and is ripe in late July and August. Although not grown extensively, it is important as an interim source of food after rice begins to run short and before funde is ready to harvest. Like most other garden crops, it is cultivated mostly by women.

Garden crops. The other garden crops are normally planted at about the same time as maize. Gardens are women's work, but if the garden is fenced, men do that.

The Farming Household

The household consists of a man, his wife (or wives), and his unmarried children. In many households other persons are attached as dependents and contribute all or part of their agricultural labor time to the household's farming activity. These dependents may include unmarried younger brothers of the household head; more distant unmarried male kin of the head; aged relatives (usually female) of the household head or of his wives; "strangers" who have come in search of cash or wives and who do some work and receive in return a sleeping place, food, and social assistance; and married daughters of the head on extended visits, especially if they are in the late stages of a first pregnancy or are nursing a first child. Although the households usually concentrate their efforts on their own farms, they usually receive some help from the household head's younger married brothers or married sons, if any. As mentioned previously, in times when labor is badly needed (when rice is planted and, to some extent, when it is harvested) help is also often available from descent group members, affines, or neighbors. Some household heads also hire unattached young men to work for wages.

This is a considerable range of persons, but few, if any, households contain people belonging to every category at any one time. The current composition of a household depends on its demographic history and on its position in the developmental cycle of Yalunka households. Briefly, this developmental cycle is marriage of a young man to a first wife and the setting up of an independent household, the birth of children, marriage to a second (and later perhaps a third) wife, the birth of more children and their maturation, the marriage of the children (young women going to their husband's households, young men setting up households nearby), and death of wives or husband (if the husband dies first, remarriage of the younger wives and probable residence of aged wives with a son). Thus a young man who has recently married a first wife may still be living in his father's or older brother's house, and he and his wife may be only partly independent of the larger household. As he grows older he will probably build a house of his own, and his household will, from time to time, contain many of the various types of persons listed above.

This is not the place to present a detailed quantitative analysis of Yalunka households and household types, but a few statistics gathered during my own census should help fill in the general picture. In one Yalunka village containing 153 married farmers, the range in farmer's household size was 2 to 24 persons. The mean number per household was 5.8 persons. The mean number of wives per married farmer was 1.84. The count included only the farmer and persons dependent for their livelihood on him.

These figures include only those in the household at the time of the census. Migration is important among the Yalunka and has important effects on household composition. Most households whose head had reached late middle age had at least one member (usually male) who was residing and working out of Yalunka country. (The ratio varied from settlement to settlement but lay between 60 and 80 percent.) Most of these migrants are young men who stay away from six months to several years before returning. Some go to the capital, Freetown, or to the other population centers, but most go to the diamond areas.

The missing labor of these young men can be important during the heavy agricultural work season. This loss is even more serious if they return at other times of the year and consume part of the household food supply without being able to make a contribution from their down-country earnings. Absent men may also leave wives and small children in their father's, brother's, or affine's households. As will be discussed later, if these migrants are able to bring or send cash to the household they are an important asset, but if they cannot they are often a serious loss or even a drain on the household budget.

"Cooperative work groups" are formed by young men who join together during the planting season to help each other with the planting of rice farms. They are usually formed in small villages or by the young men of several nearby hamlets where there is not enough male labor available locally through kinship links to get the planting done quickly enough. Such groups comprise five to ten men, and each member's fields are planted in turn.

HOUSEHOLD FOOD PRODUCTION AND FACTORS AFFECTING IT

We now take up the question of how much food a producing unit is able to raise using the traditional technology. First we shall estimate the annual needs of households and outline the potential of the Yalunka environment. After that, we shall analyze actual production figures for a number of households and conclude with a description of the factors that affect household production.

Only rice production will be discussed. While most Yalunka farmers can give at least rough estimates of rice production and consumption, few Yalunka will even try to guess their production or consumption of other crops (with the partial exception of funde). The only way to obtain figures for nonrice crop production or consumption is to be on hand every time food is gathered or prepared, an impossible task.

The lack of such data is, however, not too serious. Rice will dominate any discussion of Yalunka production, for it is the diet staple and is more important than all other crops combined. This is true in terms of the amount of foodstuffs consumed and in terms of the place rice occupies in Yalunka culture.

My observations and Yalunka statements about rice consumption indicate that if an adult ate rice every day he would consume between three and four bushels a year. Although for most Yalunka this would be the "ideal" diet, no one expects to eat this much rice. Other foods do replace rice in parts of the year. Estimating how many days of the year the "average" Yalunka household consumes rice is a bit risky. I have information on this topic for parts of the year for a few households, and I have some interviews on the subject of food needs and consumption. On the basis of these data I would say that most Yalunka can reasonably expect to consume between 70 and 80 percent of the ideal figure.

My census figures indicate that the mean size of Yalunka farming households was 5.8 persons. The mean number of wives per farmer was 1.8. If one assumes that the other members of the household were children, as they usually were, one can estimate the average rice consumption, based on 4 adults per household (2 children equal 1 adult), at from 8 to 12 bushels of rice per household per year.

Considering the character of the environment, production of this much rice is within the capabilities of most households of "average" size. No experiments have been carried out in Yalunka country to determine the productive potential of the soils there. The Agricultural Officer of the district in which the Yalunka are situated estimated that, using traditional technology, Yalunka upland farms could produce between 10 and 20 bushels of rice per acre in an average year and that swamp farms could produce between 20 and 30 bushels per acre. If the farmer can get labor assistance at planting time (as all or nearly all can), he can make large enough farms to produce this much rice.

Yalunka farms rarely approach an acre in size. Swamp farms are usually a good bit smaller than upland farms. A typical swamp farm is about one-third acre and a typical upland farm covers a little more than one-half acre. If an average household has both types of fields of these sizes it should be able to produce its minimum needs for the year.

Thus in theory a household can produce sufficient rice to meet its needs. Actual production figures tell a somewhat different story. For some households I have reasonably accurate production figures for one or two years. (Farmers' memories become too hazy to be at all reliable further in the past.) Table 3 gives production figures for 21 farmers. As inspection will show, out of a possible 42 production years there are data for only 28. The figures are approximate, but they are useful because they can be compared with each other, as all are subject to the same biases.

The remarks column of Table 1 notes whether or not a given farmer produced sufficient rice to feed his household in a particular year. Rice sufficiency is determined by comparing adjusted bushel production with the number of bushels estimated as the minimum required to feed a particular household. This last figure is obtained by multiplying the minimum adult ration requirement (two bushels, as estimated earlier) by the number of adult ration units that comprise a household (two children equal one adult).

The comparison of adjusted production and needed rations gives the following sufficiency figures. In only 5 (18 percent) of the 28 production years was there a marked surplus. Ten of the production years (36 percent) reached a level about equal to the minimum household needs, and these farmers therefore should probably be considered to have produced sufficient rice for their households.

TABLE 3
Adjusted Rice Production in Bushels for Selected Yalunka Farmers,
1965 and 1966 (Approximate)

Farmer Number	Household Size[a]	Bushels First Year[b]	Bushels Second Year[b]	Remarks[c]
1	3	?	9⅓	1-?, 2-y
2	5	19⅓	?	1-y, 2-?
3	4	?	11⅓	1-?, 2-y
4	4	7⅓	15⅓	1-m, 2-y
5	4	13⅓	8⅔	1-y, 2-m
6	3	5⅓	5⅓	1-m, 1-m
7	2½	4⅔	6⅔	1-m, 2-m
8	7	11⅔	?	1-m, 2-?
9	3	5⅓	?	1-m, 2-?
10	4½	6⅔	8⅔	1-x, 2-m
11	4	6⅔	4⅔	1-m, 2-x
12	3	?	1⅓	1-?, 2-n
13	4	?	5⅓	1-?, 2-n
14	3	?	2	1-?, 2-n
15	3½	?	3⅓	1-?, 2-n
16	5	1⅓	4⅔	1-n, 2-x
17	4	3⅓	?	1-x, 2-?
18	4½	?	3⅓	1-?, 2-x
19	4	4⅔	?	1-x, 2-?
20	9½	?	9⅓	1-?, 2-x
21	8½	?	11⅓	1-?, 2-x

SOURCE NOTE: Based on a detailed questionnaire administered to 50 farmers. For various reasons, the material pertaining to rice production was usable for only 21 of these farmers.

[a] Number of adult rations required by household.
[b] Rice needed for the next year's seed not included.
[c] Figures 1 and 2 refer to years; y = sufficient rice, probable surplus; m = marginal, probably sufficient rice; n = deficient owing to special conditions, in normal year probably sufficient rice; x = rice not sufficient.

On the basis of information in the agricultural questionaires but not shown on the chart, I would say that another 5 production years (18 percent) would have reached the minimum had it not been for extraordinary circumstances. These conditions include unusually heavy flooding of a farm, great destruction of a farm by uncontrolled cattle, unusual and unavoidable absence of the farmer during a crucial part of the agricultural cycle, and so on. In the remaining 8 production years (28 percent) sufficient rice was not grown to reach the minimum. Thus, in this group of production years, only 72 percent reached or exceeded the minimum (or would have but for special circumstances).

There are two kinds of production failure—those caused by some "outside" or "unusual" circumstances that can easily be discovered by questioning a farmer and those resulting from more subtle factors such as careless or lazy farming. In the discussion above I have lumped failures due to unusual factors in with successes to reach the sufficient-production rate of 72 percent. From the point of view of successful or unsuccessful application of a particular technology this seems proper. But in terms of self-sufficiency these people, like the others who have failures, must look to extrahousehold sources for the rice required to meet minimum needs. Both kinds of failure occur in any one year, though the same farmers are not involved from year to year.

Unfortunately the nature of this sample of farmers is such that it is difficult to generalize from it to any larger population. The 21 farmers in the sample were almost equally divided among three villages (6, 7, and 8 farmers). Two of the settlements were quite small (with populations of 90 and 55) and the third somewhat larger (with a population of 276). Half of the farmers in the two smaller villages were present in the sample, but only 20 percent of the farmers in the bigger village were included. Production information on the other farmers in these villages is not sufficiently reliable to include in the chart. Because the farmers on the chart were present only on the basis of usefulness of the data and because the sample was small, no statistical manipulation of the data seems worthwhile.

My impression of these villages is that the data are probably representative of the situation in these settlements as a whole, so that one can say with some confidence that between 25 and 30 percent of the farmers did not produce enough rice to feed their households. What is the relation between household rice production in these three settlements and household rice production in Yalunka country as a whole? My impression, based on their locations and the general appearance of the villages, is that they were a little worse off than most Yalunka settlements. Most Yalunka villages probably have a slightly lower percentage of sufficiency failures than these three. Nevertheless, the overall percentage of failures is fairly high. Allowing for the limitations of this sample, I suspect that if both of the types of failure discussed before are lumped together, in any given year between 20 and 30 percent of Yalunka farmers do not produce enough rice to supply the needs of their households.

The factors that lead to insufficient rice production fall into four groups: (1) destruction of crops, (2) late planting, (3) failure to plant enough land, and (4) inept farming.

Destruction of the crop on a farm may occur at any time during the agricultural cycle and may be partial (the usual case) or complete. Weather conditions rarely cause crop losses. There is some yearly and areal variation in rainfall, but Yalunka seldom complained of drought. Sometimes there is unusual localized flooding of streams. If this happens relatively early in the year, swamp farms nearby may be damaged. Insect damage is rarely an areawide problem either. Occasionally swarms of locusts cause widespread destruction, but usually only a few fields in widely scattered localities suffer from insects.

Much more widespread is crop destruction by animals and birds. Crops may be eaten by any of a number of pests, especially baboons, other species of monkeys, and the cutting grass, a type of rodent. Unattended cattle also wander into fields and can destroy much of a field before they are discovered. Fencing and guarding are the usual precautions taken against animals, but every year some farmers suffer considerable losses. Birds cause the most destruction. They are a problem when seed has just been planted and when the various grain crops have begun to ripen. Planting early reduces the danger from birds, as there are fewer about, but the only way to save a crop from bird incursions is to have scarers on duty from dawn to dusk. Bird scaring is usually done by small boys, but anyone may be pressed into service. Every field suffers a little from birds, but each year a few fields are particularly hard hit.

Late planting delays the rest of the crop cycle. Needed rainfall may be missed, and the bird problem is worse later in the season. If the crop has not been planted early enough to get a good start and if there is unusual flooding, the small plants may be washed away. The primary causes of late starts are a shortage of labor, illness, or involvement in a debt cycle. If a person is caught up in a debt cycle, he must often work on the planting of someone else's farm to repay the loan before he can plant his own. This late start often leads to another bad year and another loan, which perpetuates the difficulty. Also, a farmer may be late because of lack of seed to plant a new crop. He may have no seed because it has been eaten owing to an unusually bad crop the year before or because rats or fire have destroyed his stored crop. If he does not have seed, he must usually work for it or spend time borrowing it from relatives so that he is late in planting.

Some farmers do not plant enough land to produce sufficient rice to feed their households even if the bushels per acre they produce reach the technological and environmental potential. This failure can result from missing labor at the beginning of the agricultural cycle or mistakes in judgment about how much to plant.

Inept farming is difficult to pin down, and probably only a few farmers are guilty of it. It is most easily seen in poor weeding. Uncontrolled weeds choke off the crop plants, and delayed, omitted, or careless weeding causes serious loss. Other manifestations of inept farming are poor site selection, reuse of a field before a sufficient fallow period has passed, and the use of contaminated seed that germinates poorly.

If the production figures presented earlier are an indication of Yalunka household food production, then in any year between 20 and 30 percent of these households do not produce sufficient rice on their own to feed themselves. They must turn to extrahousehold sources for food. (All households do, of course, grow other food crops in addition to rice, and these are an important supplementary source of food. But in estimating rice needs, I have allowed for intrahousehold production of supplementary foodstuffs so that a shortage of rice can be considered a shortage of food in general.)

There are two general sources of extra food—the traditional social network, and persons or organizations outside this network.

Yalunka in need of food will first call on their kin. They will request food from close patri-kin (fathers, elder and younger brothers) and from genealogically more distant members of their corporate descent group who live in their own or nearby settlements. Money to buy food may come from household members who are working as migrant laborers in other parts of Sierra Leone (particularly the diamond areas). If need exceeds the ability of descent-group members to fill it, households turn to affinal kin. Efforts are made to tap all affinal links, both the kin of wives married into the household and the households of women married out of the household. Both patrilineal and affinal kin belong to a network of social obligations and interaction that involves much more than the sharing of food, though this is one of its most important activities. Food obtained from such sources is rarely thought of as a debt to be repaid but is a part of a continual set of reciprocal transactions. In later years, when the lenders fall on hard times, the borrowers will come to their assistance.

There is a final traditional source of assistance. This is the chief. In traditional Yalunka society redistribution was an important part of the economy, and the chief was the focus of the redistributive system. Today this redistributive system has broken down considerably. Nevertheless, and particularly if the shortage is due to some natural disaster, people can still turn to the chief and request rice. They will not receive enough to make up a serious shortage, but the chief's contribution will help piece out supplies from other sources.

If a shortage is very serious, or if the traditional links do not supply enough to make up the shortage (as is increasingly the case), the household must look elsewhere. This means that rice or money to buy rice must be borrowed from someone not in the reciprocity network. A formal debt is incurred. Most moneylenders in Yalunka country are either traders or cattle owners and are usually Mandinka or Fula immigrants, not Yalunka. These people lend money at high interest rates, and the loans must be paid back at the next harvest. Thus it is very easy to become involved in a debt cycle that leads to greater and greater difficulties over rice sufficiency. Even if sufficient rice is produced the next year, enough of it may have to be paid to the lender to make another loan necessary. Or often, the borrower or a significant part of his labor force may have to work for wages (or for the lender at the beginning of the next agricultural year) so that the household's planting of rice farms is delayed or reduced in size. This naturally increases the likelihood of another year of insufficient production.

HOUSEHOLD PRODUCTION IN A LARGER CONTEXT

Having considered food production by individual households, we now take up how this production fits into the context of developments and conditions in the Yalunka area as a whole.

For the Yalunka, the household is the significant unit of food production and consumption, even though each household belongs to a wider network of cooperation and reciprocity. Subsistence agriculture is the major economic activity of most Yalunka households. (In one large village the major economic activity of 89 percent of the Yalunka households was subsistence farming. This was a chiefdom headquarters town and had shops, government clerks, and so on. In most other villages the percentage of subsistence-farming households is higher.)

Cash cropping has not been important in the Yalunka area in the past. Yalunka country is well to the north of the area where Sierra Leone's export crops are grown. Since early in this century groundnuts have been carried down-country for sale. No production or sales figures are available, but though groundnuts are important from the individual Yalunka household's point of view as a source of much-needed cash, they have never been commercially important in the area. For most households, cash income from groundnuts rarely exceeds Le4.00 or Le5.00 a year (1 Leone = 10 shillings). Some farmers now grow Aureol Tobacco Company's improved varieties of tobacco. But probably less than a fourth do so, and cash income for individual farmers is not great.

For some time the most valuable commodity exported from the area has been cattle. Again, accurate figures are not available. Most of the cattle are owned by Fula, who have been migrating into the area since before World War I. The Yalunka have always held some cattle, but only a few own enough head to engage in the livestock trade.

Because of increases in field productivity owing to recently introduced mechanical cultivation (discussed below), rice has become a cash crop for some men. But most Yalunka even today do not look to agriculture for needed money. The main source of cash, at least since the diamond boom began after World War II, has been work outside Yalunka country. The published data in the report on the 1963 census are too general to allow an adequate analysis of out-migration, but they give a rough picture of the situation. According to these figures, 21 percent of the persons who identified themselves as Yalunka were living outside the three Yalunka chiefdoms. Seventeen percent of the total Yalunka population was living outside the district in which the Yalunka chiefdoms are situated. These figures include a few students studying at boarding schools, but most of these people either were working or were the dependents of workers. In one large village, 39 percent of the farmers interviewed had earned money from nonagricultural sources in the past. Most of these persons worked outside the Yalunka chiefdoms. These figures suggest high out-migration, which is not surprising when it is remembered that the Yalunka lack cash crops and that few jobs are available inside the Yalunka chiefdoms. Some of the cash brought into the area by returning Yalunka is used to purchase food, but most of it is spent on marriages, on building "pan" (corrugated iron) roofed houses, and on consumer goods.

This out-migration is not motivated by high population density and crowding, as is the case in some Sierra Leone chiefdoms. The Yalunka chiefdoms have the potential, using traditional technology, to support a larger population than they do. It would be desirable to demonstrate this by calculating the "carrying capacity" of the land using Allan's methods [6] or by some similar technique, but once again data problems intervene. No studies have been done of the distribution of soil types and related matters in the Yalunka area. Here, too, estimates based on my own limited material must suffice.

Compared with the rest of Sierra Leone, the population density of the Yalunka areas is not high. The 1963 census report gives a population of 29,000 for an area of 870 square miles; thus the density of 33 persons per square mile. The mean density for chiefdoms in Sierra Leone is 78 persons per square mile (there are 146 chiefdoms with a range of 8 to 246 persons per square mile). Even if allowance is made for the fact that the Yalunka area may have been seriously underenumerated, the difference between the two densities is still great.[7]

The population is not, of course, evenly distributed throughout the three chiefdoms. According to the 1963 census report, 25 percent of the population lived in the six villages reported to have populations of more than 500. Large tracts of the area are almost unpopulated. Not all of the land is arable, but many small swamps and a few large ones are uncultivated, and potential upland farm sites are not a part of the swidden cycle as well. I would say that Yalunka country could support a significantly larger population. (This is true even allowing for the swidden cycle and an eight- to ten-year fallow period on upland rice areas.)

There are no rice production figures for the Yalunka area as a whole, but according to an experienced observer (the Agricultural Officer whose district includes the Yalunka chiefdoms) until 1964 or 1965 the Yalunka area imported rice. Now it exports some rice to the rest of Sierra Leone. The source of this increase in production is the recent introduction of mechanical cultivation of certain low-lying flatlands. Mechanical cultivation easily doubles the yield of these rich alluvial soils. The Agriculture Department has also tried to introduce improved varieties of seed and has a small artificial fertilizer program, but the main credit must go to the tractors.

---

[6] See William Allan, *The African Husbandman* (Edinburgh: Oliver & Boyd, 1965), especially chaps. 2 through 5.

[7] If an arbitrary one-third of the reported population is added to the reported population, the resultant density would be only 45 persons per square mile. I doubt that any underenumeration was this great. Some chiefdoms contain urban centers, and if this factor is taken into consideration by omitting chiefdoms containing towns of more than 10,000, the mean density for the remaining chiefdoms is 75 persons per square mile (there would be 141 chiefdoms with a range of 8 to 246 per square mile).

Only a few farmers' swamps are plowed. Because of the great increase in yields on a few farms (and because a few large swamps have been newly opened by tractor), the area's total rice production has increased enough to make it a rice surplus area. But most farmers remain unaffected by mechanical cultivation, and if the big producers are excluded the condition of rice shortage still holds for the area. This is an important point. If figures become available for overall production in the area, readers of the figures should take into consideration that the majority of Yalunka farmers there are not a part of this recent burst of productivity.

Mechanical cultivation is a project of the Department of Agriculture. The department owns the machines and its personnel operate them. Two kinds of location are cultivated by these tractor-drawn disks. Parts of the larger swamps around the bigger villages are plowed for the farmers using them, and large, previously uncultivated swamps not near established settlements have been opened up to cultivation.

Mechanical cultivation is carried out entirely on the flat alluvial area the Yalunka call swamps. The soil is turned by disking to a depth of six inches, in contrast to the two inch depth of hand hoeing. This brings more of the soil's nutrients into the root zone and leads to an increase in yields of about 100 percent. The only technological change in farming introduced by mechanization is in soil preparation; all other parts of the agricultural cycle remain unchanged. This obviously facilitates its introduction. Other advantages of mechanical cultivation, besides increased field fertility, are encouragement of early planting and the tendency for different holdings to be brought together rather than scattered. The Agriculture Department encourages farmers to lay out their farms side by side so that plowing costs can be kept down. This consolidation of formerly scattered farms also makes bird and animal pest control considerably easier and reduces the labor and the loss spent on this problem.

The swamps that are plowed near the larger settlements have been in use since the nineteenth century. The traditional location of these big villages is near fairly sizable streams and near swamps of considerable extent, and swamps seem to have been the major source of rice for these settlements. Machine cultivation of all or part of these swamps continues this pattern and makes these fields even more important. The farmers pay cash fees to the Agriculture Department for this service.

Mechanical cultivation is performed around three of the larger villages and some of their smaller satellite villages. I have sociological and agricultural data about the farmers in one of these large villages where there were 153 Yalunka farmers. Table 4 compares users and nonusers of mechanical cultivation for four variables. Of the 153 Yalunka farmers in the town, 23 (15 percent) used mechanical cultivation in 1967.

The demographic variables in Table 4 give the mean age, mean number of wives, and mean number in the household for users, nonusers, and the farmers as a whole. The mean age was lower for users than for nonusers, and both the mean number of wives and the mean number of persons in the household were higher for users than for nonusers. A difference of means test for the two groups was applied for each of these variables. The probability that the differences between the means was due to chance is: for age, $p = .12$; for number of wives, $p = .11$; and for household size, $p = .02$. For household size, the p is less than the usual rejection level of

TABLE 4

Comparison of Yalunka Farmers in One Village Using Mechanical Cultivation with Those Not Using Mechanical Cultivation, 1967

	Cultivation Type		
Demographic Variables[a]	Mechanical	Non-mechanical	All
Mean Age	39.3	43.4	42.8
Mean No. of Wives	2.26	1.77	1.84
Mean No. in Household	8.87	5.42	5.8
Percentage Involved in Nonagricultural Cash Earning[b]			
Since 1966	34.8	11.5	15.0
Before 1966	47.8	28.5	31.4
Ever Involved	52.2	36.9	39.2
Number of Farmers	23	130	153

[a] *Tests:* Difference-between-means test, probability that the difference between the means for the two groups is due to chance; age: p-.12; number of wives, p-.11; household size, p-.02.

[b] *Tests:* Adaptation of Ellegard's test of significance for r_n expressed in percent, probability that the difference in percentage is due to chance; since 1966: $p < .05$; before 1966: $p < .05$; ever involved: $p < .05$.

$p \leq .05$, but for age and number of wives the p's are not quite this good. Even so, I would argue that the three p's taken together are fairly low and consistent and that they are good evidence that the users and nonusers are two significantly different groups of farmers when viewed from the perspective of these variables.

The rest of Table 4 gives the percentage of users, of nonusers, and of the entire group that was involved in nonagricultural earning of cash. As a part of a household census I collected wage-labor histories on each farmer. The category of nonagricultural cash earner tries to uncover those people who have or have had some involvement with the money economy in a regular fashion other than through the sale of agricultural products. Probably all Yalunka farmers have sold at least some agricultural produce for money (if only enough to raise the annual head tax of Le3). Detailed and reliable agricultural sales data in the absence of regular cash cropping were impossible to collect, but no farmer in this sample regularly sold significant amounts of agricultural produce. People categorized as nonagricultural cash earners included not only those who had worked as wage laborers in the diamond or urban areas, but soldiers or policemen, chiefdom officials with large cash incomes (Paramount Chiefs), and the self-employed (tailors, traders, traditional specialists whose income is now mainly in cash rather than in kind, and so on). To determine whether or not the difference between the percentages for users and nonusers was significant, I applied an adaptation of Ellegard's test of significance for r_n expressed in percent that has been worked out by Joseph G. Jorgensen. In all three cases (since 1966, before 1966, ever) the probability that the differences in percentage were due to chance was well below the $p = .05$ level. Thus in terms of the cash-earner variable, users of mechanical cultivation differed significantly as a group from nonusers of mechanical cultivation as a group.

To summarize the preceding analysis, the users of mechanical cultivation on the average differed significantly from nonusers in having a lower age, more wives, and more persons in their households, and in being (or having been) more involved in the nonagricultural earning of money. The larger mean number of wives and larger mean household size are indicators both of larger labor forces at the disposal of users and of their probable greater wealth. (Acquiring a wife involves considerable expense, and it is usually older men rather than younger ones who have more wives. Then too, bigger households require more resources to keep them together.) The greater participation of the users in earning money also shows probable greater wealth as a group as well as possible sources of money to pay plowing fees. Taken together with information I have that is less amenable to statistical analysis (my and my informants' impressions of the wealth of some of the farmers in the two groups), I would say that these data indicate that it was the better-off farmers who tended to make use of the mechanical cultivation scheme. (Mechanical cultivation had been introduced too recently to account itself for the users' being wealthier than their neighbors.) This is not to say that only the better-off used mechanical cultivation or that none of the farmers of the village who could be termed better-off belonged to the group that does not use mechanical cultivation, but that as a group it was the financially more able who were benefiting from the scheme.

The Agriculture Department is also opening up new alluvial areas some distance from any settlement that have rarely been cultivated before. The swamps are cleared of trees and brush and at the beginning of the planting season are disked. Again, the farmer pays for the plowing of the area he uses, but in this case he is not the traditional user of the farm but someone who has changed farming locations or added a new swamp farm to his agricultural commitments.

One such large swamp was opened up in Yalunka country in 1965, and there are plans to open several more. The project is very recent and is not located in the area in which my research was concentrated, but I do have some general information about the scheme. The Yalunka near the swamp who wished to use it pleaded poverty when it came to paying the plowing fees. (This seems to happen all over Sierra Leone when new agricultural schemes are introduced.) Government loans were arranged so that plowing fees could be advanced to the farmer. These loans were to be paid back when the crop was sold. The harvest seems to have been quite large, but it is reported that a majority of the farmers defaulted on their loans, again pleading poverty. It is a bit early to tell, but it seems that the original Yalunka users of the scheme are being replaced by immigrant farmers who are fairly reliable repayers of government loans. Thus, from the Yalunka point of view, the new swamp will probably be at most a minimal success and source of additional rice.

I can only surmise why the Yalunka who used the scheme were unable or unwilling to pay their plowing fees. A main factor was probably that most Yalunka have a subsistence orientation to agriculture, and rather than treat the money gained from sales of surplus production as a means to produce even more they handled the money as they usually handle nonagricultural income. That is, they used the money in marriage transactions, to buy cattle, to build or improve houses, and to purchase consumer goods. Other factors probably included the need to repay other debts and a lack of concern for repayment of loans from government sources.

CONCLUSION

The major difference between the agricultural technology of the Yalunka and that of neighboring peoples is in the use of different types of farmsites. The Yalunka use a greater proportion of permanently cultivatable farmsites, which have a name we have rendered as "swamps," than their neighbors.

The Yalunka are still oriented primarily toward subsistence agriculture. One reason for this is that suitable cash crops have been lacking. Cash crop opportunities have increased recently, and some Yalunka are becoming more involved in the money economy.

Perhaps the most important point that the Yalunka material brings out is that many households still do not produce enough food to meet their needs even though the area as a whole has gone from rice importing to rice exporting. This is important to bear in mind when assessing the results of "development" programs, especially those aiming at increases in food production. Not only must areal changes be looked at, but what portion of the population is responsible for and benefits from any increases must be known. In the Yalunka case, the persons who benefit seem to be chiefly those who are rather better off to begin with.

In the past twenty-five years, immigration of non-Yalunka into the Yalunka area of Sierra Leone has been considerable. Many of these immigrants have become traders and cattle herders rather than subsistence farmers. It appears that these "strangers" are coming to be among the chief beneficiaries of large-scale mechanical cultivation. In this ethnically mixed area it is the "strangers," as a group, who more readily take up the production of foodstuffs as a cash crop.

Yalunka agricultural practice will probably remain fairly traditional for some time, except for an increasing use of mechanical cultivation to grow swamp rice. And if the less-well-off Yalunka households are to receive the full benefit of the productive potential of mechanical cultivation, special efforts will probably be necessary to encourage their participation in the scheme alongside their more prosperous neighbors.

CHAPTER 6

AGRICULTURE AND DIOLA SOCIETY

Olga Linares de Sapir

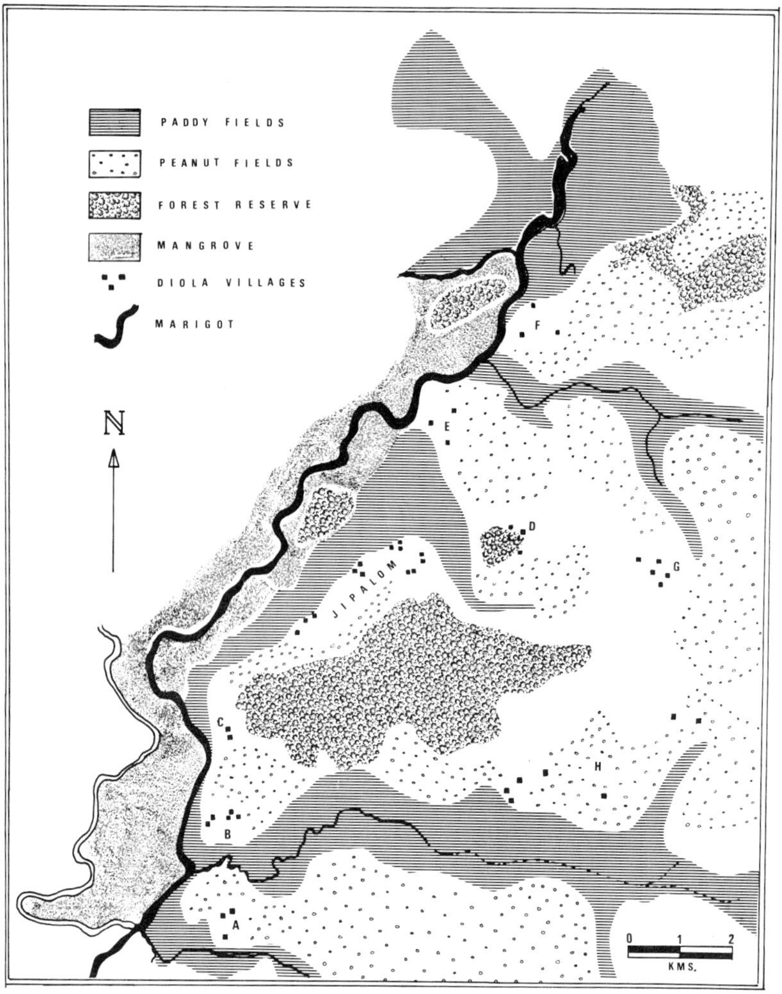
PADDY FIELDS
PEANUT FIELDS
FOREST RESERVE
MANGROVE
DIOLA VILLAGES
MARIGOT
N
JIPALOM
A
B
C
D
E
F
G
H
0
1
2
KMS.

INTRODUCTION

The Diola of Lower Casamance, Senegal, are wet-rice cultivators using intensive methods of continuous cropping with irrigation, transplanting, and fertilizing. For the past forty years the peanut (*Arachis hypogaea*), Senegal's cash crop *par excellence*, has been making inroads into Diola economy. Where peanut cultivation is feasible, the system employed is extensive or shifting bush-fallow cultivation.[1] The result, then, is that in areas of mixed peanut-rice farming two agricultural systems with different methods of land use and labor operate side by side. The two crops are also differentially integrated into the society, rice being central to Diola life, peanuts only peripheral.

In this essay I contrast the two agricultural systems along the dimensions of land classification and ownership, the scheduling and organization of work, and the channels for distribution and disposal of the products. The emphasis throughout is on how the Diola themselves conceptualize their agriculture and particularly on their categories of land and how these affect their land tenure. I also emphasize their application of traditional knowledge.[2]

The purpose of this contrast is twofold: to show how cultural factors may affect a subsistence crop as opposed to a cash crop, and secondarily, to discuss why and how agricultural production could be increased. I should like, however, to suggest at the start some general hypotheses concerning the effects of a cash crop on a traditional economy.

The first is rather obvious: that cash crops often have contradic-

---

[1] For a definition of these terms see Ester Boserup, *The Conditions of Agricultural Growth: The Economics of Agrarian Change under Population Pressure* (Chicago: Aldine Publishing Co., 1965). Although Boserup presents a theory for the transition from extensive to intensive agriculture, it is clear that she also considers this process as potentially reversible (pp. 62–63). Adoption of extensive or shifting cultivation by otherwise intensive farmers has parallels elsewhere. A particularly well-documented case is that of the Kofyar of northern Nigeria who practice intensive hillside farming in the escarpment and yet have recently opened up bush farms by shifting cultivation in the plains (Robert McC. Netting, *Hill Farmers of Nigeria: Cultural Ecology of the Kofyar of the Jos Plateau* [Seattle and London: University of Washington Press, 1968], pp. 193–224).

[2] I should like to thank my husband, J. David Sapir, for countless hours spent mapping rice fields with me and for his help in gathering this data. In many ways his knowledge of Diola society is greater than mine, and only a necessary division of labor prevents this from being a joint article. Robert McC. Netting read this manuscript and helped clarify many of its basic ideas. My father, Frank Linares Danz, gave extensive botanical and agronomic advice.

tory effects. At one level they may actually promote isolation by permitting a society to meet the demands of the outside world without altering local organization. By continuing to be one of Senegal's most isolated ethnic groups in spite of participating in the peanut market, the Diola are a classic example of this situation. At another level, cash crops may have marked social effects. This is best expressed in the Diola as a "loosening" of the social system. Social ties have been extended outside of kinship bonds in an effort to procure usufruct rights to peanut fields. Attitudes and values concerning manufactured objects and the outside world have also changed. Taken together, all these changes help create the necessary conditions for the eventual commercialization of the more basic subsistence crop.

The second hypothesis is that the creation of proper market facilities is often more important for an increase in production than technological change. The nature of the market is crucial. If it is external (that is, primarily for export) and geared to nonstaples such as tea, coffee, or even peanuts, a society that produces an abundance of a subsistence crop finds no outlet for its normal surpluses and no stimulus for increasing them. Many cash crop markets in West Africa are external; internal domestic markets have been discouraged in many areas by the rural emphasis on self-sufficiency and the lack of urban concentrations.[3] To participate in cash revenues, societies without domestic markets, though capable of high agricultural production, often have to reduce traditional crops and substitute cash crops less efficiently grown. This is the case among the Diola, who are reducing the area under rice cultivation to have more time for peanuts. Yet there is an increasing demand for rice in Senegalese cities, and to meet it 150,000 tons of rice are imported each year. If the Diola could fill part of this quota, their rice production would naturally increase without the need to interfere, at this stage, with the traditional system.

The final suggestion I should like to make is that radically different strategies for development often need to be applied to different types of crops. As we shall see, rice production among the Diola could be increased by the extension of market facilities. For peanuts, however, radical changes in technology and land tenure must be effected before they can be made more rewarding. How this can be done, and why, will be understood only after the details of Diola agriculture are discussed.

[3] John C. de Wilde *et al.*, *Experiences with Agricultural Development in Tropical Africa* (Baltimore: Johns Hopkins Press, 1967), p. 22.

Some Facts and Figures

There are approximately 210,000 Diola in the Lower Casamance region of southwestern Senegal between the Gambia and Portuguese Guinea. They live in Senegal's most fertile and best watered lands. When the Portuguese first made contact in the fifteenth century, the Diola were already prosperous rice producers. It is not certain, however, when and where they first started cultivating rice; it must have been many centuries before the Portuguese arrived.[4] The Senegambia is what Portères has called a second center of diversification of *Oryza glaberrima*, a group of rices indigenous to Africa. They are believed to have been propagated first in the bend of the Niger River absolutely independent of the Asian varieties *O. sativa* and *O. indica*.[5] Although the Diola today mainly cultivate the introduced *O. sativa*, they still raise some *O. glaberrima*.[6] The old people remember when such varieties were cultivated much more commonly.

Rice is not a major crop in West Africa today. A scattered population and the absence of large river systems may account for this. It is truly important only within a coastal belt from the Gambia to the Bandama River in the center of the Ivory Coast. In Portuguese Guinea, Guinea, Sierra Leone, Liberia, and a large part of the Ivory Coast it is grown as a major crop.[7]

In Senegal, the Sudanic complex of millet and sorghum are clearly the most important subsistence crops. In 1963–64 there were 865,000 hectares under millet and sorghum and a production of 420,000 metric tons, compared with only 71,000 hectares under rice cultivation (for a production of 97,000 metric tons).[8] Of the rice,

---

[4] Joseph Jerome Lauer ("Rice in the History of the Lower Gambia-Geba Area," Master's thesis, University of Wisconsin, 1969) has argued convincingly for the pre-European presence of intensive rice agriculture in the Casamance on the basis of *O. glaberrima*. I have proposed elsewhere that rice agriculture in the Kasa area may have started by A.D. 300 (Linares de Sapir, Olga, "Shell-Middens of Lower Casamance and Diola Protohistory," *West African Journal of Archaeology*, [University of Ibadan, Nigeria], Vol. I, in press).

[5] Roland Portères, "Berceaux Agricoles Primaires sur le Continent Africain," *Journal of African History*, 3, no. 2 (1962), 198.

[6] Of the fifteen varieties I collected in one ward, four were *Oryza glaberrima* and the rest either *O. sativa* or *O. japonica*. Roland Portères of the Laboratoire d'Etnobotanie, Musée National d'Histoire Naturelle, Paris, kindly identified the plant material.

[7] Bruce F. Johnston, *The Staple Food Economies of Western Tropical Africa* (Stanford, Calif.: Stanford University Press, 1958), p. 61.

[8] "Aperçu sur le Sénégal et son Economie," mimeographed (Chambre de Commerce d'Agriculture et d'Industrie de Dakar, 1964), p. 11.

50,000 hectares was in the Casamance, where the rainfall exceeds 1,200 millimeters and in some areas reaches 2,000 millimeters, in contrast with 40 percent of Senegal with an average of only 300 to 700 millimeters a year. The other rice-growing areas of Senegal are much smaller. The Richard-Toll project in the north and the delta and valley of the Senegal River together had 8,500 hectares under cultivation in 1963–64.[9]

Of the rice grown in the Casamance, at least three-fourths comes from Lower Casamance and is grown by the Diola. The average yields have been given as 1,000 to 1,200 kilograms (paddy, or unmilled) per hectare.[10] The reliability of these figures, however, is questionable. Rice is grown for consumption, not trade, and there are few statistics on production.[11] In addition, some figures that are published average the yields for Middle and Lower Casamance, and in the former area the lower-yielding upland rice is dominant.

If we now compare the million hectares under peanuts with those under millet, sorghum, and rice and the 120,000 hectares under maize, manioc, and other crops, it is apparent that half of Senegal's cultivated surface is under a single cash crop. In 1963–64 the million hectares yielded 930,000 metric tons of peanuts which, alone, constituted 80 percent of the country's export revenue. So much effort goes into peanuts that the nation needs to import regularly 40 percent of the grain it consumes.[12]

In the Middle and Upper Zones of the Casamance the peanut is recorded earlier than in Lower Casamance, where it became important some 40 years ago among the Diola of the drier, more Islamisized Northeastern Region.[13] About 14.1 percent of the coun-

[9] *Ibid.*, p. 12.
[10] "Rapport Général sur les Perspectives du Développement du Sénégal," mimeographed, Part one (Dakar, January, 1963), no. 26, pp. 1–3.
[11] Estimates of Diola rice yields are given in Paul Pélissier, *Les Paysans du Sénégal: Les civilisations agraires du Cayor à la Casamance* (Saint-Yrieix [Haute-Vienne], 1966), p. 759. They are higher and somewhat more detailed, but they are still approximations based on published reports and not on actual measurements: 800 to 1000 kilograms per hectare for rice fields in the drier areas of a village, 1200 to 1500 kilograms per hectare for middle-area rice fields, and 2000 to 2500 kilograms per hectare for the deeply flooded fields.
[12] In 1962, 118,000 metric tons of rice were imported by Senegal. In recent years the amount imported has risen to 150,000 metric tons.
[13] The peanut was first introduced into the Casamance in the middle of the nineteenth century according to Louis-Vincent Thomas, *Les Diola: Essai d'Analyse Fonctionelle sur une Population de Basse Casamance*, 2 vols., Memoires de l'Institut Français Noire, no. 55 (Dakar, 1963), 1, 104. Its cultivation did not surge until after the 1930's (Pélissier, *Les Paysans du Sénégal*, p. 671). In Jipalom the older folk still remember when it was first planted. For a discussion of the peanut and the Islamic expansion, see Pélissier, pp. 808–13.

try's peanuts presently come from the entire Casamance. Lower Casamance alone produces 5 percent of the national total; south of the Casamance River very little is grown.

The degree to which either rice or peanuts is important among the Diola depends to a large extent on water and soil resources. In the fertile alluvial soils bordering the estuaries south of the Casamance River, precipitation averages 1,800 to 2,000 millimeters a year. There is also little land here suitable for peanuts. This encourages a labor-intensive wet-rice economy with a population density of 35 persons per square kilometer.[14]

The Western Zone, or Bignona subdivision, which forms the setting for this essay, receives only slightly less rainfall: 1,600 to 1,800 millimeters. Thirty-five percent of the land is covered with rice fields and only a smaller area with peanut fields. The rest is mangrove swamps or forest reserve (*fôret classée*). The economy is therefore mixed rice and peanuts, and population densities average 30 persons, sometimes reaching 50 persons per square kilometer.

In the third portion of Lower Casamance, the Northeastern Region, water resources are considerably less. Rainfall averages 1,200 to 1,300 millimeters and there are no large river systems. Here the principal subsistence crops are, as in the rest of Senegal, millet and sorghum, while the main cash crop is peanuts. Population density is less than 10 persons per square kilometer. What little rice is grown is entirely women's work and serves only as an adjunct food.

Detailed discussion here is restricted to the mixed rice and peanut area north and slightly west of the town of Bignona, near the *marigot* (river) of Baila. The Diola of this general region speak the Fogny dialect and call themselves *Kujamat*. They are minimally Islamisized; although they have given up pigs and palm wine, and although they perform the major Moslem rituals, they still adhere to much of their traditional religion.

Most of the data was gathered in 1964–65 during fourteen months in a small village which we will call Jipalom.[15] Although the anthropological problems my husband and I were studying at the time were not focused primarily on the agrarian economy, it was

---

[14] These and the following figures are found mainly in "Rapport Général sur les Perspectives," pp. 24–25. These estimates do not show the range of variation, however, since in some parts of Lower Casamance population density is less than ten persons per square kilometer, while in others it is more than fifty persons per square kilometer.

[15] The resident population of Jipalom in 1965 was 102 male adults (born in the village), 8 "strangers," 132 wives (about half born in Jipalom), and 299 children (excluding infants under two years of age).

virtually impossible to understand most aspects of Diola social organization without considering their wet-rice system. If their society was to be viewed in other than static terms, then a knowledge of how peanuts affected their economy was essential. Therefore we gathered information on agriculture though, unfortunately, not enough information on yields. My main concern was the sociocultural context of Diola agriculture.[16]

PADDY FIELDS AND PEANUT FIELDS: DIFFERENCES IN CLASSIFICATION AND LAND TENURE

The layout of a rice-producing Diola village follows closely the distribution of the paddy fields.[17] If the fields are strung out along a straight stretch in the river, the living quarters (*kalolak*; pl. *ulolaw*) are strung out also.[18] If the river makes a loop, the quarters of the village are clustered in the center. These configurations are shown in the map of Diola-Fogny villages.

The fields themselves are in the alluvial land between the edge of the forest, where the houses are located, and the mangrove swamp bordering the *marigot*. There is a very slight gradient, less than 3 percent, from the higher land near the compound to the depressed areas near the river.[19] The steeper the gradient, the smaller the field. Paddy fields therefore vary in dimension from a few meters to several hundred. Their size and shape are easy to distinguish, since each plot is surrounded by a levee or bund varying in height from 20 centimeters to more than a meter. The bunds serve to impound either rain or river water.

---

[16] My observations and those of Pélissier, *Les Paysans du Sénégal*, though made completely independently, are largely complementary. Pélissier gives a general picture of Diola agriculture for all of the Casamance; I focus on one village typical of a subarea. Being a geographer, he controls better the ecological and technical data; as an anthropologist I have dealt more extensively with problems of social organization, cultural attitudes, and the agricultural system as a socioeconomic institution.

[17] Following the literature, the word "paddy" is used here in two senses: "paddy fields" refers to the rice plots; "paddy" alone refers to the unhusked rice grain after harvest and before milling.

[18] Clusters of compounds are called kalolak by the Diola, *quartiers* by the French, and, elsewhere in West Africa, "wards" by the English. Here I use either *kalolak* or ward.

[19] The Lower Casamance is so flat that the Diola have no word for mountain. Hence they use the word *montagne* even when referring to anthills. But they have many subtle ways of describing gradual dips and rises in the terrain.

Aerial view of Diola village in the Kasa or southern area of Lower Casamance, south of the Casamance River. (Courtesy Georges and Maya Bracher, photo Bracher, Dakar.)

Aerial view of the Diola *wengaw*, or deeply flooded ricefields. (Courtesy Georges and Maya Bracher, photo Bracher, Dakar.)

Diola men preparing the *biitab* while women transplant the rice. (Courtesy J. David Sapir.)

A Diola male *ekufey* preparing a peanut field prior to punch-hole seeding. (Courtesy J. David Sapir.)

Diola Categories: Paddy Fields vs. Peanut Fields

To the uninitiated Western eye the rice fields seem a confusing tangle. For the Diola, however, the *biitab*[20] belongs to a clear and logical system of categories, differentiated from each other by two important criteria: level of impounded water, dependent in turn on the location of the plot itself, and type of soil. Some of the most important categories made by the members of one ward are as follows:

TABLE 1
Paddy-Field Categories in One Diola Ward

Type of Field	General Characteristics
BIITAB: FED BY RAINWATER	
NURSERIES: RICE SEEDS BROADCAST	
Kuyolenak	Sandy soil No bunds Strong slope for fast water runoff Near compound walls to facilitate guarding from animals
RICE TRANSPLANTED	
Yentamey	Small plots Heavy, clayey soils Small bunds 10–15 cm. of impounded rainwater
Sibaafas	Larger plots Sandy soils At edge of *yentamey* on slightly raised ground 10–15 cm. of impounded rainwater
Kuyelenak (not to be confused with *kuyolenak*)	Large fields Heavy, clayey soil In depressed aresa flooded by rainwater runoff Up to 50 cm. of impounded water
Senfaas	Large, regular, flat paddy fields carved recently from mangrove Heavy, clayey soils Strongly exposed to evaporation by the sun; require periodic flushing of salts by rainwater Low bunds 25 cm. high; high dikes along the edge to regulate tidal waters Abandoned in Jipalom

[20] A word such as *biitab* has different degrees of inclusion. At one level of contrast it may include all rice fields, as opposed to peanut fields. At another it refers only to the paddy fields as opposed to the nurseries. In yet a more precise context it includes only the rainwater paddy fields as opposed to those partly flooded by river water.

MULUAM: IRRIGATED BY *MARIGOT*
RICE TRANSPLANTED

Wengaw	Flooded by a combination of rainwater and brackish *marigot* water Bunds up to 1½ m.; deeply flooded to 1 m. Women transplant at end of rains with water chest-high Extremely heavy, dark, clayey soils Large parts of it abandoned because peanut harvest impinges on their preparation

The categories mentioned so far are found in only one of the five wards in Jipalom. The neighboring wards have either different amounts of the same kinds of fields or have different types of paddy fields.[21] To complicate matters, the same type of field may be called next door by a different term. In addition, there are differences among the rice-growing villages themselves. The main distinction is between villages with only *biitab* and those that have both *biitab* and *muluam*. *Biitab* in this context refers to the rainwater paddy fields ("providence" rice in the United States), while the ones in the *muluam* receive supplementary irrigation. (On the map, villages G and H have big *biitab* but no *muluam*; villages C and E, like Jipalom, have both.)

Peanut fields are not semantically differentiated because they are uniform in location and shape, being on the better drained sandy soils in areas that were formerly forested behind the compounds. In fact, the Diola of this area don't have a word for peanut field; the one commonly employed is *karamba*, or "forest." Cleared about forty years ago by slash and burn, they revert to secondary growth and savanna when fallow. Since peanuts obviously do not require impounded water, the fields lack bunds and are much larger than the largest paddy. Thus the richness of paddy vocabulary compared with the absence of terms for peanut fields is not due solely to rice cultivation being older and more traditional. The terms for paddy fields are based on functional distinctions; different categories are planted with different varieties of rice. With the peanut, only two kinds of seed are planted, usually alternating each year.

[21] The four other wards in Jipalom vary from ward A in these important respects: Ward B has no *seenfas, wengaw,* or *kuyelenak,* except what has been borrowed from ward C. Instead it has a special field called a *woyaw* at the edge of a drainage canal, and it also has much *yentamey.* Ward C has all of the paddy field categories, but because of an excess of *kuyelenak* will not cultivate the *wengaw.* In ward D the opposite is true. It has no *kuyelenak,* so its residents must cultivate the *wengaw* intensely. Also they call the *seenfas* by a different name. Ward F, again, is like ward D.

Principles of Land Tenure

The basic residential Diola units are the *ulolaw* (plural for *kalolak* or "ward"). These are largely autonomous and, within a village, placed at a distance from each other. Each *kalolak* is made up of *silupas* or "compounds" surrounded by a fence of palm fronds and composed, in turn, of patrilocal extended families each living in a house arranged around a courtyard.[22]

Land is individually owned by each married agnate of a compound and is inherited patrilineally by his sons. Save for rare occasions, and only in some villages, women do not generally inherit land. When he reaches marriageable age, a young man is given a few paddy fields by his father or his father's brother if the father is dead, and these are added to when he marries. During the life span of the individual more fields may be distributed to him according to the size of his family. The role of redistributor will pass to the eldest son when his father dies.

If a man dies without sons, his land reverts to his brothers or, if these are dead, to their children. Thus a delicate balance must be maintained within the patrilocal extended family so that every male member has sufficient fields, in each of the categories mentioned. He must also be sure during his lifetime to reallocate them equitably among his wives. A person whose fields are all in one paddy category will be jeopardized by even the normal variations within rainy seasons.

This system is basically different from our Western concept of individual versus communal ownership. The paddy fields are individually and communally owned simultaneously. A man may not

[22] Diola social organization has been largely misunderstood in the literature. What have been called patrilineal clans are not descent groups but loose, unlocalized, named groups to which a Diola belongs through *patrifiliation*. These groups are exogamous within the village and within a circle of neighboring villages. Aside from these groups, the important units are the patrilocal extended families of three generations' depth. Two or three families within a compound will have the notion of being agnatically related, but exactly how is not important. In short, the Diola system is based on agnatic collateral groups and not on unilineal descent groups. The extension that is important is to the same-sex persons of the same generation, so that two men are "brothers" if they come from the same compound, the same ward, or, in some contexts, the same village. This kind of arrangement obviously extends ties of cooperation in wide circles. Rules of complementary filiation with the uterine collaterals also operate. There are no totemic filiations for social groupings.

The village is more a geographic than a social entity. The only time it functions as a unit is during the circumcision festival. Following the rule that you should marry someone outside your named group but who nevertheless lives close by, Jipalom is about 50 percent endogamous since it contains several named groups.

be deprived of his fields, yet if he has more than he can cultivate he is required to redistribute them or to allow their use outside his own extended family. This continuous redistribution, projected for centuries, accounts for the excessive division of the land, though the plots belonging to a single compound are somewhat clustered.[23]

Patrilineal inheritance cannot cope with the normal increase in population and the differential growth of individual households, so there must be other means to obtain land. One such way is through borrowing. Land may be borrowed by manipulating uterine rights.[24] A man has the right to use paddy fields in the compounds of his or his parents' maternal kin. These rights do not involve "ownership" but only the use of surplus fields. In some instances, uterine rights can be stretched to include far-removed genealogical kin, as when a young man has land use rights because his father's mother and a lender's mother were born in the same compound. The land to which a man has rights may be located in villages other than his own. Thus he may need to change residence to work it. If he returns to his natal village, the land lent him reverts to its owner. If he marries someone from the new *kalolak*, however, the land may be inherited by his children via their mother.

A second way of getting land is through a "pledge" of a cow, a bull, or a number of smaller animals to a close or distant agnate in the same ward or village or in a nearby village.[25] Having supplementary fields nearby is advantageous, since it does not require change of residence. Pledged fields can be passed on to the pledger's children through normal patrilineal inheritance. But they are never owned outright by the pledgee and must be returned to the original owner if he gives back animals equivalent to the value involved in the original transaction.

Inasmuch as outright alienation of land is discouraged, it has led to statements that there is no private ownership of land among the Diola. This mistaken Western concept automatically links ownership with freedom to buy and sell. But a Diola is considered the sole owner of the fields he inherits and is free to lend them, to

---

[23] Distribution of the paddy fields in relation to social groups is not random. The paddy fields of a compound will tend to be together, as will those from a single ward.

[24] Uterine or matrilateral kin are related to Ego through females. The closest are the male agnates of Ego's mother, then those of Ego's father's mother, or of his mother's mother, and so forth. These relatives live elsewhere and never in the natal compound of Ego.

[25] Agnates is the term used in anthropology to distinguish patrilineal kinsmen.

alienate them for many years by receiving a pledge, or even to stop working them for as long as he wishes—provided, of course, that there is no undue need by others for the land. He is also free to distribute them to his wives and pass them to his children in ways he considers equitable.

A third method for acquiring paddy fields is only partly effective today, as it involves gradual expansion into uncultivated areas. In the old days, when the Diola were pushing into the rich riverine areas, this was probably the most common way of getting land. Very little prime riverine land is left now in the Lower Casamance. The only expansion possible is along the mangrove swamps that line the river shores and the seacoast. Cutting the mangrove, building the dikes, and desalinating the soil is hard work. The adaptation of salt-resistant rice varieties has not proved successful so far.

A fourth method of territorial expansion is closed to the modern Diola. It involved the conquest of alien land through warfare and feuding. From the accounts of European observers, until the French pacification of the Casamance some fifty years ago, the Diola were in constant strife. Feuds are still remembered with nostalgia by the elders. From several of the accounts I have gathered it is clear that the cause of many of these conflicts was disputes over fields. They varied from conflicts between persons of two different wards of a village over ownership of a cluster of plots, leading to murder and revenge, to the outright attack of one ward on another ward of the same or of a neighboring village to gain possession of paddy areas. For this reason, if a ward had suffered population attrition through normal causes, such as absence of male progeny, they would join their neighboring ward or invite outsiders to settle there to maintain numerical strength.

Although peace was brought about by the French colonial administration and continued by the independent Senegalese government, there are still occasional disputes involving entire wards over rice fields. I know of two villages in the Fogny area that go to war every few years over the ownership of plots in their borders. Government officials come to measure the land, map each paddy, and drive stakes to establish each ward's boundaries. The officials no sooner leave than the stakes are pulled and the conflict resumed. Other Diola recall with amusement that this has gone on for decades. Claims may go back centuries.

Conflicts involving individuals are also common today, especially in areas of population pressure where the problem rises between traditional concepts and modern concepts of private property. Many of the cases I recorded hinged on claims by one party that fields they had "bought" by the pledge of cattle belonged to them, while the other party claimed the land under the traditional system of nonpermanent alienation. These disputes are today arbitrated by the *préfet* or, if warranted, may go to the governor's office.

The principles of land tenure involved in peanut fields are essentially different, even though some of the mechanisms for the acquisition of fields may be the same. The difference is that an intensive rice-growing system involves permanent yearly cultivation of the same fields while a bush-fallow system requires resting of exhausted fields. A man may have inherited two separate one-hectare peanut plots that his own father, or his father's father, had cleared. These fields are used alternately on successive years up to three or four times, then rested for four to six years and sometimes up to ten. The longer a field has been under cultivation, the longer it must lie fallow, since the Diola use little if any fertilizer on their peanut fields. Therefore, very few have enough land to tide them over the fallow cycle, especially if they want to keep yields high.

A constant search for fields goes on from year to year. Our census of Jipalom showed in 1965 that more than half the men of one compound were cultivating peanuts in other villages while not one had moved elsewhere to obtain paddy fields. The change of residence necessary for peanut cultivation is only seasonal, however—one or two months at the beginning of the rains and one month at harvest time. A man simply moves with his wife and children to the village where he is cultivating that year for the duration of each phase.

Like rice fields, peanut fields can also be borrowed through uterine ties. The seasonal displacement then involves a comfortable stay with relatives. Often a man will cultivate a peanut field jointly with a uterine kin of around his age, and they will divide the earnings. This is considered an ideal arrangement. There is very little acquisition of usufruct rights to peanut fields by the pledge of cattle. Within a single village in the Fogny area, conditions of scarcity or abundance are uniform depending on whether there is still forested land for clearing or whether the forested land has been set apart as a *fôret classée* and there is no more to be had for peanut fields. The usual pattern is for villagers coming from a mixed peanut-rice economy to borrow extra fields in *fatiya* (plateau) villages.

A unique type of borrowing applies to peanut fields. An informal partnership based on friendship is established between two unrelated individuals. The lender then becomes the "host" or *ajuerti* ("he who does not move"), and the borrower becomes the *ajaura* ("one who goes," a traveler, a stranger). The latter is lent land and the use of one or more rooms in the host's compound. He also receives protection and, in many instances, food for the period of stay. No payment in cash or kind is involved, although periodic gifts must be made by the borrower to keep the relationship in good standing. Consequently, were the host later to need some services, like a loan of rice, the *ajaura* would be under obligation to help. *Ajuerti* connections are carefully established and maintained throughout the years by periodic visits and gifts. They depend largely on ethical precepts of generosity and hospitality reinforced by Islamic ideals of brotherhood.

Searching for peanut fields often takes a man to faraway villages at the end of the dry season. How careful he is to borrow good fields depends largely on individual initiative and ability. Some visit two or three villages and, not content with the quality of the fields offered, will go on to find better conditions at still a fourth place. Others simply alternate year after year between fields they own near the forest and fields they have near their compounds until they exhaust the soil and are forced to cultivate elsewhere. Meanwhile they have harvested lower yields than the enterprising man. More than with rice, profit from peanuts depends on individual initiative, not landed wealth.

To estimate the total area of paddy fields that a man cultivates is more difficult than to know how many peanut fields he works. As I have explained, plots are irregular in shape and scattered among paddy categories. Including paddy fields acquired through matrilateral ties or a cattle pledge, a rough estimate of the land surface that an individual cultivates in rice each year varies between 1.35 and 2.09 hectares.[26] Peanut fields, being rectangular, are easier to measure. A man owns two, occasionally three fields, which he works in rotation; each field measures three-fourths to one and a half hectares. In any one year he is then cultivating one of these fields, or if these are resting he is using a field of equivalent size elsewhere.

Summary of Effects of Diola Land Tenure

We can see how the complicated system of paddy field classification and inheritance, plus the constant care required by levees and

[26] This information is based on a detailed map that we made of paddy fields covering 30.15 hectares belonging to one ward in Jipalom.

drainage canals, contributes to the localization of the Diola agnatic line. A man must either be born or spend many years residing in a village before he can master all the subtle differences in paddy field ownership and typology. Women have to know a great deal about the characteristics of different rice varieties and the conditions under which they prosper, but since this knowledge is, in a sense, transportable, they have much more real spatial mobility than men. This accords well with patrilocal residence—it is women who change residence at marriage.

The demands of peanut cultivation tend, in contrast, to disperse the agnatic line for short, specific periods of time. Men can wander over a large area and still have enough knowledge of the local conditions for successful cultivation. Friendship, not kinship alone, helps a man obtain additional peanut fields.

THE AGRICULTURAL CYCLE AND COOPERATIVE FORMS OF WORK

Timing Agricultural Tasks

The rainy season in Casamance lasts three and a half months, from the middle of June to the end of September. The dry season is from October to May. With the advent of the rains, labor demands increase to the maximum and do not let up till the start of the dry season; no farming whatsoever is done at the height of the heat. Details of the agricultural cycle are summarized in Table 2.

Clearing the peanut fields and the nurseries in the forest is by slash and burn.[27] To prepare the ground men use the *kajando*, a tool unique to the Diola and their immediate neighbors to the south, the Balanta, the Bainuk, and the Manjaku, and also borrowed by the Niominka Serer beyond the Casamance to the north. The *kajando* is a fulcrum shovel with a long handle and a curved wooden scoop at one end capped with a steel blade. Used with the knee as a fulcrum, it can lift heavy paddy soils to make furrows and ridges. Although the tool is slower in the light soils of the peanut fields than the Sudanic hoe used by the neighboring Manding, the Diola of the western area including Jipalom retained it for peanuts because the hoe involves entirely different body move-

---

[27] The only fertilizers used in the peanut fields are the burned-over brush and the dry peanut stalks after the peanut has been removed.

TABLE 2
Diola Agricultural Schedule

	Koeringoek May–Mid-June	Fujamaray Mid-June–July	Fujamaray Aug.–Sept.	Koewegen Oct.–Dec.	Furantaray Jan.–April
			Rice		
Men	Slash and burn forest for nurseries	Prepare compound nurseries, broadcast rice	Prepared fields in following order: *yentamey*, *ebaafey*, *kuyelenah*, *wengaw*	A few men prepare the *wengaw* for next rainy season	Pasture cattle in fields, labor outside, build houses, loaf
Women	Do crafts, make salt, take fertilizer to fields	Select rice seeds	Transplant in same order as plowed	Harvest in same order as transplanted	Fertilize, do crafts, make salt
			Peanuts		
Men	Slash and burn peanut fields, burn dry stalks	Prepare peanut fields		Build drying racks, pull out peanut plants, dry on racks	Both sexes thresh and winnow peanuts; time for this is flexible.
Women		Plant peanuts on ridges			

NOTE: Garden farming excluded.

ments.[28] A few border villages of Diola nevertheless use the hoe for peanuts and the *kajando* for rice.

Peanuts demand much simpler soil preparation than rice, there being only one manner of ridging followed by punch-hole seeding. There are many ways of ridging paddy fields, depending on the type of plot. *Kawanjer* involves splitting up old ridges; *eriip*, building up the ridges by digging furrows on both sides; *eboob*, turning over the surface of the ridge with the *kajando* and burying the weeds and leftover rice straw; and *kalaken*, digging earth from the old furrow and piling it up on the new ridge.

Rice seeds are broadcast on the nursery ridges. Men do this, but the wives select the varieties and carefully mark where each is put, using a complicated terminology to distinguish them. A woman may select four to ten varieties which she identifies through such features as color of the peeled grain, length of grain, shape, and placement on the panicle branches. The taxonomy is systematic so that a woman may, in addition to the varieties she uses, learn to distinguish a few more that other women grow. There is continuous trading back and forth of varieties and constant exchange of information as to their behavior under specific soil and water conditions. Such knowledge is restricted to womenfolk. A man usually has no idea of the varieties his wife gives him to broadcast. When asked for the reason why more than one variety is employed, Diola women would answer in terms of the need to space the harvest by planting different varieties. They will also emphasize the need to have fast-ripening varieties in fields that dry up fast and varieties adapted to deeply flooded conditions for paddy fields that retain water during part of the dry season. Finally, several varieties minimize the risks from a possible lack of rain.

Preparation of the paddy fields by ridging and furrowing is followed immediately by transplanting.[29] Seedlings of the desired variety are pulled with their roots and either left overnight or transplanted the same day. A rich terminology also describes the steps in the planting and transplanting. There is a term for broadcasting the seed for a nursery (*kayolen*) as opposed to broadcasting on a plot where early rices are to be grown directly without trans-

[28] Ridges for the peanut need not be more than 20 centimeters high. Ridges for rice, which is to be inundated, average 25 to 30 centimeters in height and are up to 50 centimeters wide. In the *wengaw* (or deeply flooded area) the height is more than 50 centimeters and sometimes as much as 1.5 meters.

[29] Advantages offered by transplanting, rather than broadcasting, are numerous: control of weeds, saving of the seed, increase in yields, etc. The Diola are well aware of these advantages.

planting (*eisay*). There is a general term for transplanting (*burokab*, or "work") which breaks down into *emuny*, or transplanting all of the plants from a nursery; *kapujel*, or transplanting half of the plants by thinning; *karulanken*, a delayed pulling out of the plants left in the nurseries to grow taller; and *karolangken*, a fill-in by second transplanting where the original transplanting failed. These are only a few of the many terms used in different steps in plowing, sowing, transplanting, and harvesting rice.

A strict order of rice fields is followed in all these tasks, starting with the rain-fed fields and finishing with the *wengaw*, or deeply flooded *marigot*-fed paddy fields. From the time the rice is transplanted to the time it is harvested, each rice plant has been handled individually.[30] The amount of time spent in this labor is enormous. Not surprisingly, women as well as men, who have the heavy task of ridging, often fall sick during the height of the rains.

After the harvest, cattle are systematically pastured in the paddy fields. Women also spread crushed shell, debris from the kitchen, and dung collected from goats and sheep as fertilizer on their plots. Meanwhile, men thatch the roofs and build new houses. Women extract salt by boiling crusts of soil obtained near the brackish *marigot*. For those skilled in crafts, there is pottery and basketry to be done. At the height of the dry season, men seriously loaf under shady trees. Most organized social activities—dancing, wrestling, even big funeral festivals—take place then. With the last weeks in May the cycle begins again, and the pace quickens as the rains approach.

To conclude, field tasks, though similar in some respects for peanuts and rice, show an important difference. Peanuts are mostly men's work, while rice is harder on the women. Men prepare the ground in the peanut fields, harvest the crop, stack it, dry it, do part of the threshing and winnowing, sack it, and finally sell it. Women only help in the threshing and the winnowing of peanuts but spend long, backbreaking hours transplanting, harvesting, and processing rice by pounding it and then cooking it. As a result, men pocket the money from the peanuts while the rice crop belongs to the women. This is important and will be discussed at more length later.

[30] The tool they use for harveting is a small pocket knife with which they cut each panicle 10 to 15 centimeters from its end. These are gathered into bundles weighing from 1 to 2 kilograms depending on the variety of rice harvested.

Organizing Cooperative Work

Whether it involves peanuts or rice, whether it is individual or collective, work depends on close cooperation between men and women. Individual work centers on the nuclear family. Men and their unmarried sons prepare the rice fields, while the women and their unmarried daughters do all the planting and transplanting. Cooperative work, however, extends beyond the nuclear family. It is done by informal groups that the Diola call *ekufey* and translate by the French word *société*. The various male *ekufey* in a ward roughly follow age lines. There is an *ekufey* of the children, of the unmarried young men, of the middle-aged men, and finally of those elders who can still cultivate. The *ekufey* may combine at different levels so that two, three, or even all work together, depending on the size of the field to be furrowed and ridged and the resources of the sponsoring party.

Ekufey for females follow a different principle. The main division is between the *kusekak*, or female affines (women married into the ward), and the *furimanaf*, or women agnates (women born in the ward). Of the latter, only the young girls or the unmarried young women would still live in their natal wards. As we shall see later, young unmarried women are usually away in Dakar except for a few months at the height of the transplanting season, when they come back to help their mothers. The important functioning female group in the ward then is the in-married women. They perform at least 80 percent of the female agricultural labor.

Cooperative work is remunerated. In some instances the reward may only be a good meal, as when the men and/or women of a ward work for the most respected elders and receive millet or rice beer and an abundant midday meal including meat. In other instances the pay may be money.[31] An *ekufey* holds its remuneration communally, and if it is money it will eventually be invested in sheep, goats, or cows to be sacrificed during communal propitiatory feasts, or saved until the boy's circumcision festival, which takes place every fifteen years or so. As with all transactions involving

---

[31] The entire male *ekufey* of one ward of Jipalom (22 males) were paid collectively an average of 3,500 CFA francs (240 CFA = $1.00) for half a day and twice that much for the entire day. The *kusekak* (26 females) received 1,500 to 2,000 CFA for half a day's work and twice that much for the entire day. Instead of money, either *ekufey* could get a goat or a sheep as payment, but a cow could only be earned if the entire male *ekufey* of one ward worked all day. Differential payment for males and females was based on a feeling that female work was somehow less valuable.

money among the Diola, the amount an *ekufey* gets depends on an informal agreement between the parties. There are no set standards; all agreements are subject to long and sometimes protracted negotiations where rights and obligations are carefully weighed.

The hours that a man spends at work for others will probably balance the number of man-hours that others work for him.[32] But such cooperation serves to reinforce social bonds and is more enjoyable than individual work, since it involves communal singing, drinking, and sometimes dancing into the night. But most important of all is the competition surging from working side by side; getting the task done is sped by races with the *kajando*. Careful planning during the labor-scarce season of the number of workdays he gives and gets so as to come out even or perhaps ahead is the mark of a wise Diola.

STORAGE, USAGE, AND DISTRIBUTION OF RICE; SALE OF PEANUTS

Attitudes Toward the Products

Rice and peanuts are handled differently after they are harvested. At the end of the day, paddy is taken in special baskets to the granaries for storage or early consumption. The structure of the *buntungab*, or granary, reveals many of the social functions of rice. It is a separate, room-sized, round, two-level structure of puddled adobe, with a conical thatch roof; the storage area is on the top level and the kitchen underneath. Kitchen smoke keeps out rats and other pests and dries excessive moisture from the rice. Within the storage platform, separate sections are kept for last year's crop and this year's harvest. No woman would ever mix paddy in the *buntungab* from different years. Neither, would she store in it any grain but rice. Millet and sorghum may be kept in the kitchen area, or in a different house, but never in the upper level of the *buntungab* lest the paddy be lost through supernatural causes.

The paddy stored in the *buntungab* "belongs" to the woman, as symbolized by the fact that her kitchen is under it. In the case of divorce she takes all, or as much as she can. If a man has two or more wives, each has her own granary to store the harvest from the plots allotted to her by her husband. A woman uses her rice

[32] Persons working alone may also volunteer their services for pay. A man will get 200 to 300 CFA for a day and a women half that much. This money belongs to the person who earned it and cannot be touched by anyone else in the family.

to feed her "family," that is, her husband and her unmarried children. If her relationship with her cowife is good, they may alternate in the cooking, but if their relationship is strained, then each will cook separately and take a bowl of rice to their mutual husband each meal. In any case, a woman has a large measure of control over the rice she harvested. She is nevertheless obligated to feed her husband's guests; the crop is considered partly owned by him.

The husband, if known as a generous host, may have a separate granary for himself. The paddy stored in it comes from plots that he has set aside for such use and that have been worked by *ekufey* paid by him. His wife (or wives) and his married sons may also contribute their labor. The paddy from his granary is for distribution outside the nuclear family, for guests, and for social or ceremonial obligations. A young unmarried man may also have a *buntungab* for himself or use a section of his mother's. Here he stores the paddy that will eventually start him off in his married life.

Secrecy is the pervasive attitude toward the paddy stored in the granary. The wife can open the door only early in the morning or late in the afternoon, when others are not around. Strangers may never enter the *buntungab* or the stored crop will "run away" (that is, will be bewitched). A related phenomenon is the widespread custom of amassing rice, especially in the area south of the Casamance River. Someone may have two or three tons of unthreshed paddy stored in his granary for up to fifteen years until the smoke makes it no longer edible. At first glance it may seem that he is simply hoarding it, since large quantities confer prestige. In Diola terms, however, he is saving for leaner years.

An adequate explanation of this "hoarding" pattern must take into account the nature of Diola society and the timing of its redistributive cycles. The absence of institutionalized channels for the expression of political power—even the chiefs of today are a creation of the former French administration—precludes the regular and systematic use of surpluses in big-men feasts like those of Oceania. The only big occasion for redistribution, as we shall see later, is the circumcision festival, and a village holds one of these only once in fifteen years or so. Smaller occasions such as funerals hardly absorb the rice stores of a rich man; furthermore, poorer men must give nearly as much. At the circumcision everybody's stores are depleted, but in the meantime, prestige is gained by amassing rice and keeping it hidden from the inevitable crowd of demanding relatives.

Yearly surpluses vary greatly from region to region within the

Casamance, even between villages in the same region and even between individuals of the same compound. Where peanuts have displaced rice significantly, such surpluses are not found. Since in rice areas population concentration is greater, land is overfractionalized and scarce. Some persons may have an excess of land, others a scarcity depending on the particular history of their family holdings or their own role in manipulating them. There are also persons who, in spite of large holdings, will never amass large surpluses while others, with more initiative though limited holdings, will. The difficulty in overcoming secrecy and the great regional and individual variation in productive capacity are great obstacles in obtaining reliable figures on yields throughout the Lower Casamance.

Peanuts never cross the compound walls. Everything from the plowing to the bagging is done in the fields, quite openly and publicly. Consequently there is no storage problem. Each season's crop is sold at the end of the harvest, rapidly and efficiently, and if the money made enters the economy it is not through socially important channels but simply through individual purchasing power. In contrast with rice, then, the attitude toward peanuts is straightforward and open. No one will hesitate to inform you of his earnings. Since such earnings depend on the amount sold, reliable production figures are easy to obtain.

Rice and Peanuts in Social and Religious Life

The earnings from the peanuts go to the men.[33] With the money they pay taxes, buy cattle, pay bride prices, and buy new blades for the *kajando* and new clothes for themselves and their families.[34] If a man takes a trip to Dakar to visit relatives and "see the lights," he may come back penniless. But those with foresight will save part, usually no more than 20 percent, to pay the *ekufey* next season.

Peanuts, then, mean money to the Diola, pure and simple. Rice means other things. First, it means a meal. In fact, the word *sinangas* means both cooked rice and a meal. To a Diola, be he peasant or bureaucrat, a meal without rice is not a meal. In areas where Islam forbids drinking palm wine, a peasant would have rice

[33] The average yearly peanut earnings for men in one ward of Jipalom, based on the price of 20 CFA per kilogram, were as follows: one man with the occasional help of two brothers in very good, fresh, new land, 50,000 CFA; two men (partners by friendship) on productive land, 25,000 CFA each; one man alone in fairly poor, exhausted land, 15,000 CFA.

[34] Bride prices have soared after Islamization and the introduction of the peanut. Today they average 20,000 CFA in Jipalom.

at midday; in areas where they drink it, palm wine would be the noon meal. Breakfast is with the leftover rice from the day before and the night meal is with freshly cooked rice. All meals consist of a large bowl of fluffy, long-grained rice (which, by the way, they do not parboil) and a sauce with fish, or occasionally meat, and palm oil. The nuclear family usually eats together. Strict taboos are observed between generations, who cannot share the same bowl.[35] Children usually eat together or with their mother. Guests and elders eat alone. Babies are given a kind of rice porridge until they are old enough to eat solids.

The Diola have a very definite preference for new rice, fresh from the harvest. Anyone can tell by simply smelling and tasting whether cooked rice is this year's or last or is more than two years old. Children are given old rice, while adults eat new rice. Guests should be given new rice for fear of seriously insulting them. Getting rid of old rice without giving offense therefore requires great cunning.

Peanuts are eaten, but very little compared with rice. While they are being shelled to be used for seed, women and children set aside defective ones to roast and use for sauce. In the Bignona market women sell fist-sized mounds of peanut butter displayed on short boards.

Rice is occasionally sold, but then only locally and usually to strangers.[36] Some selling takes place in the Kasa south of the Casamance River, but this is recent.[37] Where peanuts are predominant, or in areas where peanuts have lowered rice production, milled rice may be regularly bought, but it usually comes from Southeast Asia or the United States.[38] Diola values emphasize self-sufficiency, and the few in Jipalom who must buy rice will go to great lengths to keep it secret. If kin give them rice, they will do so at night unobserved.

[35] J. David Sapir, "Kujaama: Symbolic Separation among the Diola-Fogny," to be published in *American Anthropologist* (in press).

[36] On the few occasions when it is sold in large amounts, a sack of paddy weighing 75 to 80 kilograms will bring during the harvest season 2,100 CFA and during the scarce season 2,500 CFA. A sack of pounded (i.e., milled) rice weighing 100 kilograms brings 4,000 CFA during the harvest season and 5,000 CFA during the scarce season.

[37] In the Kasa village of Elinkine, where we did six months of field work in 1965, a government post had been set up to purchase rice. One family alone that we recorded sold at one time more than 1,000 kilograms of paddy.

[38] The price of Southeast Asian rice, which is generally small-grained due to fracturing in the milling process, is 3,500 CFA milled during the scarce season. If Diola rice is going to compete, milling facilities and government subsidies will have to be established, at least temporarily.

Rice enters the Diola social system at every level, not just in subsistence. It is the subject of many a conversation. Groups of women or men spend hours gossiping about who has lots of rice, who didn't quite make it through the lean season, who exchanged how much paddy for a cow, and so forth. The social usages of rice are a more important subject of discussion than the details of its production.

Predictably enough, the patterns of rice redistribution are fairly complex. Paddy is redistributed at all life crises, at a naming ceremony, a marriage, a funeral, or a circumcision festival. The last two are the most important occasions for redistribution. Guests and kin who come together in large numbers on these occasions have to be fed; it is hard to estimate too highly the amount of rice that they eat then. If a prestigious old man has died, the funeral rites may last several days; the guests must be fed by the agnatic kin of the deceased. In Moslem funerals, rice is also distributed to guests and relatives as a sweet dough mixed with sugar. All funerals require distribution of paddy as well. The people who have matrilateral ties in the compound of the deceased—that is, persons whose mother, or father's mother, or mother's mother were born there—must contribute paddy to the agnatic kin of the deceased. Part of this paddy is in turn redistributed by the agnates to the uterine kin (the mother, father's mother, mother's mother) of the deceased himself. Several basketfuls go to the deceased mother's compound, one or two to the "relatives" of the mother of the deceased's father, and so forth.

Obviously this kind of redistribution serves other than economic functions. It strengthens social ties, interweaving the different groups that are relevant to a person's existence in a web of reciprocal rights and obligations. During a person's lifetime he has inalienable rights to fruits from the trees and to chickens grown in the compound of his maternal relatives. He may also have spent several years with the "brothers" of his own mother. These privileges are, in a sense, repaid at his death by his own agnates, aided by persons who have uterine obligations in the agnate's compound.

At the time of the circumcision, another set of distributions takes place, with the uterine kin of the initiate helping his agnates by contributing rice. Literally hundreds of kilograms of rice are consumed by what may amount to several thousand guests during the ceremonies. Those fortunate enough to have had large surpluses to distribute will have the consolation of their increased prestige. In this manner, differences in wealth are equalized and the egalitarian structure of the society maintained.

Rice, then, is a symbol of wealth, but not necessarily of power.

Many a "wealthy" man will have full granaries, but if he consistently refuses to distribute it during important occasions he will be simply regarded as a miser, as someone whose "hand is dry." To be respected and have a say in the informal running of his own ward he must know when and just how much to be generous. In fact, Diola hold an ambiguous attitude of admiration and reproach for the man whose "hand is dry."

Having plenty of rice is not the only criterion of wealth. Cattle are also important. Animals may be acquired by exchanging them for paddy; generally, two or three hundred kilograms buy a heifer and twice that a cow. Much less is needed for a sheep and even less for a goat. In non-Islamic areas, paddy rice is also exchanged for pigs. Animals are mainly for prestige and ceremonial redistribution, though some may be killed to feed members of an *ekufey*. Cattle are also hoarded. Among the herds of the elders there are cows that are dying of old age.

In spite of the recurrent events of semiceremonial nature, there is no special bond between agriculture and religion. Diola traditional religion is animistic: a plurality of spirits (called *sinertas* in the Fogny area and *boekiin* in the Kasa) associated with natural forces and disease. The propitiation of these spirits is in the hands of individuals who inherit this duty patrilineally. Islam has changed this pluralism to some degree, but only superficially. At the onset of the rainy season the spirits of the compound are propitiated and asked for a season of abundance. Some villages in the Fogny area will also have a propitiatory rite for a "rain spirit" whose shrine is located in the middle of the rice fields. Propitiation always involves a simple invocation followed by the sacrifice of an animal, which is then eaten as a sort of communion. Jipalom is the center of the rain shrine serving several villages.

Bad soils, pests, and weeds do not require the interference of the spirits. These problems are handled by hard work, observation, and experimentation. In fact, the basic attitude of the Diola toward their agriculture is matter-of-fact. If a woman is asked why plants from a certain paddy field have done so badly, she invariably answers in terms of insufficient rain, fertilizers, and so forth. On some occasions she may blame providence, or even Allah, but in such cases it requires very little prodding to get an empirical explanation. If nature is to blame, it is usually the rains. A few more rain propitiations may take place, but the rest of the rainy season is given to hard work and little else.

With peanuts, even less religion is involved. The general propitiation at the beginning of the rains may include this crop, but this is the only time when it comes into conceptual contact with the supernatural. Peanuts are never used in propitiatory rites, never in communion feasts; but the money they bring may be used to pay for curing ceremonies. The Diola, then, are largely disinterested in linking agriculture and religion and keep their supernaturals functioning in other spheres besides subsistence.

Rice and Peanuts in Social Change

Rice and peanuts are involved in the "modernization" process in different ways. Rice is the symbol of ethnicity, of continuity, of all that is traditionally Diola. The Diola consider peanuts a symbol of the outside world and associate them with the new religion, Islam, and with the Manding, who introduced both. Peanuts bring cash, social change, and outside goods. Rice keeps men tied to the land, village-bound, and wholeheartedly peasant. Peanuts get the Diola out, to Dakar.

The world they learn to know in Dakar is not European but rather that of the Wolof, Senegal's dominant ethnic group. The Wolof control many of the important governmental posts and set the tone of Dakar's urban life. The young men and women who go to the capital live in the same districts as the Wolof and often rent rooms in their compounds.

This exodus to Dakar demands special attention.[39] Unmarried, girls and boys between the ages of 14 and 20 leave their families, the arduous work in the fields, and the monotony of village life for a more exciting existence. In Dakar the girls work as domestics in the households of both the Wolof and the French, who prefer them to other ethnic groups because of their clean habits and their willingness to work hard at low pay.[40] The boys have a harder time getting jobs; more often than not they are forced to join the unemployed, who in Dakar are alarmingly numerous. Their stay in Dakar is not always permanent. After a youth finds a spouse, often

---

[39] In the census we took of Jipalom in 1965, 34 of the adult males, or one-third of the labor force, had moved to Dakar, Ziguinchor, and other centers. Of these, 8, mostly young men, came back during the rains to help their fathers cultivate. In contrast, 33 of the young, unmarried women in Jipalom, or roughly four-fifths of all the girls in the village, were temporarily in Dakar. Of these three-fourths came back during the rains to help their mothers transplant.

[40] Robert McC. Netting (personal communication) has made the interesting observation that intensive cultivators often differ from extensive (i.e., shifting) cultivators in the values attached to hard work, perseverance, and frugality. There is no doubt that the Diola ethos fits this picture well.

from his own village or immediate neighborhood, both usually return home to continue marriage negotiations and, once married, settle there to farm for the rest of their lives.

Exposure to Wolof ways changes some of the Diola eating habits. Diola shift from their long-grained varieties to the coarsly-milled fractured rice imported from Southeast Asia, which is preferred by the Wolof. They justify this shift by saying that it is healthier and easier on the stomach. The truth is that they simply cannot buy Diola rice in Dakar.

The sale of peanuts introduces cash into an otherwise subsistence economy. But the economic changes money has brought so far are largely superficial. Money permits the purchase of manufactured goods, especially household utensils and clothing, and buys more durable construction materials, cement and corrugated metal roofing, for example. Because earnings go to pay taxes, money also makes the Diola aware that they belong to a larger nation; but this awareness is unwelcome. And even though the people value manufactured goods greatly, the majority of the household objects are still locally made. Furthermore, objects do not necessarily bring social change, and it is clear that the fundamental principles of Diola social organization, religion, and culture remain largely traditional.

The Fogny Diola continue to be isolated from Senegal, to oppose the dominant party, to resist use of the cooperatives, and to keep their individualistic and tradition-bound mode of life. This will eventually change, it is certain, but up to now they have been able to maintain the privileged position of being able to feed themselves and yet have a per capita cash income that varies from 15,000 to 25,000 CFA francs (roughly $60.00 to $100.00) a year.[41] They are the only ethnic group in rural Senegal able to do this.

CONCLUSIONS

If we place the Diola on a continuum from subsistence to commercial agriculture, we must find them still rooted in a traditional, "conservative" economy. Their main crop, wet rice, is produced for family consumption, and redistribution along kinship lines absorbs most surpluses. The introduction of peanuts has not altered appreciably the economic isolation of Lower Casamance. Except for the occasional purchase of construction materials, the goods the

[41] See footnote 35.

Diola buy are mostly European luxury goods, and even the cooking pots and the food items they occasionally purchase (tomato paste or cooking oil) are foreign imports. In fact, they sell peanuts to an export market and buy mostly foreign products. Neither has the transition to a monetary economy increased overall agricultural production. Everyone who produces peanuts in Senegal but the Fogny-Diola has to buy millet and rice. And more often than not, millet comes from elsewhere in the Sudanic belt and rice from the United States or Southeast Asia.

That peanuts have lowered rice production in the Fogny area is a fact that few Diola deny. Elders talk proudly about the days when two crops of rice were grown a year "so that the men had to aid the women with the harvest." We have observed large tracts of the *wengaw* and *seenfas* in Jipalom that lie abandoned to salinization and the encroaching mangrove because of labor scarcity resulting from peanut cultivation and the flight to Dakar.[42]

The future of agricultural development in Lower Casamance is encouraging, at least from the standpoint of resources. Without doubt this is the best endowed region of Senegal in terms of rainfall, irrigation, and soils. It also has a large potential labor force compared with the rest of the country, 35 to 50 persons per square kilometer being the highest density outside the urban zones. The traditional agrarian wet-rice system is productive and sophisticated, even though it places high demands on labor. The riverine Diola easily make it through the dry season, which the other rural ethnic groups cannot do, and they actually produce surpluses, even though they do not regard them as such.

Obviously their rice yields could be increased with modern technology. Mechanized cultivation, at present, is out of the question because paddy fields are far too small and have levees and furrows. To eliminate paddy boundaries and consolidate fields would be very difficult, since holdings are scattered. For the government or anyone else to force changes on one of the most complex and fundamental aspects of Diola culture would be to invite total mistrust and complete disruption.

There are, however, limited technological improvements that could benefit Diola rice cultivation. I do not mean tractors and the like; the use of small mechanized equipment for land preparation

---

[42] Pélissier, *Les Paysans du Sénégal*, mentions the same phenomenon occurring in many other regions of Lower Casamance where the deep rice fields have been abandoned because of peanut cultivation; the mangrove is encroaching upon these abandoned fields.

is feasible in the larger fields of the *ebaafei* and the *kuyelenak*, but these fields are not the most numerous, and cost and upkeep would render machines impractical. And because the Diola reserve cattle for propitiatory rites, the use of draft animals would meet resistance, at least initially.[43] A more immediate means of increasing rice production is the systematic use of chemical fertilizer. Manure is not available in quantity for use in all paddies, and there is no prejudice against fertilizer except its cost. Saline soils could be more effectively used if salt-resistant rice varieties were developed. The Diola's willingness to experiment with new varieties would make their chance of acceptance good. Double cropping by irrigation and the additional cultivation of upland rice, possibly with the use of selective herbicides, are other means of increasing yields. Widespread use of small, low-cost hand mills would also free women from the time-consuming and backbreaking daily task of pounding paddy to peel the grains before cooking and permit them to use their labor more effectively elsewhere.

Far more basic than considerations of how to increase production is the question of why the Diola should want to grow more rice if what they have is ample for subsistence and also leaves them a margin for redistributions and surpluses for leaner years. Such techniques as multi-cropping with extensive river irrigation would involve tremendous work and would eliminate the few months of summer leisure that the Diola now enjoy.[44] I am convinced that the only incentive would come from the surging demand for cash. Finding outlets for surpluses in Senegal's urban centers, which up to now have been fed on rice imports, would be met by increased production. Under these circumstances, if the necessity arises for the Diola to restructure their land tenure rules they will eventually consolidate their rice fields. But these changes must come from within a society in response to new needs and new demands. They cannot be forced on the people. Given the Diola potential for

---

[43] Boserup, *The Conditions of Agricultural Growth*, pp. 36–39, suggests that if draft animals have to be fed by produced fodder, agricultural output per man-hour may actually be reduced under plough agriculture. In the Diola case, any move to multicropping would probably reduce grazing potential since cattle feed on rice stubbles after the harvest. This would probably force them to produce fodder because natural grazing areas are small.

[44] During these months many of the Kasa Diola, who grow no peanuts, leave for the north and east to gather palmwine among Islamisized Senegalese and sell it for cash in the cities. If multi-cropping with irrigation were adopted in this region, the Diola would somehow have to be convinced to give up palmwine gathering during the summer, a far more pleasurable and less arduous task.

higher yields, and considering that the Kasa Diola can grow only rice and no peanuts, emphasis should be placed on transportation and marketing facilities. Perhaps a campaign employing young Diola from Dakar who are well acquainted with a money economy as rural *animateurs* would help to pry loose existing rice surpluses and encourage their sale. Since consideration must be given to price subsidies and protective tariffs, direct government action is required.

If the peanut market does not disappear altogether, intensification of peanut cultivation will probably also become necessary in the future. The need for land under bush-fallow cultivation cannot be indefinitely met by the desultory pattern of borrowing extra fields wherever one can. Peanut land is becoming scarce, and there is little assurance that the people who lend fields are going to continue to do so for a long time. The relative openness of the attitudes toward peanuts could facilitate consolidation of the fields a person owns. Even now peanut fields are large enough to receive farm machinery, if erosion could be controlled and the financing and servicing of the equipment guaranteed. This would be possible only through production cooperatives in harmony with Diola ways of organizing cooperative work in the fields. I suggest that peanut cooperatives have met with little success among the Diola partly because they have dealt exclusively with buying and selling, for which people have no patterns of cooperation.

The day could arrive when the Diola, who constitute 9 percent of the total population, might profitably produce rice for the entire Senegalese urban population and assume a greater share of the peanut export market.

CHAPTER 7

THE INTRODUCTION OF THE OX PLOW IN CENTRAL GAMBIA

Peter M. Weil

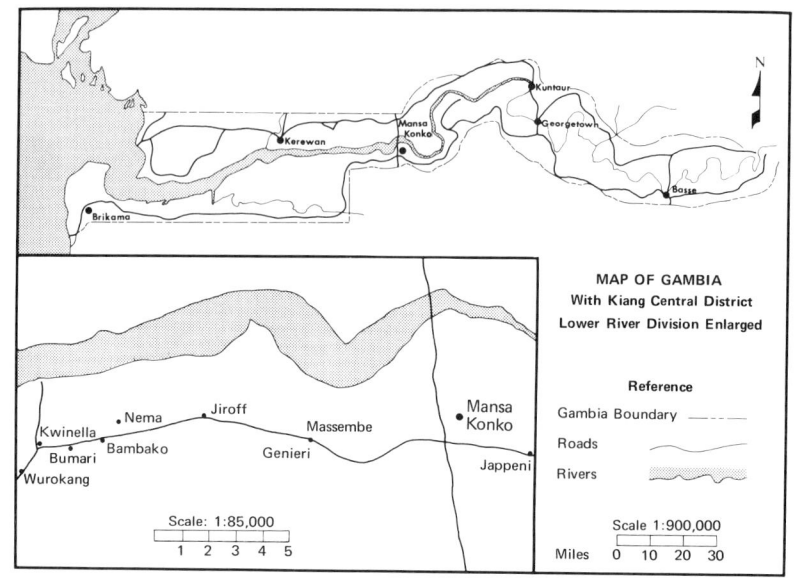

The map of the Gambia is adapted from one compiled by the Directorate of Overseas Survey and used in the Sessional Paper No. 13 of 1965, *Report on the Census of Population of the Gambia*, taken on 17/18th April, 1963.

INTRODUCTION

This chapter analyzes the social and economic effects of the introduction of the ox plow in the Gambia, which may have implications for development programs in other "third world" countries.[1]

The Gambia is a small, newly independent West African country extending eastward inland from the Atlantic coast along the Gambia River for about 200 miles.[2] This country comprises about 4,000 square miles but has an average width of only 12 miles. With a population of approximately 320,000 persons, its overall density is 79 persons per square mile. Three ethnic groups—the Mandinka, the Fula, and the Wolof—make up more than 67 percent of the population. The capital is Bathurst.

The Gambia experiences a long dry season that begins in September or October and ends in May or June. During the dry season the country is swept by desert winds from the north and northeast (the Harmattan), and temperatures hover around 97 degrees Fahrenheit with an average humidity of 50 percent. Approximately 40 inches of rain fall in the short rainy season, during which temperatures average approximately 85 degrees and the humidity around 80 percent.

Part of the Senegambian plateau, the Gambia is characterized by savanna and low, flat-topped hills. The soils are generally lateritic.

There are no known mineral resources of economic importance

---

[1] The data for this paper were gathered during a year's predoctoral research (August, 1966–August, 1967) sponsored by the National Science Foundation. Eighteen of the nineteen trainees of the 1966 class of the Kwinella Mixed Farm Center were interviewed during their training and during the first planting season afterward. Data on trainees were gathered only in Central Gambia (the eastern half of the Lower River Division on the Gambia River's south bank). Trainees interviewed were all Mandinka, the dominant group in Central Gambia and in the Gambia as a whole. While conclusions apply primarily to Central Gambia, observations suggest that the experience of the program there is similar to that in the rest of the country.

All pound figures should be converted to dollars at the Nov. 17, 1967, exchange rate of $2.80.

Appreciation is expressed to Amang Kanyi, Minister of Agriculture, to members of the Gambia Department of Agriculture, to trainees, and to sponsors of trainees, whose assistance facilitated my research.

For critical comments, I should like to thank Norman Schwartz and Edward Dodson of the University of Delaware and V. R. Dorjahn of the University of Oregon.

[2] H. R. Jarrett, *A Geography of Sierra Leone and the Gambia* (London: Longmans, Green & Co., 1964), pp. 4, 13, 25, 37.

in the Gambia. Thus agriculture is the principal source of wealth, and agricultural production is the occupation of the majority of the population. There is one cash crop—groundnuts. The Gambia Oilseeds Marketing Board (GOMB), the government purchasing and marketing agent, completely controls the export of this crop. Other dry-land crops produced for domestic consumption are sorghum, early and late millet, maize, and a small amount of fonio (*Digertaria excellis*). Almost all of the dry-land farming is carried out by men, who devote most of their efforts to groundnut production. Women produce rice, the major food crop, which is grown in rain-fed and tidal swamps. Both men and women tend small gardens for vegetables, cassava, and yams. Agricultural production is undertaken by production units which range in size from nuclear family units to extended family units that pool resources and labor. Because ox plows are used only by men and almost exclusively for dry-land crops, rice production will not be discussed here.

The Agricultural Year

The agricultural year for groundnuts begins in early May with the clearing of land and ends in October or November with the harvest. December, January, and February are spent threshing, winnowing, and bagging groundnuts for sale. As the time for land preparation and planting is quite short, any innovation allowing the farmer to plow more land between May and July greatly increases his productivity. So does any innovation permitting seeding to be completed after the first or second rain in June, for early germination of the seed leads to greater yields per plant. It is in this context that the ox plow must be viewed.

Agricultural Change

Production of both the cash crop and subsistence food crops has increased since the end of World War II. In this period the production of dry-land food crops has changed from a fairly balanced position in relation to groundnut production to a subordinate one, but swamp rice production has increased to partly fill the food gap this change has caused. The devotion of more time, energy, and land to groundnut production results primarily from an increased demand for cash to buy consumer goods.

Because possibilities for industrial development are negligible, governments both before and after independence recognized the necessity for agricultural development.[3] They observed that many of the young Gambian males, imbued with the rise in expectations engendered by independence and other forces, were leaving their farms to seek a rather small number of better paying jobs with higher status in the city of Bathurst. By introducing modern, scientific agricultural methods that would make farming more profitable, the government sought to remove the drudgery and stigma from farm labor and to make a farming career more attractive and acceptable to youth, particularly educated youths.[4]

Toward this goal the government has introduced several agricultural innovations, including fertilizers, secure seed stores, insecticides, and improved seed varieties. But by far the most important innovation has been the Mixed Farm Center Program.

THE MIXED FARM CENTER

The Mixed Farm Centers, known as Ox Plowing Schools until 1964, began in 1952 when Hector Davidson, then an agricultural officer at Masembe in Kiang East District, diverted funds intended for fence-building to construct the first training center and ox cart. Davidson's immediate purpose was to expedite the moving of crops and building materials from the farmstead as well as to teach new farming methods. By 1955 the concept was accepted by the Department of Agriculture, and the first "school" was recognized. At that time five students were attending.

By 1961 the department had increased the number of centers to 15, permitting an attendance of 149 students. Twenty-four centers with an attendance of 384 students were in operation by 1966. A total of 1,874 students had graduated from the centers throughout the country by the end of the 1966 training year.[5] Much of the program's improvement and guidance in its first 14 years must be credited to Davidson. The program has been financed primarily by Britain, but the United States signed an agreement in the summer of 1967 to provide capital to increase the number of students per

---

[3] No GNP figures are available for the Gambia. The 1965 average income per farmer was £25. In the same year there was an estimated total of 80,000 farmers in the country. (The Gambia Department of Agriculture, *Mixed Farm Centers in the Gambia: Their Impact on Agricultural Production and Improved Social Standards* [Fajara, 1966], p. 1.)
[4] *Ibid.*
[5] *Ibid.*, App. A.

center from 16 to 25. The United States also provided money for development projects related to the program.[6]

Goals of the Program

The centers' purpose has been to replace traditional tools with the ox-drawn plow, to train farmers in the scientific care of livestock and the use of farming innovations, and to increase the productivity of farmers not attending the Mixed Farm Centers through contract plowing by Center graduates.[7] The program's staff hopes to lead Gambian agriculture up a "mechanical ladder." The first rung of this ladder is the simple ox-drawn, double-moldboard Emcot plow; the second is the more complex Aplos tool-bar plow; the third is a small, inexpensive tractor; and the final rung is a full-size tractor and a completely mechanized agricultural system. According to one government official, the mechanical ladder is aimed at providing "every small farmer with reasonably accessible progressive steps in a logical sequence to advanced mechanization."[8]

The major justifications for the staged program are an infrastructure inadequate to maintain motor-powered equipment, the limited income of farmers, and the government's limited development capital. While farmers advance up the "ladder," the government plans to train mechanics, stockpile spare parts, and establish fuel depots to support mechanized farming.

The program had advanced to the second rung of the ladder by 1966 with the intensified introduction of the Aplos plow and tool bar. Operation of the Aplos as a plow, planter, weeder, and cart is seen as preparation for the use of similar motor-driven equipment. Meanwhile, beginning in the spring of 1967, the centers were supplied with a full range of spare parts for all equipment they used and sold. Literate agricultural officials were placed at the head of each center to keep accounts and make orders for more parts. The

[6] The United States also provided funds for the training of administrative and instructional personnel, for the services of an American agricultural technician, and for training tools. Under the aid agreement, no funds were provided for the extension of agricultural credit for bulls; as will be demonstrated, such funds are needed if the Gambia is to meet its social goals for the program. The United States is examining the Gambian Mixed Farm Center Program as a possible prototype for a similar program, the Casamance Project, which it has agreed to establish in Senegal.

[7] The Gambia Department of Agriculture, *Oxenization in the Gambia: An Agricultural, Economic, and Sociological Revolution* (Fajara, 1964), p. 1.

[8] *Letter from Mr. Hector Davidson, Director of the Gambia Department of Agriculture, to the Hon. Sherif M. Diba, Minister of Public Works and Communications* (Fajara: Gambia Department of Agriculture, 1966), p. 2.

Demonstration of *kedabo* (hand plow).

Emcot plow.

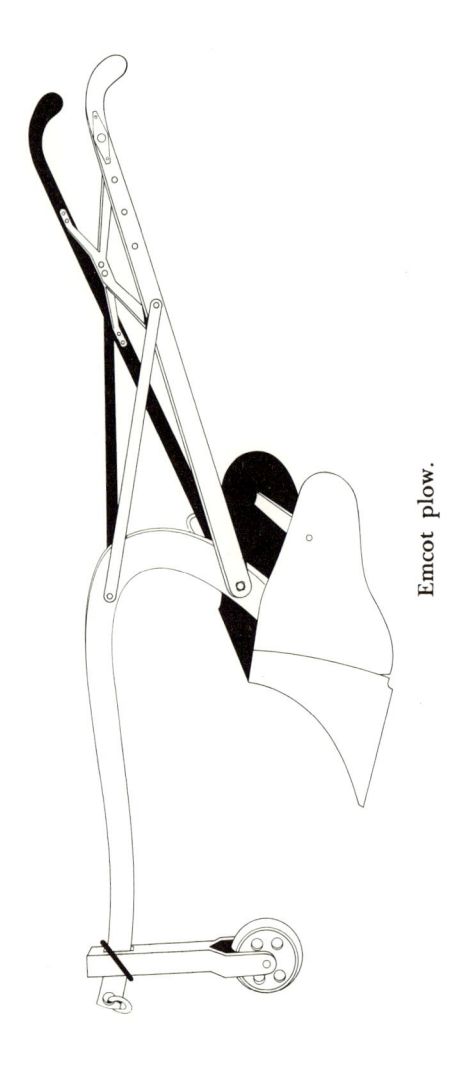

Aplos tool bar with plow attached.

Annual extension day at Mixed Farm Center (Kwinella). Here the staff members are demonstrating the Aplos tool bar with its weeding attachment.

Department of Agriculture trained mechanics to repair the Emcot and Aplos equipment, and two portable machine shops were purchased.[9] In this manner the infrastructure necessary for more advanced agricultural development was built into the mechanical ladder.

Political Opposition

There is some political opposition among a few farmers, politicians, and traders to the gradual development program. The opposition cites the Department of Agriculture's failure to provide a moderately priced small tractor to bridge the gap between ox plows and large tractors and asserts that the country needs immediate and full mechanization to develop. The department answers that even with government support, full-size tractors could be bought by only a few rich farmers who would probably undertake mass contract plowing and simply become a new breed of creditor. Moreover, the department's officials argue, the prohibitive price of full-scale equipment would kill the small farmer's incentive to improve his lot.[10] Several persons involved in the program noted the political liability of a dissatisfied and frustrated agrarian sector. As one put it, "The mechanical ladder provides for agricultural evolution and avoids or prevents the need for an agricultural revolution."

Organization of Centers

Within the Ministry of Agriculture, the Department of Agriculture is charged with supervision and execution of the Mixed Farm Center Program. The country is divided into sections, each of which is headed by an agricultural superintendent who is usually based at an experiment station. Within each section are several centers. Each center is headed today by an agricultural officer or extension agent responsible to the superintendent over him. This agricultural officer supervises all programs of the center, does some teaching, keeps accounts, and undertakes person-to-person extension duties. Under the agricultural officer are three instructors.

---

[9] The Texaco Company has begun increasing its small number of service stations in an attempt to create a complete chain along the length of the road on the Gambia River's south bank. This effort is not part of the Mixed Farm Center Program but is in line with its aim of creating an infrastructure in the agrarian sector. At first the only service will be the sale of products; later, small repair garages with mechanics will be attached.

[10] The Gambia Department of Agriculture, *U.S. Aid: Oxenization Programme* (Fajara, 1966), p. 4.

The instructors determine the basic daily program of the students and concentrate on teaching the proper use of the ox plow and the correct care and feeding of bulls. Instructors are usually recruited by agricultural officers from the farming populations within the centers' own areas.

The 24 Mixed Farm Centers in the Gambia are similar, and a description of the Kwinella Center will serve as an example. The center sits on 11 acres granted to the Department of Agriculture by the *seyfo* or chief of Kiang Central in consultation with the people of Kwinella. The center's compound consists of a large open-sided barn and fenced paddock, a wooden equipment and lecture shed, and six cement-faced brick buildings wtih corrugated roofs used to house trainees and staff. The appearance of the center is deliberately simple; expensive and specialized government housing is forgone so as not to "upset the trainee's sense of values or prevent the application at the village level of lessons taught."[11]

The mean average cost per trainee for the 1,874 men who graduated from 1955 to 1966 was £77. This figure includes not only the students' per diem allowance but also the costs of construction, salaries, and equipment. The £77 figure does not include depreciation.[12]

The usual training period is from March to November. Some students begin to register in January and February, but active recruitment and registration does not begin until March. During that month the center's agricultural officer and his staff visit villages in their area and talk to elders and farmers about the advantages of ox plow agriculture. Farmers are told that they can triple their income during the training year to £75. They are also told that attendance at the center will open up government credit for plows and related equipment. The staff members explain that trainees must have two bulls to participate in the program and emphasize the important role of an ox plow farmer in an economically developing, independent country.

Trainees arrive in April and are assigned rooms in the small dormitories. For each day he spends in residence, the trainee receives a cup of rice and the per diem pay of a shilling.

During the first week, trainees are taught how to ring the nose of the bull, how to feed and care for the animals, how to collect manure for fertilizer, and how to make a yoke from wood gathered

---

[11] Department of Agriculture, *Oxenization*, p. 2.
[12] Department of Agriculture, *Mixed Farm Centers*, App. A.

from the bush. The bulls are trained to pull a harrow, a cart, and then a plow.

After the first rains, trainees plow the center's demonstration fields. They are taught the proper depth to plow, the proper intervals at which to plant seeds, and the appropriate amount of commercial fertilizer to use. Then they are sent home to apply what they have learned to their own fields, using equipment from the center.

Trainees work on their own or their sponsor's land, or both.[13] Some trainees begin contract plowing for a relative, who usually lives outside their production unit. A center fee of ten shillings per acre for contract plowing is collected and divided equally among all trainees and staff (except for the agricultural officer). In 1966, trainees from the Kwinella Center plowed 142.5 acres on contract, or 7.5 acres per trainee.

A member of the center's staff usually follows students to their villages. He gives them advice on their area's problems of soil erosion and "safe" plowing depths. This home training period is particularly valuable, since the student can now adapt what he has learned to his own farming situation while giving the hand-cultivating farmers a vivid demonstration of the effectiveness of the ox plow.

Trainees work at home from late June to late September except for a three-day period in which they are asked to return to the center. Some return in July to weed the late millet, the others in August to weed the groundnuts.

All trainees return to the center in early October. Bulls not castrated prior to coming to the center are now castrated by veterinary officers. This month is filled with detailed lectures on crop rotation, soil conservation, seed germination, animal husbandry, maintenance of plows and equipment, crop spraying, fertilizers, and poultry care. During these final lectures, staff members explain the mechanical ladder concept to the students and discuss plans for future agricultural development.

The last month of the program is taken up with the harvesting of crops and with an open house which provides an opportunity for the center to carry out its extension and public-relations functions.

[13] A sponsor is a farmer who provides bulls so that a young man, usually related to him patrilineally, may attend a mixed farm center. In return, the sponsor receives plowing services for what is normally an unlimited number of agricultural seasons.

FACTORS WORKING FOR ACCEPTANCE

Interviews with eighteen students who attended the Kwinella Mixed Farm Center in 1966 disclosed that they have similar economic and social characteristics.[14] These characteristics were related to several economic and cultural trends that favor the acceptance of the ox plow in the Gambia.

Demand For Higher Incomes

Over the past decade, improved communication and the availability of consumer goods have triggered a demand for higher income among Gambian farmers.[15] The opening of an all-weather road in 1964 along the whole south bank of the Gambia River has greatly accelerated this trend. As Dalton points out, "In traditional society, material wealth acquisition was largely a byproduct of social status."[16] With the impetus of the new road, traders have now made the symbols of status available to all who have the cash to pay for them. Before the introduction of the plow, the agricultural technology available to those of low and high status was the same, the main difference being that men of higher status could demand *corvée* labor or hire work groups to till their fields. The ox plow offers the common farmer a new way to gain the symbols of high status, so it is widely accepted as an ideal. But to own or use a plow, a farmer must already have more wealth than other hand-cultivating farmers.

All of the Kwinella trainees said the major reason for their participation in the program was to increase their, or their sponsors', cash income. Some students emphasized the advantages of the cash that could be earned from contract plowing while others mentioned the savings possible by using an ox plow instead of human labor. Yet another factor mentioned was competition coupled with economic pragmatism. A common comment was: "I saw a man plow his entire field in half a day. It would have taken me five days to

---

[14] The 18 trainees interviewed represented 4.74 percent of the 384 farmers trained under the program in 1966. The program had trained 1,874 of the 80,000 farmers in the Gambia by the end of 1966. The data obtained from such a small sample must be treated as limited.

[15] M. R. Haswell, *The Changing Pattern of Economic Activity in a Gambia Village* (London: Her Majesty's Stationery Office, 1963), pp. 52, 86. Haswell's research in 1949 and 1962 took place in Genieri, Kiang East, in Central Gambia.

[16] George Dalton, "The Development of Subsistence and Peasant Societies in Africa," in *Tribal and Peasant Economies, Readings in Economic Anthropology*, ed. George Dalton (Garden City, N.Y.: Natural History Press, 1967), pp. 158–61.

plow the same land. Why should he do less work than I and earn more money?"

My research also suggests that the trainees indeed came from production units possessing significantly more wealth than other hand-cultivating units. In all cases the sponsors or trainees could afford to buy or provide from their herds the two plow bulls necessary to enter the program. The average plow bull costs £10-10-0,[17] and in those cases where the bulls were purchased, the sponsors could afford to do without the capital normally needed by hand-cultivating farmers to buy food and other necessities. This supports Haswell's conclusion: "... not until agricultural production has reached about double the subsistence minimum will cultivators tend to employ animal rather than human labor."[18]

Data gathered by the Wye College student team reinforces the conclusion that the trainees held wealth prior to participation.[19] The report shows that trainee compounds have significantly more livestock than those of other hand cultivators—for example, 535 percent more cows, 60 percent more sheep, 25 percent more goats, and 21 percent more poultry per working man.[20] Cattle, which in the Gambia are a major index for showing differentials in wealth, are not acquired in large numbers by any production unit in a short time.

Increasing Commercialization of Markets

Since World War II, the Gambian farmer has become dependent upon an increasingly commercialized market and production system for the bulk of his cash income, most of his credit, and a growing amount of his labor. Groundnuts are purchased by GOMB at a guaranteed price that may vary from year to year. The bulk of credit is now handled by cooperatives and is primarily based on the demonstrated productivity of the individuals and not on kinship or friendship ties. Cash labor is becoming more common. The long-term "strange farmer," who would receive a plot of land, food, and

[17] This is the mean price paid for 25 bulls by the 18 trainees or sponsors of the 1966 Kwinella Mixed Center class.
[18] *The Changing Pattern*, p. 22.
[19] Wye College Exploration Society, *Report of the Gambia Ox-Ploughing Survey: 1966* (Wye, England: Wye College, 1967), App. 3, Tables 16, 17, 18. The team sampled all the Gambia to determine the effects of the use of the ox-drawn plow. The author disagrees with the team's conclusion that all or most of the greater wealth found in the trainees' production units resulted from their use of the implement.
[20] *Ibid.*, App. 3, Tables 16, 17, 18.

lodging in return for a half-week's labor on a patron's field, is passing from the picture. Today the short-term "strange farmer" demands cash payment for his labor as well as food and lodging. Where once a chief could demand *corvée* labor, today he and other rich farmers must pay cash, large amounts of food, cigarettes, and kola to village work groups.

This situation is critical to the introduction of the ox plow. For as Dalton says, "Modern machine technology and applied science cannot be introduced into a primitive subsistence economy unless the production lines they enter are first commercialized."[21] In the Gambia, much of the hand-cultivating farmer's agricultural labor is not factored out commercially, but those farmers who can afford cash labor are factoring out their production. Sponsors of all the Kwinella trainees had previously hired work groups for planting.

Dalton makes another point concerning market dependence that is germane here: "As with hired labor or any other purchased factor, a machine represents a money cost which can be incurred only if the purchaser uses the machine to enlarge his money sales revenue from which he recovers its cost."[22] Thus it is suggested that experience in the factoring of costs through dependence on a commercialized market and the use of commercialized production lines has been an element in determining which farmers participate in the program. Perhaps greater wealth itself is not as important as how the wealth has been managed. The dependence of all farmers on a commercialized market increases the likelihood that farmers will at least want to own or use an ox plow.

Growing Scarcity of Labor

The relative scarcity of labor within production units is also a factor in the acceptance of the ox plow.[23] Since 1949, the trend in Central Gambia has been for compounds, a patrilineal family unit of varying depth, to fracture into smaller compounds or to form several *dabadalu* internally. The *dabadalu* usually have fewer members than a compound and are commonly headed by brothers whose father is too old to bind the compound together or is dead. Haswell observes that these smaller production units have the highest proportion of younger laborers, in the sixteen-to-thirty-year age range.[24]

[21] George Dalton, "Traditional Production in Primitive African Economies," in *Tribal and Peasant Economies*, p. 77.
[22] Dalton, "Development," p. 64.
[23] Eric Wolf, *Peasants*, Foundations in Anthropology, ed. Marshal D. Sahlins (Englewood Cliffs, N.J.: Prentice-Hall, Inc., 1966), p. 29.
[24] *The Changing Pattern*, pp. 27, 28, 34, 63.

Although these smaller units have proportionally more productive labor, they also have higher operating costs. During the dry season many young men drift away to participate in wage labor, and during the latter half of the agricultural year many boys go to school. Thus labor is not available to maintain traditional housing, for example, and small units are often forced to spend cash to buy metal roofs if not to build cement-faced brick houses. Thus the *dabadalu* and small compounds are pressed to make the most efficient use of their labor. The ox plow offers an opportunity to do so, and perhaps this partly explains why fourteen of the Kwinella trainees were from *dabada* production units.

Generally, the Kwinella trainees were the youngest males in their production unit who were over eighteen. Ten of the trainees were single, and of the eight married trainees only one had children. Therefore, most of the students had no immediate financial or leadership responsibilities and could be most easily spared from their unit's work force.

Fifteen of the trainees were sponsored by the head of their production unit, and eight of the sponsors were fathers of the trainees. Of the three trainees who sponsored themselves, one was head of a production unit. This information suggests that the individual sponsor wants to retain within his *dabada* the trainee's new skills, which will lead to increased productivity.

Familiarity with Plow

The familiarity of the Gambian farmer with the advantages and use of the traditional hand plow perhaps favored the acceptance of the ox plow. The farmer realizes that the principles behind the moldboard plow are much the same as those behind his hand plow. Hand plowed fields do not need to be weeded as early or as often as fields planted by other traditional methods, but the yields per acre are smaller. The ox plow shares the advantages of less frequent and later weeding but potentially allows the farmer to make up for the loss in yield per acre by plowing more land in the same time.

Demonstration Effect

Another important factor in acceptance is status. In most villages in the Lower River Division, the village headman, the district chief, and the *moro* or holy man were among the first to send a representative to the center. Not necessarily wealthier than co-villagers, the village heads are in a better position to draw both free and paid labor and so usually farm more land than other villagers. The chiefs often use their government salaries to pay laborers to increase their acreage, and the holy man who operates a Koranic school has free labor from his many students.

There is no official program policy to recruit members of an area's leadership structure first. But when a center staff member visits a district or village to recruit, he usually does so in observance of traditional etiquette. He commonly finds a receptive audience because leaders almost always want to increase their wealth to satisfy reciprocity responsibilities.

The leaders' example has probably contributed to the success of the Mixed Farm Center Program. While none of the eighteen Kwinella trainees were members of the leadership structure, all were from villages in which leaders had been early participants in the program.

Stabilized Groundnut Price

The stable domestic price of groundnuts over the last several years is a factor that has favored the acceptance of an innovation requiring so high an investment as the ox plow and bulls. In her 1963 report, M. R. Haswell noted that "the economic limiting factor to increased output substantially above the subsistence minimum has been the producer's lack of assured markets for his products at remunerative prices."[25] Even though the world price for groundnuts has dropped steadily since 1963, GOMB has maintained the price at £27 per ton, making a stable market for the Gambian farmer.[26] It may be suggested, therefore, that the stable price has favored acceptance of the ox plow.

THE POST-TRAINING PERIOD

The success or failure of the Mixed Farm Center Program is largely determined by the farming activities of the graduates after they leave a center. Some of these activities will be considered now as they relate to the program's intent (1) to increase the number of plows, (2) to introduce methods of animal husbandry, and (3) to increase general productivity through contract plowing.

1. During the groundnut season, December through March, sponsors and trainees decide whether or not to buy a plow. They have a choice of four: the Aplos and Emcot plows offered by the center,

[25] *Ibid.*, p. 76.
[26] The Gambia, Office of the Prime Minister, *Sessional Papers*, 1966. *Statistical Summary: 1965*, no. 6, pp. 12–13.

a single-moldboard plow sold in Senegal for about £10, and an £8 plow occasionally made by local blacksmiths.

The Emcot plow is sold and delivered to the farmer at the subsidized price of £16. It may be purchased on credit with one-third down and approximately 5 percent interest on the balance for the next two years. The Aplos tool bar with cart bed and moldboard cost £55 until July, 1967, when the price rose to £64. This plow may be purchased under the same credit arrangement as the Emcot. Weeders, slat sides, and other Aplos attachments may also be purchased on credit. The cost of each attachment averages around £3.

The raising of prices for Mixed Farm Center equipment was the subject of much debate within the Gambian government in 1967. Many officials said that farmers had been subsidized long enough and that limited fiscal resources made government subsidization no longer practical. Others wanted to turn foreign aid used to subsidize the price of farm equipment to general revenue. Removing the subsidy would have entailed adding 30 percent to the price of equipment and fertilizer. This would have made the Emcot sell for £20-16-0 and the Aplos for £83-4-0. A bag of fertilizer (112 pounds) that cost 15 shillings in 1967 would have cost £1-6-0. These price increases might seriously have damaged the ox-plow program and the general expansion of production. While it might not have decreased significantly the number of farmers participating and buying Emcots, it would have slowed the purchase of Aplos equipment, the second rung in the mechanical "ladder." The amount of fertilizer sold would definitely have decreased because the government had no credit system for fertilizer other than the few long-term loans given by the cooperatives. Moreover, pressure from traders for permission to sell agricultural items controlled and sold only by the centers would have increased greatly. If the traders had prevailed, they might have sold equipment at such high interest rates that the number of farmers utilizing the new equipment and fertilizers would have decreased further.

Although the Department of Agriculture calculates that the first year's earnings will allow most trainees to purchase plows, only seven Kwinella graduates did so. Six bought Emcots and one an Aplos. Twelve trainees borrowed plows from classmates or relatives. Borrowing farm equipment is possible in the Gambia because limited capital for seed, fertilizer, and harvest laborers prevents the rapid expansion of fields and the use of plows to their full potential. The reluctance of trainees to pour capital immediately into plows suggests that personal income does not increase dramatically the first year.

The trainees also exhibited some unwillingness to climb the mechanical ladder. Those buying Emcot plows emphasized that the plow was inexpensive and light and that it could be used on fields with stumps. Although fourteen of the trainees said they hoped to own an Aplos some day, twelve of these wanted to use the Aplos only as an ox cart and the other two said they would use it only on permanently cleared fields. Most trainees pointed out that the moldboard on the Aplos made the plow too heavy, and several trainees alleged that bulls died after trying to pull the Aplos.

2. Although the Mixed Farm Centers have tried to teach farmers how to care for plow bulls, many farmers do not and cannot follow their advice. Trainees are told that bulls must be fed millet in large amounts during the season of heavy work. Late millet is a major food grain for most villagers, and the instructors are asking a trainee to feed millet to his bulls when there is almost none left in his compound's food stores. Haswell indicates that it is doubtful that farmers who produce even double the subsistence level will consider giving spare grain to their livestock.[27] Consequently, a trainee either works his bulls for a short period—half a day or less—or buys more bulls. If a farmer uses his bulls for half a day, he loses two advantages of ox plowing. First, only by sowing during the short period after the first rains can he guarantee higher groundnut yields. Second, only with difficulty can his weakened bulls pull the Aplos plow, considered to be a crucial second rung in the mechanical ladder. The disadvantage of buying more bulls is that the initial capitalization costs become even higher for efficient use of equipment.

Unless the Department of Agriculture introduces new livestock feed that the villagers do not regularly eat, most plow owners will probably not feed their animals adequately and receive full efficiency from their plows. The department is now growing green graham experimentally as a possible alternative to millet.

In Kiang Central District, however, the animal husbandry program of the Kwinella Center has been fairly successful. Trainees feed and house their plow bulls adequately, though they do not yet extend the same care to their herd cattle.

3. The center has been more successful in inducing trainees to contract out their services.[28] In fact, this supplement to cash income is an incentive to participate in the program. Although friends and close patrilineal relatives and mother's patrilineal relatives pay a lower price, most plow owners charge £1 per acre for cash and

[27] *The Changing Pattern*, p. 22.
[28] Wye College, *Report*, p. 8, Table C.

10 shillings more per acre on credit. Credit terms are usually based on two months but may be extended up to nine months.

Seventeen of the eighteen Kwinella trainees said they wanted to do contract plowing. Seven trainees from *dabada* production units said they would contract plow for all *dabadalu* within their compound as well as for farmers outside the compound. One trainee said that he would plow free for his sponsor but that he would charge all other persons in his *dabada*, in his compound, or outside his compound. The ten other trainees said they would contract plow outside the compound, not charging those inside the compound.

Viewing contract plowing as an opportunity to help other farmers, several trainees said they would charge half the normal price so that the contractee could save enough money to participate in the Mixed Farm Center Program.

People who own Aplos tool bars also hire them out as ox carts to carry bricks to building sites and to bring rice from the swamps. The charge varies, but a common price for hauling rice is six bundles for every sixty bundles carried.

The supply of plows available for contract plowing includes not only those belonging to center graduates but also those belonging to other farmers who have bought them from trainees, blacksmiths, and Senegalese traders. The Wye College report suggests that most of these other plow-owning farmers reside in the eastern half of the country where Fulas and Serahulis (Soninkes) predominate. Both groups are relatively wealthy in cattle. The wealth of nontrainee compounds with plows falls somewhat below that of trainee compounds except in the area of cattle ownership (1.28 cows per capita for nontrainee compounds versus 1.08 for trainee compounds).

The Mixed Farm Center Program does not want its trainees to instruct others in the use of the plow. Its administrators clearly state that the Department of Agriculture wants to control the introduction and use of ox plows for fear that plows owned by untrained farmers will deteriorate through inadequate maintenance and that improper use of the plow will lead to soil erosion.[29]

[29] Senegal operates a few technical schools in the provinces (not part of the Casamance Project) where a full agricultural curriculum of eight months is taught. The program is somewhat similar to that taught under the Gambian program, but the training includes carpentry. Moreover, a special two-week course only on working with plow bulls is given. The Gambia Department of Agriculture opposes this type of training because farmers are not taught modern agricultural methods and because the department fears that the use of ox plows by uninformed farmers would permanently damage the land. The department also believes that such farmers would remain at the same level of development.

Nevertheless, nontrainee plow owners are becoming more common and are often assisted by trainees. One-third of the Kwinella trainees planned to train people outside their compounds without charge. The trainees pointed out that they wanted to pass along the benefits of their training to farmers who could not afford to attend the center.

Although contract plowing is intended to increase the production of the average farmer, data show that contractees are slightly wealthier and produce a lower yield per acre than hand cultivators. Farmers who contract for plowing have been shown to have 0.49 cows per capita versus 0.13 for hand cultivators in the same village, indicating again the need for wealth to own or use a plow.[30] In 1965, contractees interviewed had 24 percent more acreage than hand cultivators. Yet in the same year the contractees' yields per acre were 18 percent less than those of hand cultivators. Because contractees use only slightly more fertilizer than hand cultivators,[31] it appears that they plow additional acreage simply to maintain yields they previously obtained through hand labor. Therefore the figures for contract plowing do not display the production increases for which the program strives.

Challenges to Success

Two major obstacles to participation in and success of the Mixed Farm Center Program were observed—distrust of the government and the program as a whole and the decreased yields per acre already described.

The centers suffer somewhat from their government sponsorship. Farmers distrust governmental authority. The independent government, like its predecessor, collects taxes, sets the pattern for justice in the courts, and imposes limits on local governments—and doing so is thought to interfere in local affairs. Moreover, policemen are the government's most widespread representatives in the provinces.

A farmer who participates in the Mixed Farm Center Program enters into a relationship with a branch of this government. It is possible that many farmers who might participate in the program do not because of the government's negative image. Moreover, recruiters for the center sometimes contribute to the problem. Center staff are almost always strangers to the villages in which they are recruiting; while etiquette requires that strangers be treated civilly,

---

[30] Wye College, *Report*, App. 2, Table 11; App. 3, Table 16.
[31] *Ibid.*, Table A, p. 7; App. 6, Table 48a.

outsiders' opinions on local problems are resented. By making such comments, recruiters help create the image of a government that meddles in local affairs.

Many farmers consider the ox plow program itself undependable. This attitude is a result of a two-year lag in delivery of the Emcot plows ordered in 1965, the late payment of the trainees' contract-plowing bonus, and the requirement that trainees perform maintenance duties at the center not directly related to plowing.

The other obstacle, the loss of yield per acre when using an ox-drawn plow, frustrates both the trainee and a few farmers who may otherwise have decided to participate in the program.

There are two traditional hand cultivation methods, and both lead to higher yields per acre than the ox plow method. The most common traditional method employs the *kongkoduwo,* a small adze-like piercing tool, to poke seed holes about four to six inches apart on two sides. The other major method utilizes the hand plow, or *kedabo,* which creates rows about eight inches apart from ridge to ridge on which seeds are planted at six-inch intervals. In contrast, both types of commonly used ox plows cut rows about twelve inches apart from ridge to ridge. To prepare trainees to use mechanized seed drills, the Department of Agriculture originally proposed a planting distance of six inches along the ridges. The department also proposed the use of upright groundnut varieties that have a lower yield per plant than the traditional spreading varieties but that will not spread into the furrows and obstruct the weeder on the Aplos and mechanized equipment to be used in the future.

Yields under Department of Agriculture methods are approximately 50 percent smaller than those of traditional methods. The Department has been fairly successful—perhaps to its disadvantage—in introducing the upright variety to hand-cultivating farmers through a seed-loan program funded by the middle-level government unit, the area council. In Central Gambia most farmers mix the two varieties, although a good number plant only the upright variety. Thus in this area the decrease in the trainee's yield per acre is not so great when compared with that of his fellow cultivators. Recognizing the problem created by wider rows, the Department of Agriculture began in 1965 to recommend that trainees plant at a distance of three inches. But even so the crop yield is about 12 percent smaller. One further department recommendation is the application of fertilizer, which, if heavy enough, should more than make up for this loss.

But most trainees do not use the recommended amount of fertilizer. In 1965 the mean average acreage per working man in a trainee's compound was 2.74 acres, as opposed to 2.09 acres in a hand-cultivating compound. To supply the recommended 178 pounds of fertilizer per acre, which ideally results in a 40 percent increase in yield, four bags (no split bags are sold) of fertilizer would have to be used by the trainee farmer, an outlay of £2-8-0 at the 1965 price of 12 shillings per bag. Wye College statistics show that trainee production units use only 0.78 bags of fertilizer per acre per working man.[32] This amount should ideally lead to a 20.8 percent increase in yield per acre, which is only 8 percent higher than that of hand cultivators.

In brief, trainees can make up for the relative loss in yield per acre, but to do so they must increase the cash costs of farming. By failing to use the recommended amount of fertilizer, they do not get full value or efficiency out of their bulls and plow. Hence the ox plow program has not yet reached its goal of fully efficient use of the new methods it has introduced.

EFFECTS OF ACCEPTANCE ON PRODUCTION AND LAND USE

Groundnut production has dramatically increased in the Gambia since 1964. The GOMB's purchasing figures show that 70,000 tons of groundnuts were produced in 1963. The figure for 1964 was 93,800 tons, for 1965, 122,940 tons, and for 1966, 130,000 tons. The Department of Agriculture attributes 34 percent of the increase to the use of the ox plow, 30 percent to the use of improved seed, and 25 percent to the use of fertilizer.[33] While all the increase in production may not be the result of the department's program, a significant part has been.

During the period between 1964 and 1965, GOMB figures show an increase of 23.3 percent. In that same period the average trainee increased his yield 24.6 percent. Nontrainee plow owners increased their groundnut production 15.2 percent, and contractees increased their production approximately 24 percent. During the same year hand cultivators increased their production by 13.1 percent.[34] These figures generally support the Department of Agriculture's conten-

---

[32] *Ibid.*, App. 4, Table 27; App. 6, Table 48a.
[33] Department of Agriculture, *Mixed Farm Centers*, p. 1.
[34] Production figures in bags are found in the Wye College *Report*, App. 4, Table 27. The Department of Agriculture estimates four bushels per bag. Percentages are computed by the author.

tion that the ox plow has been a major contributor to increased groundnut production—at least for the sample year.

In the area of land use and land tenure, the plow has caused several related changes. These include (1) a tendency for each farmer to use more land for cash-crop production, with resulting land pressures, (2) a tendency for plow owners to consolidate their groundnut land, (3) a trend toward a calling back of land on long-term loan, and (4) a tendency of plow-owning farmers to reverse the general trend toward a decrease in food production.

1. Data show that farmers using ox plows utilize more acreage than hand cultivators. In 1965, trainee and nontrainee plow owners and contractees were each compared with a sample of hand-cultivating farmers in their own villages. On the whole, trainee farmers utilize 31 percent more land than hand-cultivating farmers. Nontrainee plow owner compounds had approximately 18 percent more land per working man than hand-cultivator compounds, and contractee compounds utilized about 24 percent more acres per working man than hand-cultivating compounds.[35]

The higher acreages indicated here for plow users do not necessarily mean that acreages have increased these amounts after adoption of the plow. As suggested below, those who use plows tended to have large fields even when they were hand cultivators. Observations reveal, however, that they did increase their acreage somewhat after using a plow.

Nine of the fifteen Kwinella trainees responding to questions on acreage increases said that in 1966 they had doubled the number of acres planted in groundnuts from 1965, but that their food acreage had been unchanged. The six trainees or sponsors who had not increased their groundnut acreage in 1966 said they intended at least to double their acreage in 1967. Those who had already increased their groundnut acreage said they did not intend to expand their fields further in 1967. All trainees said they had had more acres in the 1965 season than most other hand cultivators in their villages.

2. The use of more land by plow-owning units can lead to land pressure in areas where it does not exist and can increase existing pressure in such areas as the Jarra District.

The ox plow users tend not only to expand their acreage but also to utilize land in larger blocks. The groundnut fields of most hand-cultivating production units are fairly close together to facili-

[35] *Ibid.*

tate cooperation. The 1966 Kwinella Mixed Farm Center trainees planned to have the fields of their production units continguous, thus taking the traditional practice one step further to make plowing more efficient. In fourteen cases, to have continguous blocks, the trainees had to clear bushy, fallow land not cultivated for eight to twenty years, or new land. In four cases the production units planned to make new, large block fields within a year or two. This trend toward field aggregation or block plowing is not a general pattern with plow users throughout the Gambia. The Wye College team's findings indicate that trainee compounds had 6 percent more fields per working man in 1965 and 9 percent more fields in 1966 than hand-cultivating compounds. In contrast, the Kwinella trainees at least set a goal of unfragmented landholdings that, if followed by other plow users, would lead to a different and more efficient pattern of land use.

3. Plow users in Central Gambia who consolidate lands also call back long-term land loans. Among the Mandinka, a person ideally obtains the right to use land by both obtaining permission of a village headman and clearing and using it. Even though this land may lie fallow for many years afterward, the person who first cleared it may give or lend the land to anyone he chooses. Land is most often loaned to patrilineally-related male members of the extended family, but more distant relatives, close friends, and strangers—particularly those in new compounds who will remain for a long time in the village—may also receive it on a long-term basis. The lending of land usually involves some reciprocity, which may range from political support in village meetings to the reciprocal lending of land in another area.

One instance in which loaned land was called back by a plow owner occurred in a small, old village in Kiang Central. The founding family in this village had farmed land over a large area, using different plots over the years and lending out much of it. The village moved to the new road in 1962, and some of the land became more valuable, since it was closer to the new settlement. But most remained out in long-term loans. In 1963 the head of the family, a rich trader, sent a boy to the center. Since then the trader has called back nearly all of the loaned land, almost forty acres. The land is not only close to the village but also fairly clear of stumps because of its long use. The trader now has three plows and uses them to farm a good part of the land in a block year after year. His wealth allows him to use large amounts of fertilizer, which compensates for some of the depletion of the soil, but his is an unusual case.

Several farmers have noted that plow owners like this trader had asked that their loaned land be returned, and several pre-1966 sponsors conceded that they had done so. Thus land now available to hand cultivators may decrease in the future. This trend points up the weakening of a "guaranteed subsistence" system in a society where the farmer is increasingly forced to depend upon himself and his more immediate family.

4. Ox plowing is beginning to reverse an existing trend toward the greater use of dry land for cash crop production to the exclusion of food crops. The food crops most affected have been early millet and sorghum, but late millet has also been affected. In the case of the first two crops, the increasingly prevalent small production units cannot spare the labor needed to scare birds that feed on these crops. Since 1949, early millet has nearly disappeared in Genieri villages. Findings for the village of Bumari (all hand cultivators) in the same area show that of twenty-eight farm heads, only one grew early millet and only five grew sorghum. Moreover, fields devoted solely to late millet have almost disappeared in Genieri, and only four such fields farmed by sixteen of the farm heads exist in Bumari.[36]

Production units, both *dabada* and whole compounds, have traditionally pooled their labor on millet fields. The disappearance of these fields is a further indication of the breakdown of the production unit's extended family structure. With the decrease in reciprocal labor, the main activity now holding production units together is food sharing. Late millet is valued more than rice during the period of heavy agricultural labor. Consequently, it is still grown, but it is intercropped with groundnuts.

Bumari supplied figures illustrating a general trend evident throughout Central Gambia. Of the total of 83 acres farmed in 1966 by the 28 farm heads, 70 acres, or 84.5 percent, were intercropped with groundnuts. Of the 70 acres, 43 acres were intercropped with late millet only; 24 acres were intercropped with late millet and sorghum; and 3 acres were intercropped with sorghum only. In the fields intercropped with late millet only, 76 percent of the land was used for groundnuts. In the fields intercropped with late millet and sorghum, 70 percent was used for groundnuts; and in the field intercropped with sorghum only, 97 percent of the field was used for groundnuts. Only 12.9 acres, representing 15.5 percent of the total acreage, was planted exclusively in early millet, late

[36] *The Changing Pattern*, p. 35.

millet, corn, and cassava. Bumari farmers pointed out that they are now growing much less food than in the past.

In the case of farmers using plows, intercropped groundnut acreage has shown a tendency to decrease. Traditionally, a farmer intercropped late millet every fourth or fifth row, but this rate of planting, if used by plow owners, would greatly decrease their yields per acre because of the wider rows. Data from the Wye College study suggest that plow-using farmers plant more acres of late millet alone than hand cultivators and obtain significantly higher yields per farmer than do hand cultivators.[37] It is possible that ox plow users will continue to increase their production of late millet to meet the increasing demand by hand cultivators for this grain. This need is sometimes met today by Fulas living some distance from the river who trade millet for rice produced by the Mandinka farmers.

With the change from late millet to rice as a staple grain, rice has become the major cash consumption item of the groundnut farmer. Consequently, during the last few years many villages away from the river have been stimulated to move closer to the riverine tidal swamps, which are much more productive than traditional rain-fed swamps.[38] While potential tidal-swamp rice land in Central Gambia is great, especially if more causeways are constructed, this type of migration probably cannot continue much longer without great pressure being brought to bear on the dry land near the river. The farmer who hopes to expand his land by using an ox plow thus has two factors working against him: other ox plow farmers are trying to expand their acreage as well, and outside farmers, usually hand cultivators, are moving in and competing for the same dry land.

One may ask whether, if these trends continue, there will be dry land available near the tidal swamps for the hopeful ox plow user. Three possibilities exist: 1. There may be a second migration back to the farms more distant from the tidal swamps. Farmers could produce only cash crops, either groundnuts or late millet, and buy or trade for food crops. 2. Farmers may also migrate to the city or to larger trading villages to look for other work. This second possibility is becoming increasingly attractive to Gambian youths not satisfied with the cash return of farming. Even today many young men, including those with primary educations, cannot find jobs. They stay in the towns and cities as long as they can, returning home only to visit friends or to eat well. This constitutes a loss of

[37] Wye College, *Report*, p. 7, Table A.
[38] The Gambia, *Statistical Summary*, pp. 12–13.

human resources and can often lead to political problems. 3. Some hand-cultivating farmers may become agricultural laborers. But this type of labor carries low status, and the number of laboring jobs will probably always be small. As agricultural equipment improves, there are fewer and fewer jobs that cannot be performed by members of the nuclear family. Moreover, even jobs related to agriculture are decreasing. For example, a new decorticating mill at Kaur uses conveyor belts to transfer nuts to ships, whereas the old mill at Kuntaur employed laborers to carry the sacks of nuts.

It is unclear which of these or other possibilities will be chosen by hand cultivators. Unless farmers return to less densely populated areas, it seems likely that as dry land near the rice swamps becomes less available the demand for ox plows will also decrease.

SOCIAL RAMIFICATIONS OF ACCEPTANCE

At this point some of the social ramifications of the acceptance of the ox plow will be considered. We have seen that relatively greater wealth is a prerequisite for the ownership or use of the ox plow. In addition, we have noted that primary acceptors of the plow are commonly men holding leadership positions in the social structure—in particular, district chiefs and leaders in larger villages. These primary acceptors tend not only to hold more wealth than secondary acceptors, but also to have more land available to them for farming, particularly through their ability to hire field labor on a large scale. This group is becoming a capitalized oligarchy derived, except for the African big traders, from the traditional oligarchy. The rich are becoming, and will probably continue to become, richer. These same men will be in the best position to take advantage of other farming innovations such as the tractor. Thus, the traditional oligarchy is being strengthened and entrenched by its capital resources.

It would not be correct to say, however, that the poor will become increasingly poorer. Many of the poor hand cultivators of today will some day own or use ox plows on their own land; their capital will come singly or from a combination of such factors as more efficient money management forced on them by an increasingly commercialized economic environment, the influx of more capital from off-season wage labor of younger males in the production units, and perhaps loans provided by the capitalized oligarchy, whose members are beginning to search for new ways to keep their capital working.

The newest member of the oligarchy, the African big trader, is often wealthier than his fellow members and is often much more experienced in the management of cash capital. Not all African big traders participate in farming. Those who do, see farming as a form of capital investment. They commonly use wage labor, and most of those observed operated one or more ox plows. This use was part of the general demonstration effect that led to the acceptance of the concept of the ox plow in Central Gambia. Nearly all of the 1966 trainees interviewed said they hoped to invest at least some of their new capital in trading, and nearly half said they would like to become big traders. A commonly demonstrated technique to gain capital for such a career is the use of the ox plow. While most big traders who farm did not reach their present capital level through farming, ox plow farming is almost the only capital-creating mechanism demonstrated by them that is available to farmers with some surplus wealth.

Acceptance and use of the ox plow is beginning to play a role in social stratification. In Central Gambia the Mandinka traditionally have been highly stratified into three castes. Paramount chiefs, chiefly lineages, and high-caste free men form one caste; part-time or full-time specialists such as blacksmiths, griots or praise singers, woodcarvers, and leatherworkers form a lower caste of free men; and slaves form the third and lowest caste. Traditionally, social mobility existed primarily within the castes, although Islam did offer some positions of high status and influence to low-caste members.

Today, members of the lower castes, in particular the specialists, are searching for new economic roles. Their search is in part a result of the decreasing dependence on their skills as consumer trade goods replace those items that they have traditionally made. While many are going to urban areas to search for cash-paying jobs, others are turning to trading. Their activities range from common petty trading and small scale commercial fishing to big trading. Many have entered the field by operating branches for big traders or by obtaining large amounts of goods on credit from the larger Bathurst trading companies. In the latter situation surety bonds are required, and often loans for the bonds are supplied by members of the new national political hierarchy. Another mechanism to gain more capital is the ox plow. While the traditional caste system persists, members of low-caste groups attempt to move, and have moved, into the capitalized oligarchy. Many hope to take advantage of this new social mobility by first gaining increased capital from farming with a plow.

Eight of the nineteen members of the Kwinella Mixed Farm Center class were from the specialist caste. Of the twenty members of the 1965 class, 35 percent were from this caste.

Caste lines are becoming blurred in other ways and through wider use of the ox plow may become more so. In Central Gambia the character of slavery has changed greatly in the last twenty years. In most cases, although slave-caste members often still live inside high-caste compounds, they operate as *dabada* production units on a par with their fellow high-caste *dabadalu*. They no longer perform agricultural labor for their patrons, and marriage between the specialist and slave castes is increasingly common. Slave-caste members living in their own compounds have usually completely broken their bond with their former patrons; they are operating as farmers with the same economic advantages and disadvantages as the specialist-caste members. Both castes, which perhaps may now be considered one large caste with two classes, are excluded from marriage, and thus kinship ties, with the high caste. No member of the slave class has been observed to own a plow, but this group will probably come to share the higher mobility aspirations of the specialist group.

Since World War II the trend in the Gambia has been toward the use of available capital for consumer goods, e.g., machine-made cloth, radios, bicycles, and prepared food items. Haswell emphasizes that as incomes rise, consumer items and improved housing absorb most of the new income.[39] It is suggested that this trend is accelerated in the case of production units using plows. The new capital of these units is often invested in non-income producing goods for an undefined period before significantly more capital is injected into farming. This may in part account for the low rate of investment in fertilizer as well as for the reluctance of most Emcot users to invest in a second plow (the Aplos, the second rung).

The members of the new capitalized oligarchy are setting patterns of capital investment that are helping to develop Central Gambia and that will probably be copied by others, particularly those farmers becoming richer through the use of plows. All members of the capitalized oligarchy are investing capital in trading as well as in modern agricultural innovations. Many are investing in groundnut trucks, taxis, and buses. Credit operations are also becoming a major area of capital investment.

The traditional pattern has been to invest surplus capital in cattle. Investment by farmers in plow bulls may to a certain extent be viewed as an extension of that pattern. The farmer who buys

---

[39] *The Changing Pattern*, p. 76.

plow bulls, however, intends to create capital. While investment in trade and credit operations existed in the past, the scale of these operations for the African traditionally was small compared with the capitalized oligarchy's practice today. It is likely that ox plow farmers will also attempt to make such investments as well as to enter trade.

The members of the capitalized oligarchy have the capital to influence and participate in decision-making at all levels of the society. The use of capital in the form of both gifts and loans to influence decision-makers at the village and district level is not a new phenomenon.[40] Return reciprocity for gifts and interest on loans given by leaders often traditionally involved supporting the leader's ideas in village and multivillage meetings. This pattern of obtaining political support continues today, with the major difference that the much greater capital of the capitalized oligarchy increases the potential scale.

Moreover, a whole new political arena has been opened. Free, universal suffrage elections for national and local government units since 1960 have meant that all Gambians can influence policies and decision-making in new areas or in areas they could affect only to a limited extent under traditional colonial rule. All Gambians have much at stake that is affected by political decisions; however, only the capitalized oligarchy have the money to make their personal, idiosyncratic demands heard on a basis equal to those of the general population. While it is true that their individual votes count no more than those of the individual members of the voting populace, this capitalized oligarchy can influence voters without actually buying votes. In public meetings, voiced support for their opinions will come from individuals with whom they have reciprocity and loan arrangements. These persons in turn have their own networks of political support. Political support is demonstrated in meetings, as well as in the voting booth.

In addition, most Gambians attempt to influence the decision-making process through contributions to political parties and to particular campaign treasuries. The general population usually contributes to a party as a village unit; either the village head collects a small contribution suggested by the party from all the adults in each compound, or one of the village male or female work groups contributes its earnings from an agricultural job. Usually village demands are the same as those made by individuals within a village.

[40] David P. Gamble, *Contributions to a Socio-Economic Survey of the Gambia* (London: Colonial Office, 1949), pp. 98–101 and *passim*.

Few individuals have the capital to influence the decision-making process in favor of a demand not expressed or shared by their fellow villagers. Those with idiosyncratic demands usually ask party members to find them jobs or extend them credit. Only the relatively wealthy can afford the surplus cash, often at least £2, to initiate this type of reciprocity. Even fewer Gambians, usually members of the capitalized oligarchy, can afford to give enough cash to parties and candidates to demand special consideration.

A common example of this is the district chief whose position under the post-independence government is weak; he attempts to guarantee his tenure through financial and verbal support of the ruling political party. Big traders also have much at stake in policy decisions affecting taxation, minimum wholesale and retail prices for essential foodstuffs, and interest rates.

Members of the capitalized oligarchy contribute or lend wealth as individuals, and as individuals they attempt to influence parties and each other. The oligarchy is united only to the extent that its members can assist one another financially and politically. The diversity of their demands for favorable government decisions limits cooperation. As ox plow farmers increase their surplus capital, they will probably attempt in turn to influence decision-making through the capitalized oligarchy and to follow the patterns of political reciprocity it demonstrates.

CONCLUSIONS

Introduction of the ox-drawn plow in Central Gambia is a qualified success as a program of directed culture change. As such, the program may be of value to other developing countries. It is doubtful that so many farmers in Central Gambia would either have adopted or have accepted the value of the ox plow if the government had not initiated a program to introduce it. While plows are sold in Senegal, their availability to Gambian farmers, largely because of limited credit facilities, has been minimal. Moreover, governmental links with the traditional oligarchy inadvertently assisted the early acceptance of the ox plow by this key reference group in the society. Besides their value as a reference group, the oligarchy demonstrated the economic value of the ox plow on the farmers' own terms. Other farmers followed their example, illustrating the lack of risk involved in the investment.

The government intensified the program at a time when many economic factors favored acceptance of a technological innovation that would allow the increasing number of smaller production units to utilize their time more efficiently to produce more cash. Today, cash is the key to successful participation in the increasingly commercialized Gambian society. The program has been successful in meeting its aim of increased productivity per farmer and increased national production of the cash crop.

The Department of Agriculture has stated that the ox plow will be accessible to all Gambian farmers, implying a desire to create an egalitarian agrarian society. But, to date, the agrarian society that is evolving is fairly inegalitarian, and the bulk of political decisions affecting it are determined directly or indirectly by a small sector of the population. This sector is the newly entrenched traditional oligarchy, the big traders, and to a lesser extent the wealthier farmers. The use of the ox plow alone has not created this oligarchy, but it has accelerated its formation and has strengthened it. Many farmers will probably join the oligarchy after creating capital through the use of the ox plow; many who will not join it will at least influence it.

The problem, particularly important in these early stages of the program, has been the limited amount of credit for plow bulls available to the average Gambian farmer. The relatively wealthy farmer, the members of the traditional oligarchy, and the big traders have often been the only members of the agrarian society with enough capital to purchase plow bulls. The government's limited monetary resources for agricultural credit and, in particular, for loans to buy plow bulls has been a major factor in limiting capitalization to one sector of the society. Today and in the immediate future, many of the capitalized oligarchy will have sufficient surplus investment capital from which to lend to average farmers to purchase bulls. Although many farmers will take advantage of such loans, the pattern of inequality in the agrarian society is being established now. While some farmers, given time, may move into the capitalized oligarchy, most will not. The general farming population will have a higher standard of living than today, but the capitalized oligarchy will also be richer. This is a pattern that many Gambians as well as other Africans abhor and wish to avoid.

Increasing the gross national product without parallel egalitarian social development is a possibility inherent in most development programs. The Gambian program has demonstrated its ability to increase production per farmer, personal income, and GNP. At this point the Gambian experience, as observed in the central section of the country, points up the need for a major infusion of development and foreign aid capital into its agricultural credit system. Other developing countries that aim to create or adapt an egalitarian agrarian sector in the context of a modern, commercialized economy will also need to pour a significant portion of their development program's capital into credit facilities.

CHAPTER 8

THE FOOD ECONOMY OF BA DUGU DJOLIBA, MALI
WILLIAM I. JONES

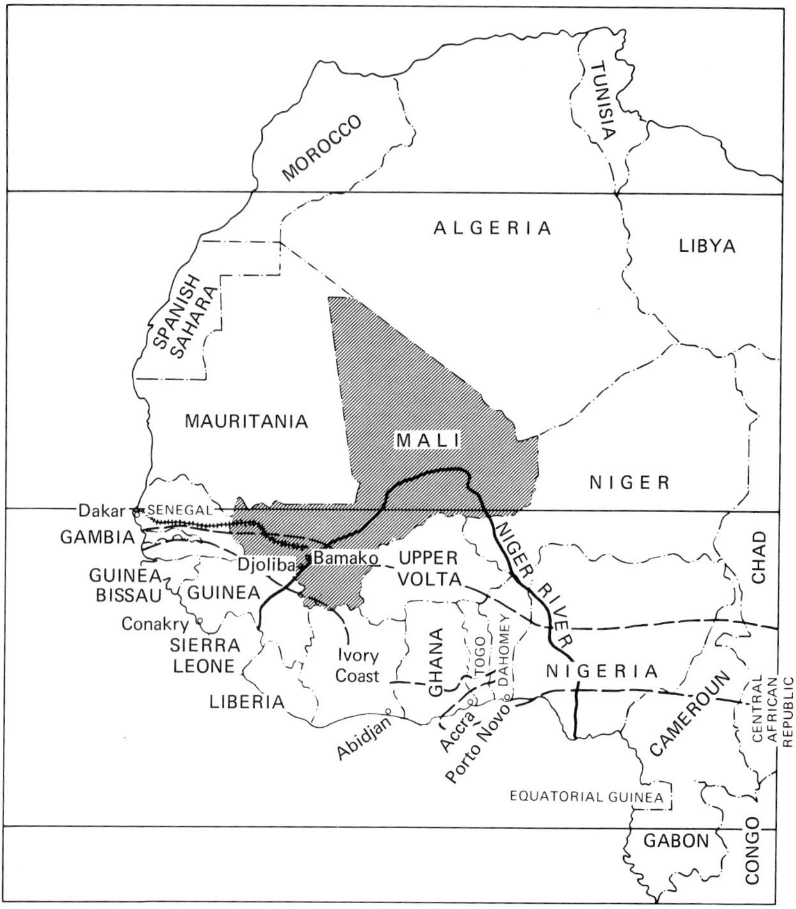

MOROCCO
TUNISIA
ALGERIA
LIBYA
SPANISH SAHARA
MAURITANIA
MALI
NIGER
Dakar
SENEGAL
GAMBIA
Bamako
Djoliba
UPPER VOLTA
NIGER RIVER
CHAD
GUINEA BISSAU
GUINEA
Conakry
SIERRA LEONE
Ivory Coast
GHANA
TOGO
DAHOMEY
NIGERIA
CAMEROUN
CENTRAL AFRICAN REPUBLIC
LIBERIA
Abidjan
Accra
Porto Novo
EQUATORIAL GUINEA
GABON
CONGO

In Ba Dugu Djoliba, food production, principally farming, is by far the dominant economic activity.[1] The only people who do not farm are the five school teachers and their families and one family of pastoral Fulbé attached to the village, which tends cattle in return for grain. These families are not really considered part of the village. Villagers may derive income from other sources—trade, French military pensions, fishing and stock-raising, minstrelsy, smithery, stipends as village chief and nurse, or remittances from relatives working elsewhere—but farming always comes first. Djoliba meets almost all of its food needs and earns some cash from sale of agricultural produce.

Djoliba is a compact village of about 1,700 people situated at the edge of the flood plain of the river called Niger by foreigners, but Djoliba by the Maninka. The village lies forty kilometers upstream from Bamako, Mali's capital, where the river runs lazily across a great plain south of the Maninka Mountains. At high water, in the summer, the village is on the river bank; in 1967 a flood even washed part of it away. During the rest of the year, the river is one and one-half kilometers away and is easily forded between Djoliba and Touréla. The river provides fish; its flood plains support rice and other supplementary crops. These strategic factors partly account for Djoliba's size—several times the average for the region—and its longevity.

In most aspects of its setting, however, Djoliba is just like thousands of savannah villages. The most important element is not the river but the rains. The yearly average is just over 1,000 millimeters, but annual variations from that average may be great. Generally, after a few useless showers in May, the rains pick up in June; two-thirds of the total rain falls in July, August, and September, before fading out in October and leaving half the year absolutely dry. Approaching the village then, one first sees the mango, silk-cotton and *néré* (*Parkia biglobosa*) trees beyond the brown fields covered only by a few stalks of last year's sorghum; next the mosque and other buildings. In the dry season, Djoliba is a very dusty place. In the rainy season, by contrast, it is virtually hidden by seas of waving sorghum, which grows right up to the courtyards.

[1] I first visited and lived in Djoliba during the first half of 1964 while doing research for my dissertation ("Economic Policy and Planning in Mali," forthcoming in 1971) with the help of a Hattie M. Strong grant. I subsequently revisited the village in March and September, 1968, during leaves from the U.S. Department of Agriculture, and in May, 1969, while on a mission for the International Bank for Reconstruction and Development. None of these organizations bears the slightest responsibility for my conclusions.

Djoliba and Environs

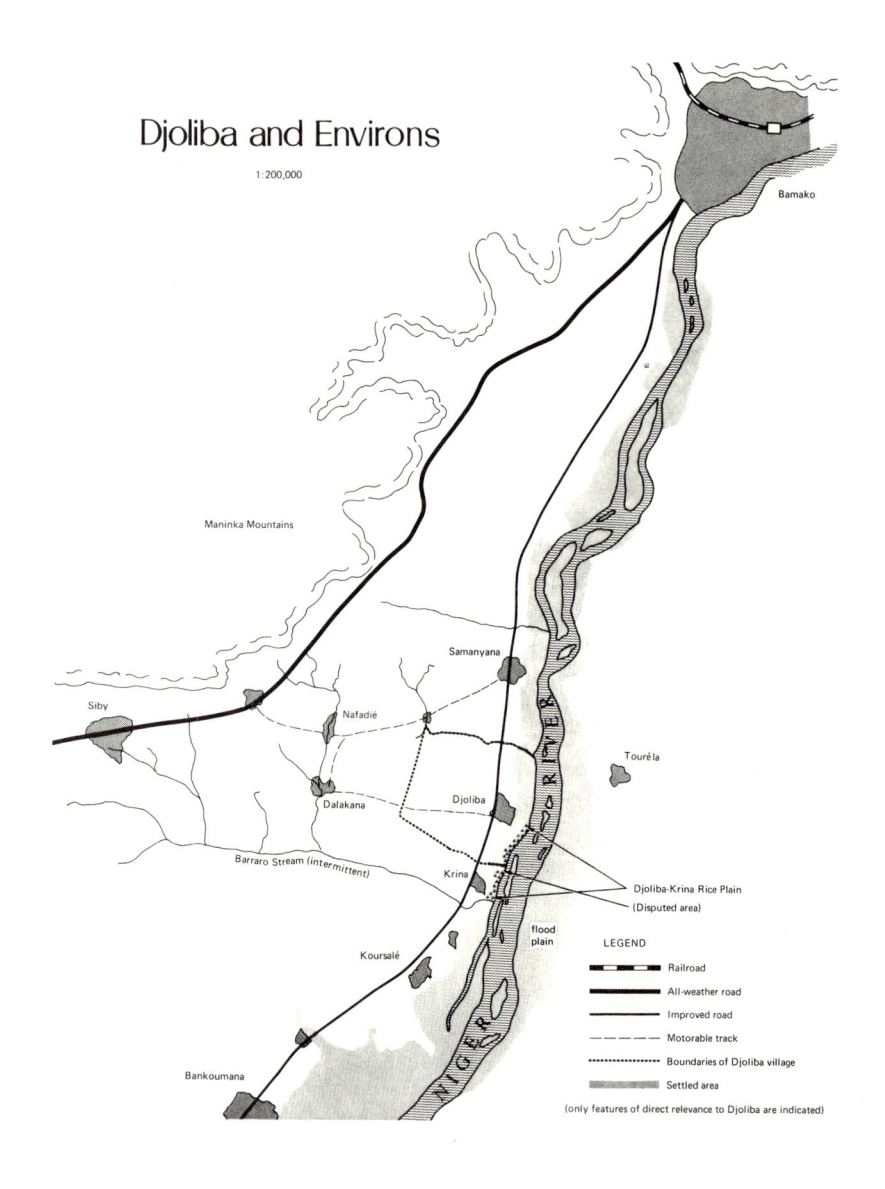

1:200,000

Bamako

Maninka Mountains

Samanyana

Siby

Nafadié

Touréla

Dalakana

Djoliba

Barraro Stream (intermittent)

Krina

Djoliba-Krina Rice Plain
(Disputed area)

Koursalé

flood
plain

Bankoumana

NIGER RIVER

LEGEND

▭▬▭	Railroad
▬▬▬	All-weather road
────	Improved road
─ ─ ─	Motorable track
•••••	Boundaries of Djoliba village
▨▨▨	Settled area

(only features of direct relevance to Djoliba are indicated)

Until recently, all structures were of sun-baked mud or mud brick, roofed with thatch. Houses were circular and joined by an outside wall to form a *lu*, the home for anywhere from 3 to 60 persons. Besides a sleeping hut for each adult, a *lu* would normally have one or more granaries, a rainy-season kitchen, a toilet area, an entrance hut, and a well, since Djoliba's water table is close to the surface. All doors but the entrance opened on the courtyard, the center of family life.

Most of the patrilineal descendants of Djoliba's founders and early residents lived in large *lu* in the center of town, inside the old defensive walls, once about three meters high but long unrepaired and now almost completely washed away by the rains. In the first half of this century, new and smaller *lu* were built north and west of the old town and away from the river. These are scattered less densely than those in the crowded center and do not all have all the features of proper *lu*. Still, the whole settled area is nowhere more than one kilometer across.

Between February, 1963, and the spring of 1966, Djolibans constructed 130 new houses on a Western model with tin roofs and enough cement in the walls to prevent erosion by the rains. The operation was paid for, organized, and administered by the United States Agency for International Development (AID) and cost more than $400,000.[2] Nevertheless, in spite of intentions stated by the Malian and U.S. governments, the project had virtually no effect on the way the village produces food or anything else. All of Djoliba's 168 *lu* took turns working on the houses, but 38 did not benefit from the result of the common labor.

The land is part of Djoliba's identity too. At low water, the village has 4,650 hectares of land; during the Niger flood, about 420 hectares are innundated. Djolibans know precisely the location of village boundaries, but these can be the subject of venomous dispute since neighboring villages do not always agree. However, land is not really scarce; in any year, less than one-fifth of the village land is cultivated.

[2] The presence of AID has generated a certain amount of literature. Some information on the project is still readily available in AID's files; the rest is in storage and difficult to retrieve, though not classified. One AID technician, Hermon Davis, made a movie about Djoliba; another, Thomas Callaway, wrote "A Countermagnet to the Capital: The Case of Djoliba," published in *International Development Review*, 8, no. 3 (1966), 18–21. These documents present the project in a very favorable light; the second contains a number of extraordinary distortions and factual errors. See my reply in *International Development Review*, 9, no. 2 (1967), 42–43. In all, this documentation is not very helpful in understanding the village.

The lateritic soils which compose the upland are rich in iron and aluminum oxides, like soils all across the savannah. Most of the area is sandy clay, highly compactible and very low in organic matter but not bad for crops. Some, though, is laterite mantle, unsuitable for cropping. Most of Djoliba's agriculture takes place on the upland.

Djoliba's food staple and by far its most important item of production is grain sorghum. A smaller amount of bullrush millet is grown—though it is less suited than sorghum to an annual rainfall of more than 700 millimeters—because it is preferred for making couscous and *degé*, a boiled porridge of millet, milk, and sometimes sugar. The village also grows rice in a semi-irrigated area along the river, some manioc at the high-water mark, and some maize and *fonio* (*Digitaria exilis*) on uplands. Part of the rice crop is marketed as paddy or after threshing, parboiling, and hand-milling.

Leguminous crops are *niébé* (*Dolichos unguiculatus*), *voandzu* or Bambara groundnuts (*Voandzeia subterranea*) for local consumption, and peanuts, mainly for sale. Some vegetables, like okra—without which no sauce is complete—and small local relatives of the tomato and eggplant are traditional. In recent years, Djolibans have begun to grow European-introduced vegetables, particularly tomatoes, which have now become the village's most important cash crop.

Other food is gathered. The most important of these crops are shea nuts, which furnish butter and cooking oil. *Sumbala*, a fermented delicacy, comes from the fruit of the *néré*, and the leaves and fruits of the baobab and other trees and bushes go into sauces and add important vitamins. During famines, wild grains are gathered. Mangoes and papayas are superabundant in season.

Cotton, practically the only nonfood crop, is of minor importance; and gathering of kapok has virtually ceased.

The diet is rounded out by fish and by small quantities of meat brought home by hunters or from the village's stock of chickens, guinea fowl, cattle, and goats.

Djoliba's food purchases are stimulants: kola nuts from the Ivory Coast and green tea now from China, with the sugar to go with it.

Large elements of Djoliba's food production are virtually the same as they were three centuries ago, when the village was founded, and represent techniques well adapted to the area and worked out centuries earlier. But Djoliban agriculture has by no means been static. Over the years, agriculture and stock-raising have been gaining at the expense of hunting and gathering. Furthermore, within the last fifty years Djoliban farmers have learned to grow several new crops to sell for money and the things money can buy; they have been adopting new tools. The food consumption pattern has even changed a little.

Recent years have shown that farmers' commitment to commercial agriculture is related to what the additional time spent growing crops will get them, as determined by the prices of produce and consumers' goods and by the availability of the latter. Except for the cash they need to pay taxes and to buy virtual necessities like cloth, Djolibans have a "subsistence alternative." The farmers also judge which of the commercial crops that they know how to grow will give them the most return for their work. To understand these changes and how they fit into Djolibans' lives, it is necessary to look at the village's past.

HISTORICAL ROOTS

Most of the food-producing techniques used in Djoliba today are part of a system evolved gradually and long ago to fit the ecology. The similarity of agricultural practices over the vast expanse of savannah from Senegal to eastern Chad proves the system's utility. Its great age is indicated by the earliest archeological evidence.[3] In the remote past the ancestors of today's Djolibans lived chiefly by gathering. Human population was sparse even by standards of that time. As lengthening dry seasons created a yearly gap in vegetable food sources, the people invented tools and turned to hunting.[4] The drying of the Sahara forced its inhabitants into oases, including the Nile Valley, where they domesticated wheat at least by 5500 B.C., and south into the savannah where the man/game ratio was more favorable and hunting long continued to be the most important way of obtaining food. Local myths attest this importance.[5]

Sudanese agriculture developed along lines different from those

[3] The best compendium of archeological and other evidence is Raymond Mauny, *Tableau géographique de l'ouest africain au moyen âge d'après les sources écrites, la tradition et l'archéologie* (Dakar: Institut Fondamental de l'Afrique Noire, 1961). See p. 251.

[4] On vegetation changes, see P. A. Allison, "Historical Inferences to be Drawn from the Effects of Human Settlement on the Vegetation of Africa," *Journal of African History*, 3, no. 2 (1962), esp. 246–49. On the invention of tools, see J. Desmond Clark, "The Prehistoric Origins of African Culture," *Journal of African History*, 5, no. 2 (1964), 166–67.

[5] Probably the best introduction is Germaine Dieterlen, *Essai sur la religion bambara* (Paris: Presses Universitaires de France, 1951). The author began her work among the "Bambara" in the Djoliba region.

of its North African analog. Hunters probably began by broadcasting local wild grains around their encampments. Gradually, selection improved varieties; experience improved techniques. Around 2500 B.C. further migrations from the Sahara taxed the supply of game and gatherable food and gave a big impetus to agriculture.[6] Sorghum and millet became the staples; other crops of local origin were domesticated during the same period. From the time the Sudanese began smelting iron, probably a few centuries before the Christian era, they used iron hoes and hatchets for farm work much as Djolibans do today.

Social organization reflected the needs of the basic economic activity—food procurement. As agriculture supplemented hunting, migratory bands formed small villages to clear land and farm it until its fertility declined. Then the village moved, unless its strategic location justified adoption of bush-fallow agriculture and the longer walks to more distant fields it implied.

From the early centuries of the Christian era to 1591, the great trading states of Ghana, Mali, and Songhai thrived in the western savannah. Their power was based on controlling the trade in gold, salt, and other items between the forest areas to the south and the merchants of the desert, who furnished the Mediterranean world with its gold. We know about this period mainly from Arab travellers, but they tell us little about organization of the countryside.

The fall of Songhai to Moroccan invaders in 1591 ended the imperial era. A high level of violence marked the next three hundred years. The strong demand for slaves for shipment to the Americas encouraged it. Djoliba was founded toward the beginning of this period, but it is only toward its end that we begin to have a reasonably good picture of life in such villages.

Precolonial Djoliba

The village was founded in the seventeenth century after the imperial period and at about the time the first Englishmen were settling North America, and it has not moved since. The present Keita village chief (*dugutigi*) is of the fourteenth generation from the founders—two brothers and their uncle, all of the Keita

[6] See Clark, "Prehistoric Origins," pp. 180–81, and also J. Desmond Clark, "The Spread of Food Production in Sub-Saharan Africa," *Journal of African History*, 3, no. 2 (1962), 212, 215, for the most likely account. The assertion by George Peter Murdock that the Sudanese "invented" agriculture by 4500 B.C.— see his *Africa: Its People and Their Culture History* (New York: McGraw-Hill, 1959), pp. 66–71—is not justified.

Kanda-si.[7] One of them is buried near the old wall. Tradition does not tell us whether they were leaders of a hunting band which settled down—the usual way old villages were founded [8]—or whether they came from a sedentary village in the Maninka heartland.

In the late eighteenth and early nineteenth centuries, the village food economy was almost completely autarkic. Prior to 1860, no overarching political authority imposed order. Any village strong enough established hegemony over its neighbors, became head of a unit called a *kafo*, and levied taxes on all trade within its reach.[9] The situation was hardly conducive to trade. Probably no agricultural goods were traded except kola and salt. Village autarky was the rule in other parts of the economy as well. Division of labor within the village assigned minstrelsy and entertainment, smithery, weaving, leather working, and woodworking to castes; farming, fishing, and hunting were the activities of free men.[10]

In the nineteenth century, Djoliba had no market. The first village market in the area was started at Samanyana, a village of Fulbé immigrants 6 kilometers downstream from Djoliba, in the early 1800's; others are twentieth-century creations.[11]

Djoliba managed to survive the violent centuries without a defensive fort and with only meager walls. Though large, it did not conquer its small neighbors and exercised suzeraignty over noncontiguous Keita villages on the basis of kinship, not conquest.

---

[7] All members of a clan are designated by the same *dyamu*, such as Keita, and are, in principle, descended from the same ancestor. In the case of the Keita, the clan ancestor—Sundiata, who founded the Mali Empire in 1235—is so remote that no one remembers the names of intervening male progenitors. The clan is divided into *si*—groups that *can* trace their descent to a common ancestor, e.g., Kanda Keita, common ancestor of the Kandasi.

[8] A large number of old villages have the names of trees plus the suffix *koro*, "beneath," indicating that they were originally meeting places for hunters. There are many Banankoro, Sirakoro, Sanankoro, Torokoro, Dialakoro, etc.

[9] Mungo Park, who traveled in the region in 1795–97 and 1805, vividly describes the situation. See, for instance, the incident at Bady in 1805 in *The Journal of a Mission to the Interior of Africa in the Year 1805* (Philadelphia: Edward Earle, 1815), pp. 148–50.

[10] See Mambi Sidibé, "Les gens de caste ou *nyamakala* au Soudan français," *Notes Africaines*, no. 81 (1959), pp. 13–17. Emile Leynaud explains the religious and noble character of farm work in "Fraternités d'âge et sociétés de culture dans la haute vallée du Niger," *Cahiers d'Etudes Africaines*, 6, no. 21 (1966), pp. 41–68.

[11] See Jean-Claude Woillet (*Les Marchés* [Paris: Bureau pour le Développement de la Production Agricole, 1962], pp. 2–3, in series La modernisation rurale dans la haute-vallée du Niger; Mission Leynaud-Roblot) regarding first appearance of intervillage markets.

Djoliba was still quite independent, though not sovereign, when the French conquered the area in 1883. It evidently survived through a supple, nonaggressive foreign policy and a willingness to pay tribute when overwhelming force required it. This was certainly the case when Samanyana was strong, or when the combined forces of Bamako, Mourdiah, and Segou defeated Samanyana and pillaged the whole area in the 1840's,[12] or when troops of El Hadji Oumar Tall's Tukolor Empire garrisoned the Touréla ford in the 1860's. But Djoliba had not succumbed to direct outside rule as neighboring Samanyana and Nafadié had—certainly a factor in the village's intense feeling of solidarity.

The French presence introduced new rules. The Maninka, including Djolibans, with fresh grievances against the Bamana and Tukolor, did not form a grand alliance against the French. But Djoliba's men did join their fellow Maninka, Almany Samory Touré, when his army fought the French at Ouéyako, 35 kilometers downstream, in 1883.[13] The Maninka lost, Samory left the area to the French, and Djoliba was quick to make its peace with the new masters. When colonial administration was organized in 1888, Djoliba was made the seat of the Balaouléna canton (*kafo*) composed of the scattered Keita villages already attached to it. Having the canton chief in the village helped get better treatment from the foreign rulers.

Foreign Rule

French rule lasted from 1888 to 1960. It brought taxes and peace, both of which altered Djoliba's food economy. Peace radically lowered the cost of moving goods. It brought foreign merchants and more foreign goods, and it permitted Djoliba's leather workers and weavers to move to Bamako.

The railroad, built for military needs and commercial hopes, also facilitated movement. In 1904 it was opened from Bamako, its closest point to Djoliba, to Kayes, where goods were stored and shipped on the Senegal River at high water. The system was not satisfactory. By 1905, authorities realized that agricultural products were not moving westward by rail. They cut the rates for such

---

[12] See Claude Meillassoux, "Histoire et institutions du *kafo* de Bamako d'après la tradition des Niaré," *Cahiers d'Etudes Africaines*, 4, no. 14 (1963), 193–94.

[13] Although Djoliba's unfriendly neighbors insist that the village sent emissaries to the French the night before and offered to switch sides in mid-battle.

products to practically nothing[14] and still had to build a rail line from Kayes to Dakar, completed only in 1924.

Direct taxes furnished only a minute part of the colony's revenue; their chief purpose was to incite villages like Djoliba to produce and market agricultural products that French industry could use. Besides taxes, Djolibans had to contribute to the Bamako district Native's Provident Society, through which the government collected reserves of food on the theory that only such measures would save the improvident natives from starvation. Djoliba's contribution generally took the form of work on the "commandant's field" to grow sorghum for the reserve, a task which was much resented because the labor demands conflicted with the people's own farming schedule. The people assert that they never saw the food again. Djolibans didn't mind communal labor on roads during the dry season nearly as much, but all forced labor was resented. Fortunately for the village, it was far from French plantations, so forced labor disrupted its economy very little.

Djoliba and its neighbors needed cash crops to pay their taxes and to be able to buy the new French goods. The French tried cotton, but failed.[15] Even the small, indigenous culture died out as imported textiles undercut local artisans. Peanuts were the answer. The new culture was easily learned because the plant behaves much like the Bambara groundnut.[16] Soon after the railroad was opened, Djoliba was producing fifteen or more tons of unshelled peanuts per year.

After World War II, the French began, for the first time, to invest sizable amounts of money in their colonies. Because Djoliba was head of a canton, it was singularly able to take advantage of these investments. In the 1950's, the government built a two-room school and an infirmary. It also spent $24,000 building a small dam on the Barraro stream near Krina, a canal, and a dike along the Niger to permit water control for growing irrigated rice on 250 hectares of

[14] See discussion and figures in Gouvernement Général de l'AOF, *Les chemins de fer en Afrique occidentale; Notices publiées à l'occasion de l'Exposition Coloniale de Marseille*, 2 vols. (Corbeil: Crété, 1906), 2, 120–31.

[15] There is an extensive literature on attempts to increase the production and staple length of Sudanese cotton. Any one interested should begin looking in Paule Brasseur, *Bibliographie générale du Mali* (Dakar: Institut Fondamental de l'Afrique Noire, 1964), under the headings "Cotton," "Office du Niger," and "Auguste Chevalier."

[16] Bambara groundnuts are native to the area. They have a lower oil yield than peanuts but are richer in protein and digestible carbohydrates. On the average, they yield 250 kg./ha. (partly because they are frequently intercropped) compared with an average of 1,000 kg./ha. for peanuts under present techniques.

land, 190 of them allocated to Djoliba.[17] Machines did most of the earth-moving, but they were supplemented by village labor, for which the people were paid in cash. As we shall see, the consequences of this project on Djoliba's food production were not all one might have expected.

Since Independence

Mali's break with Senegal at independence meant that Djoliba's peanuts were trucked to the Ivory Coast from Bamako for the next three years and the imported consumers' goods it bought were trucked back. Djolibans did not bear the increase in cost directly. Mali lost its protected Senegalese market for rice, however, and had to cut the producers' price for paddy by 25 percent,[18] which substantially reduced the Djoliban farmers' enthusiasm for the hard labor involved in growing semi-irrigated rice.

Mali's Five-Year Development Plan promised a new deal for rural Mali: new socialist structures to end exploitation by private merchants, more technical assistance, and loans to finance purchases of fertilizer, pesticides, plows, carts, and the like. In return, the primary sector was supposed to generate over half the total growth of output, projected at an extremely high 8.9 percent per year.[19] In view of the results expected, planned government investment in agriculture for villages like Djoliba was quite modest.[20]

Actually, the plan years—1961-66—saw Djoliba's farmers reduce their dependence on commercial agriculture and increase their reliance on their subsistence alternative. New institutions were set up, but they did not particularly benefit the villagers. Djoliba already had an extension worker nearby, so the government's failure to expand the extension service nationwide was of no import.

But Mali's commercial difficulties, resulting from the government's large deficits and its ambitious investments in state transport and industrial enterprises, did hurt Djoliba's farmers. Imports were

[17] See M. Guillaume, "Les aménagements hydro-agricoles de riziculture et de culture de décrue dans la vallée du Niger," *L'Agronomie Tropicale*, 15, no. 2 (1960), 143.

[18] See Modibo Keita, "Discours à l'Assemblée Nationale, 20-I-1961," in *Modibo Keita: Discours et interventions* (Moscow: Progress, [1965?]), p. 25.

[19] The Malian plan has been revised several times and the full details have never been published. Pending publication of my book (note 1 above), the most complete treatment is by Samir Amin in *Trois expériences africaines de développement: le Mali, la Guinée et le Ghana* (Paris: Presses Universitaires de France, 1965).

[20] For every unit invested in dry-land agriculture during the plan, 2.5 units of increased production were supposed to result; investments in small irrigation schemes were to produce increments of 0.4 units per unit investment.

scarce and expensive when available, and the prices farmers received for their commercial crops did not rise, so their terms of trade declined greatly. Just about every *lutigi* (head of a *lu*) in Djoliba paid $5 for a share in the village cooperative in hopes of obtaining farm equipment on credit, but none was available.[21]

The central authorities urged Djolibans to convert from family and individual cultivation to farming by the village collectivity on the theory that this would represent a return to an earlier socialistic condition that had been distorted by colonial rule. This was a serious misreading of the traditional order, and the villagers, as we shall see, treated the collective field with suspicion.

As construction of new houses under the model-village program moved ahead, AID attempted to give Djoliba some productive facilities. These and an attempt to save the situation with a vocational school ended in failure. In 1960 the French Agricultural Production Development Office (Bureau pour le Développement de la Production Agricole, or BDPA, a state development corporation) had begun studies of the region aimed at developing it, but implementation of the program got off to a false start in 1965. Even after development efforts took a more reasonable turn in 1967, the principal effect on Djoliba was to make available the inputs needed to grow cotton, though it should be noted that Djolibans were still paying for their plows.[22]

In 1966, the government spent another $2,000[23] to improve the Djoliba-Krina rice area, but this did not seem to solve the technical or economic problems. The biggest impact on Djoliba's farmers seemed almost inadvertent. The state cannery at Baguineda, across the river and downstream from Bamako, which began operations in 1964, was supposed to get its tomatoes from a state-run irrigated plantation that Bulgarian agronomists were setting up nearby. Instead, the cannery (SOCOMA) ended up providing a guaranteed market for tomatoes at $60 a ton with pickup at the village, even though the factory was running at a substantial loss. Djoliba and its neighbors began growing tomatoes and marketing them in a big way.

The changes in the food economy that did and did not occur

---

[21] I have analyzed the effects of planning in Mali in somewhat more detail in "Mali: The Economics of the Coup," *Africa Report*, 14, nos. 3 and 4 (April–May, 1969), 23–26, 51–53.

[22] As of September, 1968, a fact confirmed by records of the BDPA in Bamako.

[23] Five hundred thousand Mali francs equaled $2,000 in 1966, $1,000 after devaluation in 1967. By 1966 the franc's overall purchasing power, though skewed by controls, actually reflected the post-devaluation rate. We will use the pre-devaluation rate throughout.

may seem a bit mysterious unless we understand the institutional nature of Djoliba and something about the techniques and economics of producing food.

VILLAGE ORGANIZATION

Djoliba is not a simple collection of 1,700 individuals. As one might suspect, relations between individuals are mediated by a host of institutions, many of them based on lineage. For food production and consumption, there are few things the 1,700 Djolibans do as a village; the people who live in one *lu* usually act together for such purposes. Failure to understand this doomed the government's program for development through collective agriculture.

Clans

Djoliba and other large villages in the savannah zone are alliances of clans. Clan members are called by their *diamu*, for example, Keita, Berté, Koné, Koïta. All members are supposedly descended from a single male ancestor. In fact, there are a variety of ways to acquire a *diamu*. For instance, the descendants of captives born in a Koné *lu* become people of unfree status but ultimately with the *diamu* Koné. Militarily successful families could grow large indeed.

Djoliba is a Keita village; the Keita first cleared the bush and covenanted with the local gods. Now about half of the inhabitants are Keita.

Everyone's status is defined by how his ancestors came to Djoliba, particularly whether as free men of no caste (*horon*), as captives (*dyon*), or as men of caste (*nyamakala*). Everyone is linked to the Keita founders by the chain of hospitality or by master-captive relationships, even though the non-Keita's ancestors may have arrived at a remote date. Every free or caste settler becomes the guest of some *horon* already established there; he owes his host respect, while the host arranges things for his guest and looks after his interest in village affairs and quarrels. It would be unthinkable to exploit this relationship for gain.

Such relationships are quite relevant today. Moriba Koné is a particularly dynamic farmer, a veteran of French campaigns in Tonkin and Algeria, recipient of a large pension, and head of the Djoliba cooperative (Groupment Rural de Production et de Secours Mutuel, or GRPSM). In 1964, he was also taking a leading role in organizing house construction under the model-village program and in dealing with the Americans, who sent him on a trip to the United States. By 1964, Djolibans began to feel that he was usurping the leadership prerogatives of the village chief, by tradition and election the eldest male of the descent line from the Keita village founders.

The problem was solved tactfully. People repeatedly reminded Moriba Koné of his family's arrival in Djoliba over a century before. His male ancestor, a hunter, decided to settle there and became the guest of the Keita, who arranged for him to marry a Keita. "Therefore," people kept telling Moriba, "you are half Keita —one of us," thus also reminding him that the Keita are Djoliba's founders and the Koné's hosts.

Traditional Village-wide Institutions

The alliance of the clans is also expressed in the *ladjé*, a council with representatives of all *horon* lineages that discusses and settles village-wide problems. The Mali government formalized the village council and set up free elections, but actually this changed nothing. The elected chief and councillors have always been the men with the traditional right to represent their sublineages. Since the officially prescribed number of councillors did not accommodate all those with rights to representation on the *ladjé*, the others come anyhow but are known officially as "notables." A head of the Koïta clan, musicians-entertainers-historians of the *dyéli* caste, represents the castes and serves as the village chief's spokesman and interlocutor.

Common experience, integration into agricultural life, and political training—all across clan and caste lines—are provided by the youth society, or *ton*. The traditional role of these societies among the Maninka included dancing, agricultural work, and initiation into and instruction in traditional religious values and social customs.[24] The form and functions have evolved in recent years. Prior

---

[24] The best sources on the *ton* are Solange de Ganay, "Le *to*, société d'entr'-aide chez les Bambara du Soudan Français," *Actes du Ve Congrès International des Sciences Anthropologiques et Ethnologiques* (Philadelphia, 1956); Emile Leynaud, "Fraternités d'âge"; and Claude Meillassoux, *Urbanization of an African Community: Voluntary Associations in Bamako* (Seattle: University of Washington Press, 1968). Meillassoux discusses the village roots of existing voluntary associations in the capital. The relationship between the relatively secular *ton* and the relatively sacred *kari* is complex and unclear to me. Leynaud discusses it. I found Djolibans reluctant to discuss vestiges of the traditional religion, including circumcision and the *kari*.

to independence, possibly as early as 1930, the *gumbé* drum and dance style were introduced from the coastal regions;[25] Djoliba's *ton* adopted the name Banankoro Gumbé Ton, indicating that they met under the silk-cotton tree, though they did not actually use a *gumbé* drum. In 1961, the ruling party decided to integrate the organization as its youth wing; it became the Mali Ton.

When the BDPA mission surveyed Djoliba in 1960, the Banankoro Gumbé Ton had 69 members, most of whom were in their early twenties. It held dances and engaged in agricultural work strictly on a contract basis and for compensation, which was used to sponsor big parties. That year, the *ton* fielded most of its members for ten days of farm labor to clear three old sorghum fields and mound the soil to receive the seed in five more fields covering about 50 hectares. The *ton* received money equivalent to 10 cents per person per day, plus two kola nuts per person per day, plus tobacco and food.[26]

Traditionally, many Maninka *ton* were devoted primarily to agricultural work and labored not only for compensation but also to help old people without children and others who were victims of misfortune. In the years prior to independence, Djoliba's *ton* was not operated on a basis of altruistic village solidarity and performed an insignificant portion of the village's total agricultural work. This was the organization that politicians tried to turn into an engine of political education and agricultural collectivization.

With the change in name to Mali Ton, Djoliba's youngest schoolteacher—an outsider, but more nearly acceptable because he was a Keita—became party youth commissar of the village and adviser to the *ton*, a role traditionally reserved for an adult man and woman of captive ancestry. Membership was broadened to include all village youth of relevant ages. From the young people's point of view, the *ton*'s purpose was still mainly recreational. Many of the songs were in praise of Mali, the party, or party heroes like Modibo Keita, Mamadou Konaté, or Oussein Coulibaly, but the dance steps remained entirely as before. The party was mainly interested in getting *ton* members to work on the village collective field and to do other work of general interest—called human investment or work for honor by the government and *fasobara* (father's place work) by the villagers.

[25] Meillassoux, *Urbanization*, discusses some Bamako *gumbé* (pp. 116–30). He believes that the name *gumbé*, which does not belong to any local language, comes from the English "company" via Sierra Leone.

[26] Leynaud, "Fraternités d'âge," p. 60.

New Village-wide Institutions

Mali's political parties were organized in 1946. They had supporters in Djoliba, but no real organizations there until after independence. Moriba Keita, as canton chief a servant of the colonial administration, supported the Sudanese Progressive Party, then the party favored by that administration. But Braima Keita, the next oldest descendant of the founders and the village chief, backed the Union Soudanaise-RDA. The rivalry between the two men and their factions is a classic one, ultimately based on dissension between a man's wives.[27] When the RDA came to power in 1957, the canton chiefs were eliminated; Moriba Keita lost face, his faction was reduced, and Djoliba turned to the ruling party.

After the RDA had absorbed and eliminated its rivals, it worked to reinforce its village support. Djoliba got a village party committee with an executive bureau of secretary general, political secretary, treasurer, and commissioners for conflicts, propaganda, youth, women, and so on, just like the party organs at higher levels. The party committee was composed of members of the *ladjé* from Braima's faction.

The government was making a variety of demands upon villages, including urging them to cultivate one-fifth of the cropland as a village collective field. In October, 1961, the president called on them to set up collectives with an area of one hectare for each family in the village and to form collective work teams to cultivate the *foroba*—the fields of each *lu*—in turn during two days per week.[28]

Village leaders were torn between defending Djoliban traditions against outside interference and acceding to the government's notions of progress and modernity in return for such expected benefits as public investments in schools. As is frequently the case, the school principal, Madani Traoré, was political secretary of the party committee and a key man in pressing for the changes the government wanted. His insistence on reforms led to resentment and his transfer after his wife died in circumstances some thought to be suspicious.

Moriba Keita's fortunes were so low that the *ladjé* attempted to deprive him of his rights in the rice plain by claiming that a tra-

---

[27] *Fa-den-ya* ("rivalry") comes from *fa-den* (sons of the same father, but of different mothers).

[28] Modibo Keita, "Appel à la Nation," *Modibo Keita*, p. 80 (a radio speech launching the plan October 1, 1961).

ditional cattle trail ran across his section. In 1961, an armed confrontation occurred when the dominant faction tried to drive cattle across Moriba's land and Moriba's *lu* determined to stop them. Outside authorities had to be called to mediate. The *ladjé* presented the dispute as an action against reactionary elements, but the strong overtones of traditional rivalry tended to compromise Djoliba's reputation as a progressive village.

In 1962, Moriba Keita used the Bamako currency riot as a pretext to convert to the RDA. A new and more diplomatic school principal, Arouna Dembelé, arrived. A new party committee was elected. The new group, a combination of younger men, the old canton chief (now a militant), the teachers, and the male nurse, had fewer members who were also on the *ladjé*. With Dembelé as political secretary and Moriba Keita as conflicts commissioner, the new committee presented the *ladjé* with a serious and supple challenge. It vigorously supported the model-village project and, in food production, the collective field.

The "progressive" elements persuaded the village in 1963 to try growing cotton on a small collective field. The land was ill suited, the field was ill tended, and the harvest was negligible. Nevertheless, from then to the coup of November, 1968, the village had a collective field. It was considered a political obligation—a price to be paid for the benefits expected from being considered progressive. Working it devolved mainly on the Mali Ton; the results improved after 1963 but remained much worse than those on family or individual plots. In 1967, the collective field covered 23.5 hectares: 15 of rice, 5 of sorghum, and 3.5 of cotton.[29] Proceeds from sale of the harvest constituted the "profits" of the cooperative or GRPSM, with a part going to the Mali Ton.

The cooperative was the government's principal institution for revolutionizing food production and marketing. Djoliba's success in setting up its GRPSM early and in getting its families to buy shares gave the village its principal claim to being progressive and a chance to be considered for the model-village project and others. However, the GRPSM itself did not affect farming operations except insofar as it supervised the collective field. It did not succeed in getting any credits from the government for purchase of plows, carts, fertilizer, or anything else; the government was short of funds and particularly of foreign exchange to import these items. The

---

[29] Information from unpublished BDPA survey. I am indebted to Coulibaly and de la Chappelle, heads of the BDPA upper-valley project, for their cooperation.

GRPSM did, however, have its own budget from sales of collective-field produce [30] and from handling sales of consumers' goods over which the state trading company had a monopoly—matches, salt, sugar, lamp oil, and others. The GRPSM dealt with the state company and represented it in Djoliba, storing goods in the Mali Ton's new building, built by human investment,[31] or in Moriba Koné's *lu*, which also served as the store.

The GRPSM can be headed by a non-Keita because it is a nontraditional organization and because Koné is recognized for his honesty and ability to deal with outsiders. He sells kola nuts and other nonmonopoly items on the side for his own account. The GRPSM also handles sale of agricultural products to the government, but this is in principle only. Moussa Drabo, the extension worker in Krina, and government commercial representatives have the scales and run the operation.

The *lu*, or family compound, is Djoliba's basic institution for the production and distribution of food. The major clans are far too big to function together as farming, eating, or even tax-paying units. For these purposes, the people who live in one *lu* act together. Occasionally, one man pays the taxes of more than one *lu*; he is *carton tigi* because he has the government tax card. Occasionally, due to space restrictions, relatives who farm together must live apart, or, more often, the inhabitants of one *lu* will keep separate granaries and kitchens and have separate meals. But these are exceptions.

Today, the average Djoliban *lu* is made up of ten people: typically a man, two wives, four children, a younger brother, and his wife and child. Sometimes there will be an unmarried young brother or surviving parent. Composition and size vary widely. The

---

[30] These proceeds were called "profits," though they were virtually the entire return to the collective-field operation. The bank account of the GRPSM was made up of its share capital, these "profits" from the collective field, a very small percentage of turnover on goods sold to villagers for the government commercial monopolies, and, starting late in 1964, the proceeds from the AID-sponsored egg-production operation (see below). In 1965, when *L'Essor* interviewed Moriba Koné, he reported GRPSM bank assets of $2,280 ("Fruit du travail communautaire; Djoliba village modèle temoigne de notre effort de développement," *L'Essor* [Bamako], June 14, 1965, p. 4).

The egg operation was highly profitable (AID bore establishment costs and furnished a guaranteed market and transportation) and accounts for over half the assets. The cooperative was unable to buy farm equipment with its funds and was not free to dispose of them to its members.

[31] The *ton* provided most of the labor. Purchases of galvanized sheet for the roof and of wood beams were paid for by the GRPSM with subsidies from government and party (see *L'Essor*, "Fruit du travail").

older *lu* of the Keita founders and their early guests were in the old central village until 1965 and include a wider variety of relatives. The largest of all—with 60 members—is the Kanté clan which specializes in fishing. Its members have not moved into the new houses because they cannot get a block of houses big enough to permit them all to live together. The newer, smaller *lu* are formed of more recent arrivals or disgruntled younger brothers who have broken off from their old *lu*. Still, more than 90 percent of the males in 1964 continued to live in the *lu* of their birth, even after marriage.

The *lu*, like the rest of Maninka life, is ruled by the principle of *fasiya*, domination of the younger generations by the older and of younger brothers and cousins by older ones. When the *tigi*, or head, of anything dies, the prerogatives pass not to his son but to younger brothers, if any, then to the oldest male of the next generation. *Fasiya* means that *lutigi* are generally old men. They possess the agricultural implements, the farming rights to land accorded by the *dugutigi*, the harvest resulting from the *lu*'s efforts, and any cattle the *lu* may own. They are responsible for organizing the farm work and making the management decisions, even for distributing grain to the women for cooking.

The common farming efforts of the *lu* take place on the *foroba* ("big possession").[32] Once a *lu* has acquired the right to use land, it retains that right for the duration of use, and the possessions of a *lu* cannot be divided. This is less than crucial, since reasonably fertile upland is not scarce, though variations in fertility and nearness to the village set a premium on some land and generate controversy.

The *foroba* is devoted chiefly to growing sorghum. Intercropping is widely practiced; all possible associations can occur, but the most popular are sorghum-*niébés* and sorghum-peanuts. Millet and Bambara groundnuts are also grown on the *foroba*.

Individual farming is also part of the system. Women have their individual plots (*dyomforo*) near the *lu* to grow the ingredients of the sauces, which will make a Djoliban cook famous—or infamous. These plots are often fenced to keep out goats and other small predators. Men, too, may have *dyomforo* to raise crops that will help pay the bride price or buy a bicycle. This eases the great de-

---

[32] Leynaud misleadingly calls *foroba* a "common village possession" ("Fraternités d'âge," p. 41). In an earlier work he made it clear that the *foroba* "belongs" to the *lu*, not to the village. See Emile Leynaud, *La modernisation rurale dans la haute-vallée du Niger; Mission Leynaud-Roblot*, 8 vols. (Paris: BDPA, [1962]), 1, 8.

pendence of the younger males. Work on the *foroba* comes first, however; any other efforts may come only after the *lu*'s survival has been looked after.

There are indications that *fasiya* is eroding, that the role of *dyomforo* is increasing at the expense of the *foroba*, and that *lu* are getting smaller. Perhaps this is not so surprising as the fact that the traditional system got there in the first place. Why should able-bodied and vigorous men turn all power over to the *tigi*, though they are frequently beyond the height of their powers?

Claude Meillassoux has suggested that the power of the old men may, in fact, derive from their contribution to the productive process.[33] Except for recently introduced plows and carts, the physical factors a man needs to produce food are readily available. Land is abundant, "capital" goods—hoes and axes—are cheap, and the wood and iron for making them are abundant. The crucial factors of production are the family's labor, of course, and "technology": knowing when the rains will be regular enough to make it safe to plant, when soil depletion makes it advisable to switch to a less demanding crop or to abandon a field, which part and how much of a crop to save for next year's seed, and much other knowledge that can spell the difference between feast and famine.

Before the French introduced new crops, research, and extension activities, such skills were acquired principally as a function of age. So it was probably rational to put the oldest man in charge. A senile *lutigi* could continue to hold the title while operational decisions were made by a younger kinsman. Braima Keita, Djoliba's village chief, was entering this kind of semi-retirement in 1964.

But since the French conquest, the *lutigis'* preeminence in agricultural techniques has eroded. The new commercial crop, peanuts, and expertise for growing it did not come from them but from the colonial government's agricultural service. This was rudimentary until the very end of the colonial period; the first agricultural agent located in Djoliba's vicinity and in regular contact with it was Moussa Drabo, assigned to Krina, four kilometers upstream from Djoliba, in 1957. But even before that, one turned to the government, not to the *lutigi*, to find out why the peanuts were not doing well. Erosion of the *lutigis'* technical preeminence means that their role in food production has become less important than their social status and control over economic processes.

Institutions have been adjusting to the new realities. Nobody

---

[33] See Claude Meillassoux, "Essai d'interprétation du phénomène économique dans les sociétés traditionnelles d'auto-subsistance," *Cahiers d'Etudes Africaines*, 1, no. 4 (1960), 38–67.

knows how big Djoliba's average *lu* was a century ago, but everyone agrees that *lu* are getting smaller. There were 130 in 1964; by 1968, these had split into 168. The trend is definitely toward *lu* composed only of nuclear families and embracing old people and unmarried young relatives.

An examination of Djoliba and other Malian villages suggests that *lu* are not necessarily smallest in the villages most involved in commercial agriculture. Rather the trend appears strongest in villages like Krina that have the most intimate contact with the bearers of new agricultural expertise.[34]

Djoliba's new housing may have accelerated this trend, but it is not yet possible to so demonstrate. The government intended that house design and allocation be used to break down lineage affiliation, but this amounts to an attempt to alter social patterns without changing the underlying patterns of production. Djolibans complain that the new houses are inflexible, preventing *lu* members who want to live together from doing so, and they miss the privacy of their own *lu* courtyards.

PRODUCTION TECHNIQUES

The Sorghum Cycle and the Foroba

Life in Djoliba revolves around growing the main food crop, sorghum, which in turn depends on the rains. Growing other crops and nonagricultural activities fit into the schedule for the principal crop. In general, building and repairing houses, hunting, trips, and parties are reserved for the dry season, when staple crops cannot be grown. One can generally find Djolibans around the village then. During the crop season, the village is often empty during the day except for small children, the sick, and the aged. When timely work is most pressing, able-bodied Djolibans are hard at work most of the time and often sleep in temporary shelters near their *foroba* to save time.

Preparation of the *foroba* for the sorghum crop (or for whatever is grown with it either in the same year by intercropping or in different crops as part of a rotation) begins before the first rains. Usually in February or March, an old field is cleaned of whatever encumbers it or the brush is cleared from a new one after a fallow

---

[34] I present the evidence in "Economic Policy and Planning in Mali" (see note 1), chap. 8.

of several years. Small brush is placed around the bases of small trees (except the useful ones) and burned; larger trees are left.

No further work is possible until enough rain falls in May to soften the rock-like soils. Until recently, at that time the thin layer of topsoil and ash was heaped into mounds with a broad-bladed, short-handled hoe. This preparatory tillage was hard work; obviously it had to be performed within a short period, especially when the first steady rains were late. In recent years the simple metal plows have almost completely replaced the hoes for preparatory tillage, enabling the work to be performed more quickly and less onerously. In 1960 there were 22 plows in Djoliba; in 1964 and 1966 there were 51; in 1968 villagers told me there were nearly 100, though I was unable to verify this.[35] The BDPA's presence helped Djoliba's *lutigi* turn their cash into plows.

The timing of planting is crucial. A break in the rains which leaves the young plants without moisture for ten days means crop failure and the expense of time and seed to do the work all over again. But if the operation is postponed, so is the harvest, part of which the family may need for immediate consumption if its reserves are low. Excessive delay could also expose the crops to drought at the end of the rains in September and October. French administrators generally thought that Malian farmers planted too late, but in view of the high stakes involved if one plants too early and fails it would be hard to prove that Djoliba's farmers are either lazy or stupid.

The farmers sow sometime in June, making holes in the mounds with narrow hoes and inserting the seeds. Sowing is not time consuming, but its timing is crucial. The next operation is just as important and takes much more time. Unless the *foroba* is weeded at about the sorghum's second week, the crop will be choked out.

There seems to be a tendency for families to till and plant more ground than they can effectively weed; one sees sorghum and millet fields that have more weeds than crops. This probably results from the introduction of the plow for preparatory tillage. In the days of the hoe, a family could weed as much as it could prepare and sow; now it cannot, and the adjustment to the new situation is not yet complete.

The crop is weeded a second and sometimes a third time. The days are humid then, and the people work alone in the midst of the tall plants. It is considered lonely work. The people are happy

---

[35] See Leynaud, *La modernisation rurale*, 4, D-2; *L'Essor*, "Fruit du travail"; and BDPA/Bamako unpublished records.

when the group work of harvest begins in October or November. In this work, in particular, different *lu* trade off labor in order to work together; the work is festive, performed rhythmically to a drum beat. Up to 45 man-days per hectare may be spent harvesting the *foroba*.

The result is 500 to 800 kilograms of grain per hectare, depending on the rainfall. Other factors affecting yield are association with other crops, quality of weeding, and soil fertility.

Several of Djoliba's other crops are intimately associated with sorghum. The legumes, Bambara groundnuts, *niébé*, and maize are often grown between the sorghum plants in the *foroba*. Needless to say, this intercropping makes it difficult to calculate yields per hectare. Other staples—millet, *fonio*, and sometimes manioc—are also part of the sorghum cycle. They tolerate lower soil fertility and replace sorghum in the later years of the cycle on any piece of ground.

The Djoliba farmer knows his soils well and pays close attention to them in an effort to maximize the returns to his family's labor. Upland soils are not scarce; there is no land rent and access is virtually free. There is therefore no reason to expend additional labor and capital, as such, just to increase yields per unit of land. However, planting crops inappropriate for a soil or its state of fertility would mean wasting labor.

The rotations are complex and various—intimately adjusted to soil characteristics. Edmond Bernus explains for Kobané, a rice staple Maninka village 200 kilometers upstream in Guinea, that:

The Maninka farmer knows how to tell that a given soil, worn out, needs to be abandoned. When, after many years of cropping, the yields drop, plants appear which indicate soil exhaustion. After a fallow, shorter or longer according to the nature of the terrain, new plants appear, indicating the renovation of the soil.

Each soil is treated according to appropriate methods.... [The variety of rotations] shows that the peasant knows how to make the most of the different sectors of his land and to use his experience to best advantage.[36]

The statement applies to Djoliba, too. Soil is used to maximize the returns to labor, not vice-versa. Since rotations are so closely tailored to microconditions, it is dangerous to generalize. If the average upland parcel bears crops for 7 years at a time (a low-fertility crop like *fonio* for the last two) and requires 10 to 15 years

[36] "Kobané, un village malinké du Haut Niger," *Cahiers d'Outre-Mer*, 9, no. 35 (1956), 254, 256 (my translation).

to recover its fertility afterwards, then Djoliba can be farming from a third to two-fifths of its noninundated lands at any one time. This means that, if 10 percent of Djoliba's noninundated lands are unfarmable laterite mantle, about 1,200 to 1,550 hectares could be farmed in any year without long-run damage to soil fertility. The best guess is that the village now farms about 700 to 800 hectares of upland, most of it in the sorghum cycle.

Rice

In the old days, Djoliban farmers supplemented their sorghum-cycle agriculture by growing rice along the river banks. There is not enough rain to make pluvial rice-growing safe. During most of its life, the rice plant depends on the water from the Niger flood. The harvest can be over one ton per hectare in a good year and the work is not too onerous, but variations in the water level can drown the rice or desiccate it. The risks in inundated rice culture are high, so it is not surprising that Djoliban farmers have kept it a supplementary activity. This they could afford to do because the rice could be planted after the crops of the upland *foroba* and harvested later, too; preparatory tillage was sometimes done after the flood at the end of the wet season.[37]

The Djoliba-Krina irrigation project was supposed to give the farmers water control over 250 hectares of the Niger flood plain and make high-yield rice-growing possible and profitable. The cost, about $100 per hectare, was certainly not too much to pay for good irrigated land. But irrigation turned out to be less than optimal and the area that could be farmed less than 250 hectares.

The rice plain's first crop—50 tons for both villages—was harvested on 100 hectares in 1959.[38] In ensuing years, it turned out that about 150 hectares were farmable (115 of them belonging to Djoliba). After $2,000 was spent on improvements in 1966, the farmed area rose to 200 hectares (about 150 for Djoliba). Yields were also far below expectations. They never exceeded a ton per hectare, were usually about half a ton, and were zero in 1967 when the Niger flood was much higher than usual. Thus average yields on the irrigated rice plain were no higher than what Niger valley farmers achieve by traditional methods of inundated culture. As a

[37] Additional description of this cultural method as practiced in Niger and Upper Volta (the same as the old culture of Djoliba) may be found in W. I. Jones et al., *Rice in West Africa* (Washington: U.S. Department of Agriculture and Agency for International Development, 1968), pp. 113–14 and 178–79.

[38] Guillaume, "Aménagements hydro-agricoles," p. 143.

result of the project, Djolibans shifted from inundated culture to rice culture inside the project and cultivated a larger area of rice than before.

The project had technical shortcomings that largely account for the disappointing results, but there were sociological problems as well.[39] The irrigated area was not level, so that irrigation water did not reach some parts and was so deep on others that only *"floating"* rice could be grown. Figuring out which variety to grow on which parcel of land as a function of water depth was a complicated, technical matter beyond the competence of Djoliba's farmers, to whom the situation was novel. Drainage was deficient. Water had to be let into the whole area at once; there were no secondary canals or dikes for family holdings. Therefore if one *lutigi* used chemical fertilizer (a few tried at first), he would end up fertilizing adjacent plots.

The worst problem was a limited ability to vary the admission of water. The plain could not be irrigated until the Barraro stream had filled up after the new rains, which was not long before the Niger flooded anyway; waters from the Barraro instead of rainwater saw the rice through its first few weeks. Thus the project did not make it possible to cultivate rice in a new season but assured, for the traditional culture, that young rice plants would have adequate water until the Niger flood arrived and that the maximum inundation would be known in advance.

This alone should have enabled the farmers to do better. But Djoliba and Krina could not agree on the date to let the water in. The two villages have a history of quarrels antedating the French conquest. Furthermore, rice lands in the project were allocated by the government according to the populations of the villages; this gave Djolibans some land that had belonged to Krina, a decision Krinans still do not recognize. Finally, when it comes to agriculture, Djolibans get started a bit earlier than Krinans (the Djolibans say this is because Krinans, who are *dyéli*, waste their time singing and having a good time).

Djolibans have been willing to plow or hoe the rice land in the fall and plant immediately after they finish planting the upland *foroba*, then turn to weeding their *foroba*. They are ready to have water let into the project on the government-appointed date;

[39] There were still other factors. The rice plain had been invaded by *Oryza glaberrima*, a semiwild rice originating in and better adapted to the area than Asian *Orysa sativa* but giving lower yields. Since the two plants are so similar, getting rid of the red *glaberrima* is a knotty technical problem.

Krinans are usually not. Moussa Drabo, the extension worker who controls the sluice, however, lives in Krina and has always held up the water until the Krinans could plant. In 1960, the Krinans and the introduction of the water were so late that Djoliba's rice was seriously damaged. The extension worker was *persona non grata* in Djoliba for about a year until Djoliba's leaders realized their need for his services and arranged for him to take a Djoliba girl as his second wife.

The Dyomforo

In addition to the sorghum cycle on the *foroba* and agriculture on the rice plain, Djolibans grow food crops for their own needs on individual plots, usually near the village. Most of these plots are farmed by women. The agricultural style is more intensive. Natural fertilizer and household wastes are often used, crops are usually watered from a well, plots are usually small and fenced with pickets or thornbush. They usually grow sauce ingredients, onions, vegetables, or tobacco.

In recent years, more men have tended to farm *dyomforo*, particularly when they need cash for personal purchases the *lutigi* will not cover. Such fields, though individual, may be just like small *foroba*. Nevertheless, the *dyomforo* are supplementary to other agriculture. They fill marginal needs. Much work on them comes in the off season, when it will not conflict with work on the *foroba*; they have served to introduce commercial tomato culture.

Animal Food Sources

Fishing is the principal source of Djoliba's animal protein. One large *lu* specializes in this activity. I discovered while giving the school children swimming lessons that all boys from this *lu* already knew how, but that none of the rest did. At certain times, however, all village women participate in a big communal fish. Who has the right to fish where and when is intimately regulated by custom that I, certainly, do not understand. But it appears that the yearly increase in the river's fish population is caught without unduly depleting the stock.

The importance of hunting is far from what it must have been when population density was lower. When the railroad was opened, the Sudan's most important export was ivory, but there are not many elephants left today.[40] Hunting is practically reduced to a

---

[40] Gouvernement Général de l'AOF, *Chemin de fers*, 2, 128. Vine rubber led in volume, but ivory in value.

sport; the antique rifles look as though they might be more dangerous to the hunter than the hunted. Keeping animals is more important. The village houses an unknown number of goats, eaten on the occasion of special feasts, and fowl.

In late 1964 the village cooperative began a project to produce eggs for the Bamako market. The United States AID provided the high-quality laying hens, purchased inputs, a power-driven feed grinder, and technical advice. After the project began to function, AID, in effect, transported the eggs to Bamako and marketed them to egg-hungry Americans or other foreigners. The model-village project's trucks plying the Bamako-Djoliba road were easier and cheaper to use than the outboard motor the Americans gave the cooperative. The GRPSM was responsible for the lucrative project and received all returns after the old people who looked after the hens were paid.

When the last American technician left in January, 1966, transportation and marketing arrangements ended, too. The outboard motor was unusable. In 1967, an attack of the Newcastle disease wiped out all Djoliban chickens, including the birds in the egg project. Villagers knew about such diseases and tried to eat what chickens they could before they died. As Nambala Keita, the village nurse, explained: "The plague started on the chickens at one end of the village, and we did at the other. When we met it in the middle, they were all gone."

In 1960, Djolibans had 162 cattle, of which 53 were trained to plow.[41] The increase in the cattle population since then has been in animals for draft purposes, not for eating. In 1965 there were 71 draft animals; in 1968, 145.[42] This increase reflects the adoption of plows for preparatory tillage. Meat remained a strictly minor production item.

Peanuts

The products mentioned so far have been traditional and, except for rice, destined largely for local consumption. The rice scheme, though it permitted Djoliba to sell rice, represented an upgrading of a time-honored culture. Djoliba's peanuts, cotton, and tomatoes, however, are grown principally for sale.

We have mentioned French efforts to force Sudanese into the money economy. For villages with relatively good access to the rail-

[41] Leynaud, *La modernisation rurale*, 4, D2.
[42] From *L'Essor*, "Fruit du travail," and unpublished reports from BDPA/Bamako.

road, like Djoliba, peanuts became the principal cash crop. The plant was brought to Africa from Brazil by the Portuguese and to Mali by the French, who encouraged its adoption. This proved to be rapid; the transition from Bambara groundnuts to peanuts was easy. They have similar growing seasons, the plants are similar, and both develop their fruit in the ground after the plant flowers and the ovary penetrates the soil. By the 1930's, Djoliban farmers were devoting about 50 hectares of crop land to peanuts and harvesting 35 tons in a good year, at least 25 tons for sale.

Bambara groundnuts were and are grown interspersed with the major staples on the *foroba*. Peanuts were first grown in the same way, but the colonial administration generally persuaded Djoliban and other farmers to give peanuts their own year in the sorghum cycle. Farmers were happy to get their seed from the Natives' Provident Societies and to have a guaranteed market for the crop (except during part of World War II), but they did not follow the government's advice concerning practices that would have doubled yields without current inputs that required cash, such as chemical fertilizer.

Djoliban farmers were advised to harvest peanuts later to increase the weight and raise the oil content of their product. They generally received the same payment for peanuts regardless of quality, however, and waiting too long would have meant the hard job of hoeing up the peanuts out of hard soil after the rains had stopped. Djoliban farmers plant peanuts too far apart for maximum yield per unit of land, making weeding harder. Since land is not scarce, farmers apparently have not got used to the need to cultivate more intensively, even to save labor on weeding. Djoliban farmers have failed to use mulch and manure; for those without draft animals and carts, the labor requirement would be very heavy. Djoliban farmers were advised to grow peanuts at the head of the rotation. But the people's food needs come first; sorghum is grown on the soil that has fully recovered its fertility by lying fallow.

Cotton

Djoliba participated in early, unsuccessful French efforts to find a formula for commercial cotton production and in the independent government's efforts to spread the formula the CFDT (Compagnie Française pour le Développement des Fibres Textiles, a mixed-enterprise development corporation) pioneered in the Koutiala region. But cotton has not yet caught on in the village.

The 1963 effort of the politicians to introduce cotton on the collective field failed. These efforts have persisted with results that have been less disastrous but still not good enough to convince many *lutigi* to try cotton. Spreading the CFDT cotton system has been the principal objective of the BDPA's action program for Djoliba's area, but its chances for success were compromised by the unrealistic ideas of the first head of the operation from 1965 to 1967. Disregarding time-honored tenure patterns he did not understand, he tried to reassign all the land in the Barraro basin of Djoliba and several other villages. He urged its division into long strips to be devoted to staple crops, cotton, and peanuts, separated by strips of forest reserve. Villagers ignored the scheme, though a number of *lu* were helped by the BDPA's involvement to buy plows (but generally without credit).

The new BDPA chief has more practical objectives and methods but has found Djolibans quite unresponsive. The villagers object to the work involved in cotton growing, particularly to the number of insecticide sprayings required and to the fact that the labor comes when they are already quite busy with other crops. Extension workers consider Djolibans lazy and spoiled by the American "gift" policy.

Tomatoes

Within the past five years, Djolibans have substantially reduced their plantings of peanuts, for which the producers' price was low, and largely spurned efforts to get them to grow cotton, turning instead for cash to a crop that can be grown at the end of the crop season. Djolibans have known about tomatoes for some time; they are reported to have grown 21 tons in 1962.[43] Bamako, with its market for exotic vegetables, is close enough to try for, but marketing there is fraught with difficulties. An incident will serve to illustrate. In 1964, Moriba Koné's *lu* harvested a good tomato crop. During a trip to Bamako, Moriba made arrangements with a merchant to sell them. He then engaged a young man from the fishing *lu* to pole them to Bamako by pirogue. When they arrived, the Bamako market was glutted; the merchant insisted that the tomatoes had not been delivered when promised; the Somono felt overwhelmed by the situation; the tomatoes rotted; Moriba Koné absorbed the loss.

SOCOMA, the government owned cannery, began to operate in 1964 and was guaranteeing a market for tomatoes at the roadside

[43] *L'Essor*, "Fruit du travail."

in 1965. Djoliba's production rose to more than 100 tons.[44] The AID model-village program has claimed responsibility for this success; the AID small-industries expert helped Djolibans with tomato packaging in 1965. But government figures show that the other villages in Moussa Drabo's rural-development sector grew and marketed about the same volume of tomatoes as Djoliba per head.

The tomato revolution took place on the *dyomforo* at first. Tomato culture is really little different from growing the other crops usually cultivated there, such as peppers and okra. As the advantages of the culture became evident, more men began growing tomatoes on *dyomforo,* and the *lutigi* have begun to make tomato culture a *lu* operation. Often, land will be sown early to an early maturing crop of maize, which is then followed by a crop of tomatoes.

CONSUMPTION AND MARKETING

Eating Habits

Djoliba's agriculture provides its people with a pretty good diet. The principal malnutrition is caused not by food shortage but by custom: children after weaning are fed almost exclusively on starchy staples. Preharvest famines, which apparently racked the area in the late nineteenth century, seem to be a thing of the past. Studies by the Food and Agriculture Organization and other agencies show a shortage of calcium and certain vitamins, but these leave out diet items like fish bones and leaves that are gathered; Djolibans do not manifest the symptoms that should be associated with the alleged deficiencies. The great bulk of Djolibans' protein is from vegetable sources, but this merely means that they must eat more to get enough. Should they wish to supplement their present diet of animal protein, principally fish, raising more chickens presents an obvious opportunity.

Eating habits have changed very little. The evening meal consists of *to*—a grits-like preparation made from sorghum—and sauce, which sometimes includes fish or meat. More than enough is prepared, and the leftovers are often eaten for breakfast. A midday meal, particularly when field work is going on, often consists of

---

[44] From Moussa Drabo's agricultural survey and BDPA/Bamako figures. AID sources indicate that Djoliba marketed 150 tons of tomatoes in 1965 and 260 tons in 1966 (see, for instance, Callaway, "Countermagnet," p. 20, who put the total at 300 tons per year!), but these figures are bald exaggerations.

millet *degé*. There are variations. Cooked rice (*kini*) may be substituted for *to*; a feast calls for a couscous; there is a great variety of sauces.[45] About the only nonlocal items are tea, sugar, and kolas.

The Village Market

Djoliba's market, organized by the *ladjé* in 1954, plays a minor role in the village's commercial contact with the outside world. Nevertheless it is a vital social institution and facilitates distribution of food within Djoliba and between it and its immediate neighbors.[46] The market has changed very little since the BDPA surveyed it in 1960; since it never played a role in any sale of Djoliba's farm products to the outside, government control has not affected it.

Sunday morning at about 9 o'clock, roughly one hundred sellers arrange themselves and their wares around a big mango tree between the school and the old town center. About 80 percent of the sellers will be women; more than half will be from Djoliba, about 40 percent will come from the adjacent villages of Krina, Dalakana, Nafadié, and Samanyana, and the rest will hail from other places in the region, including Bamako. Most people of the village will congregate at the market to buy or at least to look; any participant from another village will probably have something to sell. Almost all of the clientele and merchandise arrive on foot. Djoliba's market is the smallest in the immediate area, so not many big merchants, repairmen, or artisans come. Those who do are probably making the rounds of village markets in the area and come on foot or by bicycle.

By the time the market closes a little after noon, about $50 to $70 worth of goods (at the old exchange rate) will have changed hands. Obviously, no big transactions take place; one buys important items like cattle, plows, cloth, and kolas elsewhere. Cloth and kolas are apt to come from itinerant merchants on bicycles; to get something like a lantern or transistor radio, one would make arrangements with someone going to Bamako or, better yet, outside of Mali.

[45] For some basic recipes for *to, kini*, couscous, *degé*, and the sauces to go with them, see Leon Pales, *L'alimentation en A.O.F.; milieux-enquêtes-techniques-rations* (Dakar: Office de Recherche sur l'Alimentation et la Nutrition en Afrique, 1954), pp. 296–308. Djoliban wives effectively kept me out of the kitchen, but I surmise that these recipes are approximately accurate for Djoliba.

[46] Information in Djoliba's market in the following section comes from Woillet, *Les Marchés*, supplemented by personal observations.

About 75 percent of the goods exchanged in the Djoliba market are of local origin; almost all of the rest—salt, oranges, lemons, ready-made clothes, bicycle parts, or sandals—are bought in Bamako by the sellers. Most of the several dozen items for sale are either products destined for sauces—peanut cake, peppers, dried okra, Baobab leaves, fish—or are prepared foods bought as a sort of luxury—millet pancakes, for instance. About one-third of the items originate from crops usually grown on the *dyomforo*, another third from fishing or gathering of tree leaves or fruit, and the final third from products grown on the *foroba*.

Unprocessed sorghum, millet, peanuts, and parboiled rice are sold, mainly for the benefit of the teachers who don't grow their own, but this trade is small. Most items are processed products of the primary sector. A wife can indulge in the luxury of saving herself a little work by buying them on Sunday. The ability of most wives to do so, however, is quite limited by the amount of money they have to spend. The 1960 survey found that women came to the market with from 20 to 30 cents and usually spent it all. Men might arrive with 60 to 80 cents. So most wives have to gather their own shea nuts to make butter and soap, make their own couscous from millet, grow their own spices, and gather their own *néré* fruits to prepare their own *sumbala*. The sales of the average person offering goods on a given Sunday amount to less than $1 at pre-devaluation rates.

Agricultural Exports

Agriculture contributes to Djoliba's cash income, not through the village market, but through the state commercial sector and through sale to the Bamako market through private channels, which was illegal before the November 1968 coup. Agriculture is overwhelmingly the predominant economic activity, but it does not net the village half of its cash. A combination of salaries for the teachers (the school had been expanded and there are now five teachers and a male nurse), war veterans' pensions, and money sent back by Djolibans who have jobs elsewhere easily outweighs the proceeds from sale of farm products. Still, more money comes from the latter than from any other single source.

Djoliba's 1968 agricultural sales to the government are shown in Table 1.

The total amounted to about $5.50 per Djoliban, but this is mis-

TABLE 1

Agricultural Sales of Djoliba to Mali Government, 1968

Item	Amount (MT)	Price (MF/kg)	Amount of Sale (MF)	($)
Sorghum	1.0	16	16,000	$ 64.
Milled rice	2.581	35	90,500	362.
Cotton	1.7	36	61,200	244.
Tomatoes	120.8	15	1,810,000	7,240.
Peanuts (est.)	15.0	24	360,000	1,440.
				$9,350.

NOTE: MT = metric tons
MF = Mali francs
SOURCE: BDPA/Bamako, from Moussa Drabo and state trading companies.

leading since 1967 was not a typical year in two respects: the rice crop was nearly wiped out by the flood, and farmers had cut back on commercial production, particularly on peanut production, in response to low producers' prices and high prices and shortages of everything else. In a more typical year, Djoliba might also sell 70 tons of rice (primarily as paddy; the labor involved in parboiling and hand-milling such an amount would be great indeed) and would grow and market more peanuts if the price were right. Cash income from agriculture would then be about 50 percent higher than in 1968.

This income is not evenly distributed. The differences are a function of how much land a *lu* farms per member, which, in turn, is a factor of how much labor it can field, whether it can engage labor (for example, the *ton*) at key times, whether or not it has a plow, cart, and trained cattle, and of its land assignment in the rice plain. As a result of the differences, some *lu* are barely growing enough food to feed themselves and pay their taxes; others have a nice surplus available to sell for the goods they need.

A few examples will illustrate. In 1967, the common land farmed by four Djoliba *lu* was as shown in Table 2.

The figures do not include the *dyomforo*. The amount of land the *lu* are cultivating on their *foroba* ranges from a very high 3.7 hectares per worker for the Bassi Keita operation to 0.73 hectares per worker for Diamori Koné and his wife. The physical maximum an able-bodied adult can cultivate using a hoe is thought to be about 1.5 hectares, and the national average is about 1 hectare.

TABLE 2
Size of *Foroba* of Selected Djoliba *Lu*, 1967

lutigi	Number of Adults	Number of Able-bodied Workers	Area in: sorghum and millet (ha.)	rice (ha.)	maize (ha.)	peanuts (ha.)
Bassi Keita	5	3	3.8	5.3	0.67	1.4
Tourou Traoré	6	4	3.4	5.8	0.35	—
Mamadou Cissé	13	8	5.0	2.7	0.47	1.3
Diamori Koné	3	2	0.75	0.42	0.04	0.26

Let us compare a *lu*'s bare subsistence needs with what it gets from its *foroba*. We shall assume an average year with average yields and that each *lu* has as many children as adults, that each adult will need 165 kilograms of sorghum and millet and 85 kilograms of other staples per year just to stay alive, and that each child will need 90 kilograms of rough grains and 45 kilograms of other staples.

The Koné *foroba* does not produce enough to feed the family. The Cissé family does not have much margin above bare subsistence. The two others would normally have quite a bit of rice to sell; Bassi Keita's *lu* also grew peanuts on the *foroba* for sale and the Traorés probably grew tomatoes for their cash crop.

The difference correlates closely with the agricultural equipment the familes use. Both the Keita and the Traoré have a plow, a harrow, and three pairs of oxen. The Cissé have a plow and one pair of oxen for a large *lu*. Diamori Koné has none of these and has to trade his labor or other assets to get someone with a plow to do the preparatory tillage on his *foroba*. Koné's plight is not desperate, however, because he has a pension from his service in the French army, which enables him to do less farming than he probably would otherwise.

CONCLUSIONS

The Nature of the Constraints

Djoliba's agricultural system works. It feeds the people pretty well and provides a surplus that is sold and helps Djolibans buy what they cannot produce. But Djoliba is far from "developed"— its people put a great deal of time into agricultural pursuits and have little to show for it beyond what they eat. What constraints determine their level of production?

When one looks at the situation of villages like Djoliba around the time of the French conquest, it seems plausible to argue that, in an environment certainly not prodigally endowed with natural resources, it was all hard-working people could do to stay alive. A short rainy season limited agriculture to a few months; villagers worked very hard at the key periods of that time, yet there were regular famines. Land was not scarce, but the population was too dense to allow people to get most of their food from hunting. It seemed that, given the techniques and the environment, Djolibans were producing food to their physical maximum.

This was never the dominant view of the French rulers. The conquerors generally considered Malians lazy, but as time passed, more Frenchmen began to wonder whether new techniques and not simply more stimulus might not be needed to expand commercial agriculture. After all, Djolibans, like their neighbors, found commercial agriculture sufficiently onerous that they preferred to send their young men away to the towns to earn much of the cash they needed.

In either view, the constraint was labor. But was the labor limit due to laziness or to physical constraints under existing technology? Were Djolibans hard-working people in a niggardly environment or slothful people in an abundant one? Obviously neither simplistic, moralistic view is right.

In the first half of this century, virtually without changing techniques, Djolibans added about one-tenth to the area they farmed to grow peanuts, the new cash crop. They also contributed requisitioned labor (though admittedly that was called for mainly in the dry season) and grew some sorghum for government stocks. So the labor constraint was not absolute and physical, but was related to demands for what that labor would ultimately supply. French taxes, goods, and commercial infrastructure called forth from Djoliba enough agricultural work to produce 20 to 25 tons of peanuts and other work from village boys who went off to jobs in Bamako, the French army, the peanut fields of Kaolack, or the plantations of Ghana and the Ivory Coast.

By the time Djoliban farmers had integrated the peanut into their farming patterns, they were obliged to work hard indeed during the critical stages of the crop year. During preparatory tillage after the onset of the rains and during the first weeding of the sorghum, all hands might work from dawn to dusk with little time for rest. Even so, labor use had not quite reached the physical limits. Djolibans are motivated by pride in being good farmers, by desire to pay their taxes and avoid outside harassment, and by desire for the things money can buy. However, they have other uses for their time, too. Long before the Djoliban farmer would farm to the physical labor maximum—denying himself all time for leisure and social activity—he would seek nonagricultural ways of getting cash.

This, of course, is exactly what happened. Therefore, in recent times, to increase Djoliba's agricultural production, changes in technique have been needed. The only alternative would have been to turn the terms of trade in favor of Djoliban agriculture by, for instance, subsidizing transport costs or producers' prices. The French did this to some extent, but for independent Mali there is no other sector that can pay such subsidies to agriculture.

Building the rice plain changed the physical givens for Djoliban farmers. It spurred them to cultivate a larger area of rice, but did not greatly affect yields. For the technical and sociological reasons mentioned, the development did not fulfill French expectations; it was useful to Djolibans, but not the bonanza that had been expected.

The greatest technical change has been the introduction of plows. Almost all preparatory tillage is now done by plow; in 1964 this was not yet the case. Cattle are not just kept for feasts now, and farmers have had to learn a new way of doing things. At present, oxen are not ideally trained and are not very robust; the plowing operation takes two oxen and three people. But the change has caught on; Djolibans prefer the new way.

Jean Gallais has argued for Malian villages farther downstream that adopting the plow for preparatory tillage did not, in fact, remove a production bottleneck but merely served to create social distinctions between families.[47] Djoliba is different. In the Niger central delta wetlands Gallais describes, preparatory tillage may be spread out over 150 days from January to May; a man with a hoe could prepare far more land than he could care for later. In Djoliba, soils are too hard to plow or hoe before the rains; preparatory tillage normally has to be concentrated in three to five weeks or crops seeded too late may be wiped out by drought at the end of the wet season.

[47] See Jean Gallais, *Le delta intérieur du Niger; étude de géographie régionale*, Memoires de l'Institut Fondamental d'Afrique Noire, no. 79, 2 vols. (Dakar: IFAN, 1967), 1, 240–42.

Preparing a hectare of land by hoe requires 20 to 40 man-days. By plow, ideally, it takes about half that. Therefore government agriculturalists have reasoned that introduction of plows ought to enable farmers to double their cropped land.[48] But, in Djoliba, with puny oxen and farmers who are still perfecting their techniques, plowing is not twice as efficient as hoeing. Moreover, while preparatory tillage was the prime bottleneck before the plow, it was not the only one. Once it is removed, Djolibans soon encounter the two other bottlenecks mentioned by Gallais: the first weeding and harvesting. A *lutigi* who has the members of his *lu* plow up all the land they can quickly finds that they are not able to weed it all in time to keep the sorghum or millet from being choked out. As a rule of thumb, the new bottleneck is reached when the *lu* has increased the size of its *foroba* by about 20 percent.

Within these constraints, agricultural expansion can take two directions: (1) increase in yield per hectare on the *foroba* or (2) increase in other agricultural activities that do not conflict with the *foroba* sorghum cycle. Djoliban farmers have consistently rejected the former because changes that have been suggested either involve more labor than they are worth (such as transplanting rice) or higher risk of failure (for example, planting sorghum earlier or harvesting peanuts later). And the farmers have refused new integrations into the sorghum cycle since the adoption of peanuts. Other recent developments have been acceptable because they have little overlap with the peak labor-demand periods of the sorghum cycle. Thus, more rice land could be farmed on the new plain because it could be fit into the existing cycle. Tomato culture, of course, is a perfect example because its labor overlap is so slight. Cotton, by contrast, definitely does compete for labor with staple food crops.

Prospects

How might Djoliban agriculture develop? Djolibans are already pretty well fed. They may choose to increase the animal protein in their diet, but most increase in agricultural production per head ought to be in commercial farming, designed to fulfill other wants that can only be met by purchase. Of course, Djolibans may choose to fill these needs in other ways—by exporting manpower to wage jobs elsewhere, for instance—but we are interested only in the prospects for commercial agriculture.

---

[48] Estimates vary widely. See, for instance, Leynaud, *La modernisation rurale*, 3, 49–70, which overstates labor saving from adoption of the plow.

At present, Djoliba does not have a comparative advantage in producing any agricultural product sufficient to justify its giving up its food self-sufficiency. Its resource endowments are not that different from those of thousands of other Malian villages, and in view of Mali's chronic and critical foreign-exchange shortage, the country could hardly allow its villages to begin eating imported food. Therefore, developments in commercial agriculture will need to respect Djoliba's system of producing food for itself.

At present, this system is the sorghum cycle. Sorghum and rice are roughly equal in food value; labor requirements per hectare of rice are considerably higher than for sorghum even when the rice is not transplanted. Therefore, as long as yields per hectare are similar for the two crops, as they now are, it will make sense to count on sorghum for a staple food. Djolibans express a slight preference for sorghum over rice but like rice for variety. They grow it to vary their diet and for sale to the government to the extent that they can do so without disrupting the dominant sorghum cycle.

Most of the actions that would stimulate Djoliba's commercial agriculture can be taken only by the central government and are, frankly, beyond the competence of the villagers. They involve changing the village's terms of trade with the outside. Quite clearly, in recent years the margin at which Djoliban farmers are willing to trade leisure or other activities for work in commercial agriculture has fallen. Villagers are not working as close to their physical limits during the labor-bottleneck periods of the sorghum cycle as they did just before or after independence. They are disgruntled because the same amount of labor in commercial agriculture now brings less cloth.

Of course, if the government were willing to pay more for Djoliba's products, subsidize the prices of consumers' goods, or provide free transport, villagers would make the sacrifice to work harder and grow more peanuts, cotton, tomatoes, and rice. But outright subsidies would have to be paid by someone. In Mali, where almost everyone is in the primary sector, the government cannot afford to subsidize that sector as rich countries usually do.

Though the government must avoid paying Djolibans such high prices for their cash crops as actually to lose money exporting them, this is far from the case at present. Peanut and cotton exports are heavily taxed and contribute significantly to government revenues. In view of the high responsiveness of suppliers to changes in price, it would obviously increase the country's exportable peanut and cotton crops (hence also its access to foreign exchange and imports) if farmers like those in Djoliba could receive a higher proportion of what their farm products fetch on world markets. Reduction of export taxes would oblige the government to raise the revenue foregone in some other way. Also, anticipated declines in world prices for these goods should inspire caution lest too high a price encourage too much resource allocation to such crops. Nevertheless, subject to these caveats, Mali's foreign-exchange situation justifies paying the producers all the export market will bear.

Other government policies affect Djoliba's terms of trade. As a part of Mali's planning, import licensing and various duties have been used to direct foreign exchange to the importation of investment goods needed to fulfill the plan. From 1962 to 1968, while the Mali franc was nonconvertible, the imported things Djolibans and other villagers wanted to buy were either not available or very expensive. As the money paid for cash crops lost its purchasing power, farmers showed less interest in producing for sale. They probably resented the mounting prices less than the vagaries of supply. A *lutigi* could not know in advance whether a plow or cart would be available at any price once he had the cash to buy one. Nationwide, declining farm production for export meant still tighter restrictions on imports and a vicious circle of cumulative causation. Even investment goods for farmers (plows and carts) and imported inputs (fertilizer) were frequently unavailable.

This situation was ameliorated by the devaluation of 1967, followed by the restoration of convertibility in 1968. Djolibans who could accumulate the money could buy carts and plows, even fertilizer, cloth, and transistor radios. Prices were higher than official prices had been earlier, of course, but the government recognized the close connection between certain farm purchases and production for export. It used some of the foreign aid it received to hold down the prices of plows, carts, and fertilizer to farmers. Djoliban farmers have been buying the plows and carts but are reluctant to adopt fertilizer, even at subsidized prices. They are well aware of how unreliable the market that supplies such commodities can be.

Since the monetary reforms, the government has some room for maneuver; the country's major farm products can be sold on outside markets without subsidy. Yet the prospects for increasing the returns to the Djoliban farmer's labor on commercial crops are quite limited. Mali is far and expensively removed from outside markets. Her farmers are not desperate; they have a subsistence alternative and can practically abstain from commercial agriculture if the terms do not suit them. Beyond what the government can do to improve the terms by not raising its revenues on farm exports, improvement must come from changes in technique and organization.

Djoliba is capable of producing more sorghum and of marketing it, given what farmers consider an attractive price. At present, not only is the producers' price the lowest in West Africa in terms of foreign purchasing power, but the market for sorghum is thin—confined pretty much to what Mali's towns will buy.

At these low sorghum prices, or even at slightly higher ones, Mali ought to be able to use its sorghum to put weight on cattle for slaughter and export to coastal countries. Meat export is badly mismanaged at present, but recent government reforms are promising.

The sorghum market would also be broadened if FAO research on increasing the percentage of sorghum in bread turns out to be feasible; then sorghum from villages like Djoliba could displace part of the wheat imports of Africa's coastal cities. Djoliba's sorghum would be quite competitive even at a slightly higher price needed to stimulate the additional production. However, such developments are out of the hands of the villagers.

One technical innovation might help Djolibans to increase their cash income and the efficiency of their sorghum growing. It requires integrating cotton into the sorghum cycle, putting it at the head of the cycle, and using chemical fertilizer. Cotton is a good investment of labor if it is grown reasonably well, even after the cost of fertilizer, pesticides, and rental of sprayers is deducted. Moreover, the carry-over effect of the fertilizer is remarkable on sorghum grown the following year. This last effect is important, for it permits an increase in *yield* for sorghum, yet the improvement is paid by a cash crop.

The yield increase is not important in itself. The present sorghum-production bottleneck is the first weeding, which consumes labor as a function of area. Growing cotton with fertilizer ahead of sorghum decreases the amount of weeding time per unit of sorghum production and breaks the labor bottleneck.

Few of Djoliba's *lutigi* have been persuaded to grow cotton. They have seen the unexciting results on their collective field, and putting anything ahead of the staple crop in their principal rotation is a radical move requiring much confidence. Furthermore, Djolibans are relatively well off as a result of income they used to make selling eggs to Americans, and they are still digesting the tomato revolution. However, some neighboring villages are now integrating cotton into the sorghum cycle with success. Djoliba has the plows and the know-how to make the shift; it can count on technical advice and supply of the necessary inputs from the government and the BDPA.

Djoliba could radically increase its rice production if the technical problems of the scheme it shares with Krina could be solved. But establishing complete water control, including drainage, with secondary canals and drains for individual plots, individual diking, and leveling, would be expensive. Considering the cost of getting Malian rice to growing markets in Dakar, Abidjan, and Monrovia, plus what new Asian "miracle varieties" are now doing to world prices, planners should think twice about spending money on Djoliba's plain unless there is a guaranteed and protected market for the prospective product. Furthermore, Djoliba's is only one of many underutilized rice developments in Mali and far from the most underutilized.

Prospects for the continuation of Djoliba's tomato boom are precarious. They depend on the government's finding some way of selling the canned products at a profit. Once more, success or failure will be decided outside of Djoliba. The BDPA is investigating the possibility of growing vegetables—particularly green beans, onions, and eggplants—to be flown to Europe for the winter market. The keys are regularity and quality of supply, and timing to beat other producers in Morocco, Senegal, and the Canary Islands. Since any successes could be imitated by farmers within striking distance of any savannah airport with flights to Europe, windfall gains would be shortlived. The prospects for success are again beyond the means of Djoliba's *lutigi*.

Djoliba's vulnerability to outside forces need not cause surprise or alarm. Agricultural villages everywhere tend to be perfect producers, unable to affect the market by themselves and unable to keep windfall profits for long. In learning to grow peanuts and tomatoes, to use the plows, and to change the way they grew rice, Djoliba's farmers demonstrated their willingness to change. Indeed, the rapidity with which they exploited the favorable circumstances for tomato production was impressive. Their willingness to adopt changes has, of course, been contingent on compatibility with their major economic activity, growing sorghum and other food for themselves. It has been facilitated by similarity of the new techniques to time-honored ways of growing Bambara groundnuts, African rice, and sauce crops like okra. There is every indication that Djolibans will continue to be able to exploit advantageous techniques and commercial opportunities offered them. But their survival is not at the mercy of such opportunities; they can be highly self-sufficient if they need to be.

CHAPTER 9

CONCLUSIONS

PETER F. M. MCLOUGHLIN

This concluding chapter will analyze briefly what these seven case studies tell us about the nature of tribal food production systems. What characteristics do they have in common, and what general lessons do they offer for increasing productivity in Africa?

One common economic characteristic that emerges quite clearly is that each of these societies is absolutely dominated by production of food crops. Without any question all other economic affairs take second place. This does not mean that there is not a whole range of other activities; there is. Nor does it mean that these other activities are not carried on along with food production. They are, and usually by the same people. Unfortunately, merely glancing at these societies, as many developers have done and continue to do, may lead one to conclude that some of these other activities take precedence.

The official and unofficial literature is crammed with statements to the effect that a particular set of religious, or social, or political activities seems paramount in a particular society. Such practices certainly may be more colorful or even bizarre than herding or farming to a member of an urban society that has learned to protect its livelihood from the whims of Dame Nature. Basic food production is dull, routine, grubby, and very much a background activity. In any case, a visitor to a more traditional economy probably talks mainly to the men who are a bit better off and who have, by and large, much more time on their hands than the common villagers. He thus misses the evidence of the absorbing occupation of the mass of people.

I am not sure that this point really needs further examination. As a matter of logic, as Marx recognized a century ago, you eat or you don't have a society because you don't have people. This is particularly the case in the more closed societies like the Azande.

It is evident in all these studies that relationships within the immediate family, within the extended kinship group, and within the broader community have developed over time to guide and regulate the decision-making systems for food production. These relationships—the cultural, social, and political systems—have been analyzed, classified, and theorized about. They nevertheless are the superstructure, which every society must have, over the set of basic activities that sustains the society. The more complicated, specialized, and sophisticated the technology, the more complicated the institutional framework of decision-making and the allocation of output. In highly industrialized societies, including those with considerable central planning, it is sometimes extremely difficult to chart the decision-making process for production and distribution because these functions are so complicated.

This difficulty does not hold for our case studies. Production and consumption are very close together in time and place, and the technology of production is relatively uncomplicated. Even so, the formalism, the institutions themselves, are often so attractive to analysts and students that they may not render the basic and historical rationale of a particular set of institutions immediately apparent. And because a political or behavioral scientist usually does not place a very high priority on research into food crop production, he naturally does not spend much time on it. Therefore he usually does not try to trace relationships between whatever he is studying and food production and distribution systems.

The International African Institute, London, has sponsored for twenty-five years a most varied and pioneering series of ethnographic studies. But it is remarkable how little space the studies devote to the production systems of different societies or to the relationships between these systems and the political, religious, social, and other institutions that receive detailed attention. As a result it is nearly impossible to use these studies for practical development work and for the devising of rural development theory, as is explained in chapter 1.

Another way of identifying the paramountcy of food production, at least by inference, is to notice a number of other basic features of these economies. For example, innovations normally are much more easily effected for cash crops than for household food crops. The cost of gambling with cash crops is less severe. The Jones, Linares de Sapir, and Priscilla Reining studies bring this out most clearly. The Azande repudiated a development scheme primarily because their new food crop system was less reliable and productive. It is also noticeable that the scheduling and the time spent on social, religious, and other "noneconomic" affairs are generally functions of the cycle of production activities, not the other way around.

There is also a general tendency in these societies to attempt to obtain maximum output per unit of labor input. They are in the first phase posited by John W. Mellor, as described in chapter 1. Another way of putting this is to say that a given desired level and composition of output is sought with a minimum input of labor power.

A similar characteristic is the emphasis placed, other things being equal, on activities that feature a lower level of labor consumption. This pattern manifests itself in a wide variety of ways. To save the heavy labor of bush clearing, several crops per year may be grown on the same land, even though newly cleared land would give higher yields. Crops may also be interplanted for the same reason, though there may be other reasons as well. Another clear example is the tendency to devote much less labor to crops grown for sale than to crops grown for subsistence. We saw in chapter 6 that the peanut (cash crop) cultivation of the Diola in Senegal is much less labor intensive than their rice cultivation (subsistence crop).

Much of this propensity to minimize labor inputs results from the delicate nature of the timing and the amount of rainfall over the year. Food production systems are intimately connected to the rainfall regime. This point is fairly well recognized in the more academic literature. It is apparently not so well appreciated in practice when attempts are made to introduce innovations that ignore this dependence on the timing, amount, and capriciousness of rainfall.

In this connection, one inference from these cases seems to be that the greater and more reliable the rainfall, the more complicated the food production system. Comments by some agronomists and other technicians as to the "laziness" of food crop farmers working under these conditions often reflect an incomplete awareness of the labor-timing problem.

On the basis of these cases (especially chapter 8) and material in other recent works, one also wonders if rural people regard basic food crop farming as a much more "noble" occupation in much of West Africa than they do in parts of East and Central Africa. In drier regions, food crop systems are less complicated and less reliable, animals become significant providers of basic food needs, and a tendency appears to abandon farming entirely or partly at the first opportunity.

This is a terribly complicated issue, and generalizations must not be stretched too far. But food crop selection (under given storage conditions) is geared to (1) security of supply, so that each season has something, (2) sufficiency of supply, and (3) variety. Under the relatively more secure rainfall conditions in much of West Africa, where several of these cases were studied, it is not surprising that more complicated and stable societies develop.

The technology of storage alone has a significant bearing on the system. As is brought out in chapter 3, the Karimojong cannot store surplus sorghum for more than a year. In years of bumper crops, the surplus gets distributed through such means as ceremonies, trading, and begging—social devices that may be viewed as products of the conditions of the food production system. But bumper years are not too common, so the frequency and extent of these devices vary considerably. The Azande social structure (chapter 4) is also influenced markedly by storage capabilities.

Related also to seasonal labor availability, which in turn is connected to the rainfall pattern, is the capacity to introduce new crops into the production system. The cases in this volume describe the overwhelming role of women in food crop production. This is well recognized, and we discussed it in the introduction. But new crops, such as manioc (cassava) in Djoliba, are often introduced by women in their household gardens (see chapter 8). The crop was suitable for the labor availability cycle. So was the peanut in the same case study; it could be sown after millet and harvested before the year's critical labor period. Peanut yields have not been greater in this area, however, because of other demands for labor at particular times. But in case after case, such as among the Azande, we see that societies will indeed change their food crops when conditions require it.

Yet another general inference from these cases is that many hands are needed to meet seasonal peaks in labor demand or to carry out successful livestock nomadism. Large families are essential. It is generally held that the migration, especially of adult males, from the land to wage employment in mines and cities results from deteriorating production and income conditions back on the farm. This is the "push" and is rather well documented across Africa. But the inference is often made that the "push" is caused by a community's inability to provide sufficient good land for its young men. This is not always the case. Among the Yalunka, work in the diamond fields attracted many young men who could have had land (chapter 5). Their absence exacerbated the shortage of labor at peak periods.

It may be that mechanization progresses more quickly where labor is relatively scarce, whatever the reason for the shortage. Innovations are generally more welcome, at least where the social structure permits, where they save labor and open production bottlenecks. Among the Djoliba, bullocks and plows provided to grow cotton as a cash crop were used for rice, millet, and peanuts, the most important crops. It also seems clear that rigid social relationships may retard mechanization. Those pertaining to land tenure among the Diola precluded mechanization (chapter 6). Farmers who mechanize traditional crops might sometimes even be considered "traitors," as among the Yalunka.

Perhaps this is why, in these cases and others, those who mechanize successfully in a given area may not be the people native to it. This is so among the Yalunka, for example, where "stranger" businessmen turned to mechanized rice production and account for a large percentage of it. They are more well-to-do and may export their crop from the area while others are importing it. There are scores of cases across the continent where the wealthy and the entrepreneurs outside agriculture are becoming a significant element in transforming at least part of the system.

There are a number of other important points regarding technological change brought out in these cases. One has to do with the effects of the diffusion of technology. The more adult males with a command of the technology, the greater the emergence of nuclear families with their own farms. This trend is accompanied by the nuclear family's increasing desire to make its own economic and production decisions. The implications, of course, are enormous, even at the ideological level. The case here that brings this out most strongly is that of the Djoliba and their ox plows. The trend may also be affecting the Haya (chapter 2). I know numerous other examples of this pattern in East and Central Africa.

Nor should one ignore the interrelationships of technological improvements. In Djoliba, the advent of grain mills gave the women more time to grow tomatoes for the new canning factory to bring in some cash income.

There are also several considerations regarding the relationship between productivity and distribution. As Priscilla Reining in particular brings out for the Haya, the subsistence productivity of different families is roughly similar. But the level of income from other economic activity, such as cash cropping, fishing, and trading, is extremely varied, and distribution of wealth is skewed. This is also noticeable in several other parts of Africa.

Perhaps an inference is that the lower the average productivity (subsistence plus nonsubsistence), the less polarized the distribution of income. Is improvement of subsistence food production therefore necessary at all for development?

Some of the implications for development policy of these characteristics have been touched on in chapter 1. Here I would simply like to emphasize that development policy must recognize that African food production systems are both unique and complicated. Far from being simple, as is so often assumed in policy-making and model-building, the systems are finely attuned to their diverse and often unstable constraints. Thus the solutions to these multifaceted food production problems must be equally complicated and diverse. Very little can be generalized. Research into these systems must therefore be conducted by teams of different professionals whose work is integrated into meaningful and multidisciplinary wholes.

There is also a need for decision-makers to achieve a powerful sense of urgency regarding problems of food crop production. Some officials need no prodding; they are affected daily by an agricultural sector that is failing to respond to the demands made upon it. The effects include the undesirable and often dangerous urban unemployment inflated by a continuing flow of men (and increasingly women) from the rural areas, rural landlessness or near landlessness (though the less fortunate may have claim to a meager supply of produce from the family land), and deep intertribal (and in places interracial) tensions over farming and grazing land. These tensions tend to permeate every facet of group and even personal relationships. The decision-making process is constantly being threatened with suffocation by these pressures.

Money, of course, is in short supply. Perhaps more important, so is skilled and highly motivated manpower, especially at the ground level where it really counts. Who wants to work in the bush? The institutional structure, by and large still carrying the stamp of colonial regimes, tends to be cumbersome and sluggish. It was designed to control and regulate, not to promote rapid development. Usually there are no big profits in farming, and the national and international private sector is not helping much. International lending agencies such as the World Bank are only recently becoming involved in "soft" loans to agriculture in the really productive areas—educational facilities, extension, and so on.

The whole process of articulating these agricultural economies with effective credit and marketing institutions, research on improved farm systems and new technology, markets, and the like is wearyingly slow, administratively enervating, and utterly difficult. The constant frustration is one of the most important psychological hurdles now facing rural development. It is small wonder that one finds considerable cynicism and skepticism among planners and other officials. Much of the sense of urgency has been dulled by repeated toe-stubbing. Dullness and pessimism have become institutionalized in many countries. Yet a sense of urgency must be generated, or Africa will quickly slip from its relatively good position in the race between food production and population. I believe that it is critically important for researchers and theorizers to see food production systems through the eyes of the planners, policy-makers, extension personnel, and others actually involved in the process of altering them. To these people, changes in the "subsistence" economies we have been talking about often come very near the bottom of the list of operationally possible objectives.

A typical list of objectives for an African country's agricultural sector includes expansion of agricultural exports. More volume of more crops is the aim. "Diversification" of the agricultural sector is a basic and consistent element in the planning vocabulary.

National self-sufficiency in food is also stressed. In an essentially agrarian economy, there is perhaps nothing that galls a planner more than the food import figures, especially when they are rising. The need for domestic agriculture to supply the nonrural populations with cheap basic foodstuffs is viewed as particularly important.

In addition, economic planners call on agriculture to provide food and nonfood inputs for processing and manufacturing facilities to supply domestic markets (industries of this type export very little). The bulk of Africa's manufacturing involves the processing of agricultural commodities. Industrialization programs concentrate more on this type of industry than on other lines of resource exploitation, except for a few countries like Zambia where minerals are important.

This is how government leaders and senior planners tend to view the agricultural sector. Those who must implement more detailed policies to achieve these goals are mainly civil servants in the natural resource ministries and research establishments. There is also a plethora of agencies, bureaus, and institutions responsible for more specialized aspects—credit, marketing, supply of inputs, water development, cooperatives, information, and so on. The splintering of activities is one of the more serious problems inhibiting the expansion of production. At the lowest levels of operation, each agency's representative has, as they say, only one piece of the elephant.

But here is our farmer looking at a range of strange faces. Each talks to him about a different aspect of his farming problems. The extension officer (usually at the lowest level and underqualified) is probably interested in only one or two things at a time—those practices or inputs his agency is currently promoting, perhaps fertilizer or a particular kind of crop rotation.

Each agency, then, views the farmer or herder in terms of its own objectives. But the farming family looks after its food supply first, and this tends to interfere with the achievement of the agency's objective. The farmer assesses the costs and benefits of a suggested change in terms of how it affects his existing production pattern, which is geared to provide his food requirements. Time and time again a farmer rejects a suggestion because it requires an amount or a schedule of labor or a cash outlay that would interfere with the requirements of his subsistence.

In conclusion, it seems to me that, given the characteristics of these food production systems and the typical national institutional framework:

1. Researchers must detail the more important of these systems in a manner akin to the case studies in this volume.

2. Researchers must identify in each case those points at which that particular community is open to development.

3. Researchers must present their analysis and their operational policy conclusions in a manner suitable for use at the lowest administrative levels.

4. Administrative operations must become an integral part of local development plans as they are drawn up. Such plans must be coordinated between agencies and departments. Unified extension and rural development services should receive urgent consideration nearly everywhere.

5. Planners at higher levels must view more sympathetically plans submitted from below.

6. Research results and case studies must be integrated into the training curricula for personnel destined for natural resource and development agencies.

7. Foreign experts, academic and operational alike, must digest these detailed local materials before advocating policy or other changes.

8. Technical researchers must also inform themselves more fully of the economic and social constraints of the milieus for which they are attempting to develop new physical inputs and systems. They, too, should read the results of social science research.

These are not new suggestions. Most people will agree that they are central issues needing resolution. Yet little seems to happen to put them into effect. Perhaps the central issue is the need to convince the political leadership that the political repercussions of *not* taking these steps may be frightening in the long run.

INDEX

Bush foods, 117–18, 155–57, 269

Cash crops, 139–40, 169, 184–85, 269, 292–94; versus food crops, 4, 7–8, 310–11
Collective farming, 276
Commercialization of markets, 119, 196, 243–44, 276, 291, 296–98
Credit and debt, 182, 184; and the class structure, 262–63
Cropping patterns, 114–15, 141–42, 171–76, 200–207, 212–15
Crops: diversification of, 9, 312; dominance of subsistence, vii, 7–8, 191, 309–11, 315–16; inter-cropping, 142, 146, 169, 255–56, 283, 311; main subsistence, 44–45, 114, 129–40, 168–69, 197–200, 232, 269, 285–90; and modernization, 223–24; rotation of, 287–88; storage of, 217–19, 311–12; yields of, 69–70, 116–17, 179–84, 251–52, 287, 288; *see also* Cash crops; Production systems/Farm management; Rural development policy; Technological change/Innovation

Data: problems of, 144–49, 178
Debt: *see* Credit and debt
Demography: *see* Population/Demography
Diet/Nutrition: adequacy of, 9, 113, 137–39, 178; bush foods (collecting), 117–18, 155–57, 269; eating habits, 137–39, 294–95; fishing, 153–54, 269, 290; food distribution systems, 118–19, 183–84, 217–19, 221, 223; hunting, 117–18, 151–53, 290–91; and occupations, 84; and soils, 69
Draft animals: *see* Livestock

Eating habits: *see* Diet/Nutrition
Ecology: *see* Production systems/Farm management, ecology and

European influences, 128–29, 197, 273–75
Extension services, 6, 8, 12–13, 27, 186, 233, 284–85, 314, 315; and mechanization, 12, 246–47; unified, 15–16

Family development, stages of, 54–65
Farm management: *see* Production systems/Farm management
Fishing: *see* Diet/Nutrition
Food distribution systems: *see* Diet/Nutrition

Holdings, size of, 55–56, 61, 65–66, 211, 253
Household composition: *see* Population/Demography
Hunting: *see* Diet/Nutrition

Income: cash, 27–32, 297; diversification of, 31; household, 27–32, 219, 250; other sources of, 5, 86–89, 185–86, 188–89, 267, 313–14
Inter-cropping: *see* Crops
Irrigation, 121, 226, 288–89

Labor migration: *see* Population/Demography
Land tenure, 13, 207–12, 283
Land use, 6–8, 100, 169–71, 197–99, 254
Livestock: as capital, chap. 3, 259–60; diseases of, 122–23; draft animals, 226, 233–34, 239–41; improvement of, 121; integration with agriculture, 68; *see also* Production systems/Farm management, livestock management

Marketing: *see* Rural development policy, and marketing; Commercialization of markets
Mechanization: 121, 186–91, 225, 312; *see also* Extension services, and mechanization

317

Nutrition: *see* Diet/Nutrition

Population/Demography: and food relationships, 3–4, 30–31, 93–94, 107–9, 185–86, 314; household composition, 176–79, 188–89, 207, 282–85, 312; labor migration, 5–6, 13, 177, 185–86, 233, 256–57, 312; village organization, 13–14, 177–78, 277–85, 312

Population-food relationships: *see* Population/Demography

Price stabilization: *see* Technological change/Innovation, and stabilization of prices

Production systems/Farm management, 5, 140–43; adaptability of, 142–43; allocation of fields, 143–44; cropping patterns, 114–15, 141–42, 171–76, 200–207, 212–15; ecology and, 6–7, 10, 45, 93–100; labor requirements, 7–8, 10, 46–54, 147–49, 244–45, 299–301, 310–11; livestock management, 66–68, 100, 107–10, 150–51, 185; and organization of work by sex, 7, 13, 46–54, 79–86, 143–44, 157–61, 212–15, 216–17, 232, 283–84, 312; and productivity, 8, 85–86, 115–17, 179–84; relationship to social and other systems, 10, 310; and stages of family development, 54–56; subsistence versus cash crops, 4, 7–8, 145, 196, 205–6, 225, 275, 301, 310–11

Productivity: *see* Production systems/Farm management, and productivity; Crops, yields of

Rainfall, 10, 52–54, 96–97, 148, 171, 212–15, 311

Research: anthropological, 21–27, 44, 71–79; economic, 14; priorities for, 37–38, 316; technical, 14–15, 150–51, 304, 305; tools and equipment for, 226

Rural development policy, vii, 5, 18–21, 27–32, 119–23, 162–63, 191, 224–27, 301–5, 316; ineffectiveness of, in the past, 162–63, 313–14; and marketing, 4, 6–7, 196, 224–25, 243–44; problem of isolation, 128, 195–96; *see also* most of chaps. 1 and 9 for indirect references

Rural development theories, chap. 1, esp. 9–11 and 32–37; anthropological, 21–27, 44, 71–79; economic, 18–21, 32–37; geographical, 37; need for long-term studies, 10, 28, 38; need for rapid survey techniques, 28, 38

Storage: *see* Crops, storage of

Subsistence croppings: *see* Production systems/Farm management, subsistence versus cash crops

Technological change/Innovation, chap. 1, esp. 11–17; cash crops versus food crops, 4, 7–8, 310–11; constraints on, 9, 11–16, 239, 298–301, 312–13; effects of, 255 ff., 257 ff., 312; and demand for higher income, 27–32, 242–43; increasing commercialization of markets, 119, 196, 243–44, 276, 291, 296–98; and scarcity of labor, 244–45; and stabilization of prices, 246; traditional tools and implements, 114–15, 141, 169, 212, 213, 215

Village organization: *see* Population/Demography

Water use: *see* Irrigation

Yields: *see* Crops, yields of

DATE DUE	
~~DEC 0 8 1994~~	

DEMCO, INC. 38-2931